# Interpretive Lenses in Sociology

*Series editors:* **Thomas DeGloma**, Hunter College, City University of New York, and **Julie B. Wiest**, West Chester University of Pennsylvania

---

The *Interpretive Lenses in Sociology* series provides a unique forum for scholars using a wide range of interpretive perspectives to explore their approaches to uncovering the deep meanings underlying human actions, events and experiences.

---

### Forthcoming in the series:

*Interpreting Subcultures*
*Sense-Making From Insider and Outsider Perspectives*
Editor **J. Patrick Williams**

### Out now in the series:

*Interpreting Contentious Memory*
*Countermemories and Conflicts over the Past*
Editors **Thomas DeGloma** and **Janet L. Jacobs**

*Interpreting the Body*
*Between Meaning and Materiality*
Editors **Anne Marie Champagne** and **Asia Friedman**

*Interpreting Religion*
*Making Sense of Religious Lives*
Editors **Erin Johnston** and **Vikash Singh**

### Find out more at
bristoluniversitypress.co.uk/interpretive-lenses-in-sociology

## International advisory board:

**Jeffrey C. Alexander**, Yale University, US
**Marni A. Brown**, Georgia Gwinnett College, US
**Giuseppina Cersosimo**, University of Salerno, Italy
**Lynn S. Chancer**, Hunter College, City University of New York, US
**Erica Chito-Childs**, Hunter College, City University of New York, US
**Manase Kudzai Chiweshe**, University of Zimbabwe, Zimbabwe
**Jean-François Côté**, University of Montreal, Canada
**Emma Engdahl**, University of Gothenburg, Sweden
**Veikko Eranti**, University of Helsinki, Finland
**Emily Fairchild**, New College of Florida, US
**Gary Alan Fine**, Northwestern University, US
**Stacey Hannem**, Wilfrid Laurier University, Canada
**Titus Hjelm**, University of Helsinki, Finland
**Annemarie Jutel**, Victoria University of Wellington, New Zealand
**Carol Kidron**, University of Haifa, Israel
**Krzysztof T. Konecki**, University of Lodz, Poland
**Joseph A. Kotarba**, Texas State University, US
**Donileen Loseke**, University of South Florida, US
**Eeva Luhtakallio**, University of Helsinki, Finland
**Lisa McCormick**, The University of Edinburgh, Scotland
**Neil McLaughlin**, McMaster University, Canada
**Beth Montemurro**, Pennsylvania State University, Abington, US
**Kylie Parrotta**, California Polytechnic State University, US
**Laura Robinson**, Santa Clara University, US
**Andrea Salvini**, University of Pisa, Italy
**Susie Scott**, University of Sussex, UK
**Cristine G. Severo**, Federal University of Santa Catarina, Brazil
**Xiaoli Tian**, University of Hong Kong, Hong Kong
**Vilna Bashi Treitler**, Northwestern University, US
**Hector Vera**, National Autonomous University of Mexico, Mexico
**Gad Yair**, The Hebrew University of Jerusalem, Israel
**J. Patrick Williams**, Nanyang Technological University, Singapore
**Eviatar Zerubavel**, Rutgers University, US

## Find out more at
bristoluniversitypress.co.uk/interpretive-lenses-in-sociology

# INTERPRETIVE SOCIOLOGY AND THE SEMIOTIC IMAGINATION

Edited by
Andrea Cossu and Jorge Fontdevila

First published in Great Britain in 2024 by

Bristol University Press
University of Bristol
1-9 Old Park Hill
Bristol
BS2 8BB
UK
t: +44 (0)117 374 6645
e: bup-info@bristol.ac.uk

Details of international sales and distribution partners are available at bristoluniversitypress.co.uk

© Bristol University Press 2024

British Library Cataloguing in Publication Data
A catalogue record for this book is available from the British Library

ISBN 978-1-5292-1174-0 hardcover
ISBN 978-1-5292-1175-7 paperback
ISBN 978-1-5292-1177-1 ePub
ISBN 978-1-5292-1176-4 ePdf

The right of Andrea Cossu and Jorge Fontdevila to be identified as editors of this work has been asserted by them in accordance with the Copyright, Designs and Patents Act 1988.

All rights reserved: no part of this publication may be reproduced, stored in a retrieval system, or transmitted in any form or by any means, electronic, mechanical, photocopying, recording, or otherwise without the prior permission of Bristol University Press.

Every reasonable effort has been made to obtain permission to reproduce copyrighted material. If, however, anyone knows of an oversight, please contact the publisher.

The statements and opinions contained within this publication are solely those of the editors and contributors and not of the University of Bristol or Bristol University Press. The University of Bristol and Bristol University Press disclaim responsibility for any injury to persons or property resulting from any material published in this publication.

Bristol University Press works to counter discrimination on grounds of gender, race, disability, age and sexuality.

Cover design: blu inc, Bristol
Front cover image: pixabay/kkortmulder

# Contents

| | | |
|---|---|---|
| Series Editors' Preface: Interpretive Lenses in Sociology—On the Multidimensional Foundations of Meaning in Social Life *Thomas DeGloma and Julie B. Wiest* | | vi |
| Notes on Contributors | | xi |
| Introduction: Interpretive Sociology and the Semiotic Imagination *Andrea Cossu and Jorge Fontdevila* | | 1 |
| 1 | Marked and Unmarked: A Semiotic Distinction for Concept-driven Interpretive Sociology *Wayne H. Brekhus* | 31 |
| 2 | Blumer, Weber, Peirce, and the Big Tent of Semiotic Sociology: Notes on Interactionism, Interpretivism, and Semiotics *J.I. (Hans) Bakker* | 52 |
| 3 | Collective Agency: A Semiotic View *Rein Raud* | 74 |
| 4 | Theorizing Side-directed Behavior *Paul McLean and Eunkyung Song* | 96 |
| 5 | Cultural Syntax and the Rules of Meaning-making: A New Paradigm for the Interpretation of Culture *Todd Madigan* | 118 |
| 6 | Memory, Cultural Systems, and Anticipation *Andrea Cossu* | 140 |
| 7 | Stigma-embedded Semiotics: Indexical Dilemmas of HIV across Local and Migrant Networks *Jorge Fontdevila* | 158 |
| 8 | Supremacy or Symbiosis? The Effect of Gendered Ideologies of the Transhuman versus Posthuman on Wearable Technology and Biodesign *Elizabeth Wissinger* | 181 |
| Index | | 205 |

# Series Editors' Preface: Interpretive Lenses in Sociology—On the Multidimensional Foundations of Meaning in Social Life[1]

Sociology is an interpretive endeavor. Whatever the approach taken to study and explain an aspect of social life—qualitative or quantitative, micro or macro—sociologists work to interpret their data to reveal previously unseen, or to clarify previously misunderstood, social forces. However, within the broad field of sociology, and under the purview of its kindred disciplines, there are many scholars who work to unpack the deep structures and processes that underlie the *meanings* of social life. These interpretive scholars focus on the ways that social meanings constitute the core structures of self and identity, the ways that individuals negotiate meanings to define their shared situations, and the collective meanings that bind people together into communities while also setting any given group or context apart from others. From this perspective, meaning underscores social mindsets and personal orientations in the world, as well as the solidarities and divisions that define the dynamics and mark the boundaries of our social standpoints and relationships. Furthermore, such scholars are concerned not only with how the individuals and groups they study actively make and remake the definitions that are central to their lives, as well as how those understandings influence their behaviors, but also how they seek to impact the world with their meaning-making processes. In this regard, meaning is of paramount significance to both the extraordinary moments and the routine circumstances of our lives.[2]

In their efforts to illuminate the deep social foundations of meaning, and to detail the very real social, political, and moral consequences that stem

---

[1] An extended series introduction is available for open access download at bristoluniversitypress.co.uk/interpretive-lenses-in-sociology. Shorter and slightly modified versions appear as prefaces to the different volumes of this series.

[2] On the centrality of meaning in interpretive social analysis, see Reed's (2011) important work on interpretation and knowledge, especially his discussions of the "interpretive epistemic mode" (pp. 89–121) and the "normative epistemic mode" (pp. 67–88).

from the ways people define and know the world around them, interpretive scholars explore the semiotic significance of social actions and interactions, narratives and discourses, experiences and events. In contrast to those who take a positivist or realist perspective and see the world—or, more precisely, argue that the world can be known—in a more direct or literal light,[3] they use various approaches and draw on different interpretive traditions to decipher their cases in order to better understand the deep social, cultural, and psychic foundations of the phenomena they study. From such interpretive perspectives, a fundamental part of any social phenomenon is not directly evident or visible. Rather, the core foundations of meaning underlying the cases scholars study need to be unpacked, analyzed, and interpreted—and then rearticulated—to comprehend their deeper essences.[4] And they do this work of interpretation from various angles and perspectives, using different "lenses." It is with such interpretive lenses, in sociology and beyond, that we concern ourselves here. How do the people we study make sense of the world? How do they cooperate with others to construct shared understandings, and how do such actors define their situations for various audiences? Furthermore, how do scholars understand their sense-making processes and interpret their actions and experiences? How do they get at the deep social forces, culture structures, and relationships underlying the topics and themes they study?[5] Finally, how do their interpretations allow scholars to construct new and powerful explanations of social phenomena? How do they "possess explanatory torque" with regard to various topics of widespread significance (Reed, 2011, p. 11; see also Garland, 2006, pp. 437–8)?

This is the perspective from which we organized a unique conference, The Roots and Branches of Interpretive Sociology: Cultural, Pragmatist, and Psychosocial Approaches, in Philadelphia, Pennsylvania, in August 2018. From this endeavor, we learned that many scholars were excited by our

---

[3] See Reed (2011, p. 52), especially on the "realist semiotic and the illusion of noninterpretation."

[4] Indeed, this is what Clifford Geertz (1973) meant when he called for "thick description" in ethnographic analysis.

[5] Alfred Schütz ([1932] 1967, pp. 205–6; 1970, p. 273) recognized the layers of interpretation we point to here when he argued: "The thought objects constructed by the social scientist … have to be founded upon the thought objects constructed by the common-sense thinking of [people], living their daily life within their social world. Thus, the constructs of the social sciences are, so to speak, constructs of the second degree, namely constructs of the constructs made by the actors on the social scene." Geertz (1973, p. 9) made a similar distinction when he argued "that what we call our data are really our own constructions of other people's constructions." Also see Reed (2017, pp. 29–31) on "interpreting interpretations." Such a distinction also informs the fundamental premises of psychoanalysis, as the analyst is always in the business of interpreting interpretations and unpacking layers of symbolism.

call to bring them to the table to discuss their interpretive lenses with one another. Many almost intuitively grasped the distinctions we made among traditions and camps in the field (the cultural, the pragmatist/interactionist, the psychosocial, and others) that could be gathered under the umbrella of a broader "interpretive" agenda in sociology. And why not? We make such distinctions between different camps, with their various theoretical and methodological traditions, when we teach. This is how we organize many of our journals, our professional societies and their sections, and other scholarly institutions. We also often use such categories to explain our scholarly identities. In line with these distinctions, qualitative interpretation has developed simultaneously along different paths and among a field of factional communities, and the proponents of these different camps make various claims to distinguish their respective approaches from others.

However, despite the fact that we use such distinctions to delineate our disciplinary field, they rarely sync neatly with the work scholars actually do when they interpret the cases, communities, and issues they study. Rather, in their practices of social research and in their acts of interpretation, scholars combine and integrate elements of different traditions and programs in various ways that help them to focus on and make sense of their experiences as scholars. In other words, the process of interpretation comes alive in the practice of research and, more particularly, in research situations that demand a range of theoretical and methodological tools to illuminate and articulate the social foundations of meaning central to the case at hand.[6] Thus, over the course of their work, scholars develop interpretive lenses that help them find answers to the questions that drive them. While this may not come as a surprise to many readers, we rarely interrogate or compare the nuances of these lenses explicitly.

The purpose of this series is to interrogate, explore, and demonstrate the various interpretive lenses that scholars use when they engage their areas of interest, their cases, and their research situations. Each volume is centered on a substantive topic (for example, religion, the body, or contentious memories) or a particular interpretive-analytic method (for example, semiotics or narrative analysis). The editors of each volume feature the work of scholars who approach their central topic using different interpretive lenses that are particularly relevant to that area of focus. They have asked each author to explicitly illustrate and reflect on two dimensions of interpretation in their work, and to explore the connections between them. First, they asked authors to address how the individuals and communities they study assign meanings and achieve shared understandings with regard to the core topic

---

[6] See also Tavory and Timmermans (2014, p. 35), who advocate engaging the process of research and interpretation armed with "multiple theoretical perspectives."

of their volume. In doing so, authors address the social and cultural forces at play in shaping how people understand their identities, experiences, and situations, as well as how they frame their accounts, motivations, and purposes while acting, communicating, and performing in the world. Second, volume editors asked contributing authors to explicitly reflect on their interpretive processes and approaches to unpacking the meanings of the social phenomena they study. Some authors present new material while others provide a reflexive overview of their research to date, but all illustrate and discuss the work of interpretation and the central significance of meaning. Such conscious reflection on our interpretive traditions and lenses—on how they shape our analytic foci (in terms of what cases we explore, at what levels of analysis, and with regard to which social actors) and the ways we find meaning in our cases—can illuminate underrecognized or unspoken choices we make in our work. Furthermore, it can expose blind spots and suggest new frameworks for dialogue among scholars. This reflexive dimension, along with the diversity of lenses featured together in each volume, is what makes this series unique. In this vein, and to these ends, we hope the volumes of this series will present arrays of interpretive lenses that readers can use while working to make sense of their own cases and to develop new perspectives of their own. In the process, we also hope to advance the dialogue about interpretation and meaning in the social sciences.

In this volume, Andrea Cossu and Jorge Fontdevila present a collection of essays written by a diverse group of scholars who use the tools of semiotics to elucidate the meanings of social life. As the collection makes evident, those who apply a semiotic analysis to address sociological questions might do so from formal, cultural, pragmatist, interactionist, narratological, feminist, materialist, poststructuralist, and other perspectives, as well as different combinations of these and other sociological frameworks. Furthermore, their essays variously illuminate themes relevant to cognitive sociology, the self and identity, theories of agency, communication, memory, emotion, network analysis, performance, and more. Above all, however, contributors to this volume show how they combine the various tools of semiotics and sociology in creative ways to develop unique interpretive lenses with which they reveal the important meanings of their cases. The sheer diversity of the interpretive lenses illustrated in these pages highlights the profound promise of a semiotic imagination for interpretive social analysis. Due to this diversity of perspectives and approaches, this volume outlines new and rich frameworks for dialogue around the themes that emerge in each chapter, frameworks that inform the arguments that Cossu and Fontdevila advance when they tie the collection together with their important introductory essay. Scholars and students working from the wide variety of perspectives that fall under the umbrella of interpretive sociology will find this book to be an important and refreshing statement on the ways we can use semiotics to explore and interpret the meanings of the social issues, interactions, events, and experiences that mark our lives. We are thrilled to feature this important book as part of our *Interpretive Lenses in Sociology* series.

*Thomas DeGloma*
*Hunter College and the Graduate Center, CUNY*

*Julie B. Wiest*
*West Chester University of Pennsylvania*

**References**

Garland, D. (2006) "Concepts of Culture in the Sociology of Punishment," *Theoretical Criminology*, 10(4): 419–47.

Geertz, C. (1973) "Thick Description: Toward an Interpretive Theory of Culture," in C. Geertz, *The Interpretation of Cultures*, New York: Basic Books, pp. 3–30.

Reed, I.A. (2011) *Interpretation and Social Knowledge: On the Use of Theory in the Human Sciences*, Chicago, IL: University of Chicago Press.

Reed, I.A. (2017) "On the Very Idea of Cultural Sociology," in C.E. Benzecry, M. Krause and I.A. Reed (eds) *Social Theory Now*, Chicago, IL: University of Chicago Press, pp. 18–41.

Schütz, A. (1967 [1932]) *The Phenomenology of the Social World*, Evanston, IL: Northwestern University Press.

Schütz, A. (1970) *On Phenomenology and Social Relations*, Chicago, IL: University of Chicago Press.

Tavory, I. and Timmermans. S. (2014) *Abductive Analysis: Theorizing Qualitative Research*, Chicago, IL: University of Chicago Press.

# Notes on Contributors

**J.I. (Hans) Bakker** is Professor of Sociology at the University of Guelph (Canada). His academic career involves applying Weberian insights to the study of colonialism and imperialism. Alongside his interest in neo-Weberian comparative historical sociology, he continued a focus on philosophical approaches to metatheory in the sciences. This focus led him to Peirce's semiotics, which then linked up with an interest in symbolic interaction and qualitative methods. He has published ten edited books, including *Rural Sociologists at Work* (Routledge, 2015) and *The Methodology of Political Economy* (Lexington Books, 2015), as well as over one hundred articles and reviews.

**Wayne H. Brekhus** is Chair and Professor of Sociology at the University of Missouri. His research analyzes social perception and constructions of social difference. He is author of *The Sociology of Identity: Authenticity, Multidimensionality, and Mobility* (Polity, 2020), *Culture and Cognition: Patterns in the Social Construction of Reality* (Polity, 2015), *Peacocks, Chameleons, Centaurs: Gay Suburbia and the Grammar of Social Identity* (University of Chicago Press, 2003), and co-editor of *The Oxford Handbook of Cognitive Sociology* (with Gabe Ignatow) (Oxford University Press, 2019) and *The Oxford Handbook of Symbolic Interactionism* (with Thomas DeGloma and William Ryan Force) (Oxford University Press, forthcoming).

**Andrea Cossu** is Associate Professor of Sociology at the University of Trento (Italy). He works mainly in the areas of sociological theory and cultural sociology. He is working on a project on the emergence of interpretive social science in the 1960s and 1970s. Previous publications include articles on semiotician Umberto Eco and social theory (*Thesis Eleven*, 2017), on Clifford Geertz and the concept of cultural system (*American Journal of Cultural Sociology*, 2021), and on the scripting of social distancing (*Poetics*, 2022).

**Jorge Fontdevila** is Professor of Sociology at California State University, Fullerton. He received a PhD in Sociology from Columbia University. He has conducted extensive socio-behavioral research among US populations affected by HIV/AIDS. His current research examines stigma-related semiotic barriers to HIV biomedical interventions among Latino gay men. He produces theoretical scholarship on semiotics and networks to understand HIV risky decision-making mechanisms. He has published widely in edited volumes and leading peer-reviewed journals, including *Sociological Theory, Sexualities, Poetics, Archives of Sexual Behavior, Social Theory & Health, Journal of Urban Health, Sex Roles, AIDS and Behavior, Journal of Phonetics*, and *Speech Communication*.

**Todd Madigan** is Visiting Assistant Professor of Sociology at the University of North Carolina, Greensboro. Much of his research is an exploration of how social narratives can both shape and shatter collective identity. Specifically, he has theorized what it means for a social group to be traumatized. Recent publications include "Epimilitary Culture: Vietnamese-American Literature and the Alternative to Paramilitary Culture," in B. West and T. Crosbie (eds) *Militarization and the Global Rise of Paramilitary Culture* (Springer, 2021) and "Theories of Cultural Trauma," in C. David and H. Meretoja (eds) *The Routledge Companion to Literature and Trauma* (Routledge, 2020).

**Paul McLean** is Professor of Sociology at Rutgers University. His interests include social networks, comparative-historical sociology, political sociology, and cultural sociology. In work on Renaissance Florence and early modern Poland, he has explored connections among multiple social networks (marriages, contracts, political patronage), explaining how internetwork relationships cascade to catalyze significant social and political change. His published work includes *The Art of the Network* (Duke, 2007) and *Culture in Networks* (Polity, 2017), plus articles in journals such as the *American Journal of Sociology, Social Networks, Poetics*, the *American Journal of Cultural Sociology*, and the *Journal of Modern History*.

**Rein Raud** is Professor of Asian and Cultural Studies in the School of Humanities at Tallinn University (Estonia). His research interests are broad, ranging from comparative and process philosophy to cultural theory, social ontology, and semiotics. His most recent books include *Being in Flux: A Post-Anthropocentric Ontology of the Self* (Polity, 2021) and *Asian Worldviews: Religions, Philosophies, Political Theories* (Wiley-Blackwell, 2021).

**Eunkyung Song** is Lecturer in Data Analytics and Computational Social Science at the University of Massachusetts, Amherst. Her research interests include social movements, cultural sociology, and relational inequality, in addition to computational text analysis and social network analysis. Her work has been published in *Applied Network Science*. She earned her PhD in Sociology from Rutgers with a project that examines how digital interactions shape collective action such as mass protests. She is currently working with sociologists and law school professors on a project that examines the impact of networking on diversity and relational inequality in law school.

**Elizabeth Wissinger** is Professor of Sociology at City University of New York, the Graduate Center and BMCC. Her research focuses on technology, fashion, and embodiment. Her book *This Year's Model: Fashion, Media, and the Making of Glamour* (NYU Press, 2015) examines media technologies and embodiment, including "glamour labor," work to make one's physical presence resemble one's highly filtered and edited presence online. She has published articles on cultural, aesthetic and affective labor, celebrity culture, and wearable technology. Currently, she is working on a monograph exploring how the worlds of fashion and biodesign might fruitfully combine in the design of wearable technology for every body.

# Introduction: Interpretive Sociology and the Semiotic Imagination

*Andrea Cossu and Jorge Fontdevila*

Perhaps we are, somewhere, the deep impulse which generates semiosis. And yet we recognize ourselves only as semiosis in progress, signifying systems and communicational processes. (Eco, 1984, p. 45)

Like many tales of interdisciplinarity, the one of the encounter between sociology and semiotics has its share of multiple and surprising beginnings, abrupt separations, and fights about boundaries and primacy. Indeed, sometimes the relationship between the two disciplines could be taken as an exemplar case of everything that goes wrong when disciplines get into mutual contact. Since we, as editors of this volume, write from the point of view of a double fascination—with sociology and semiotics, simultaneously—the point is how to achieve some degree of cross-disciplinary integration, despite the fact that the relationship can be often characterized as "ambivalent," "frustrating," and yet overall "exciting."

Behind those difficulties—and that is a convenient starting point—lie indeed very deep theoretical and conceptual reasons, not least because both semiotics and sociology have always aimed very high, and very ambitiously, at reaching some *intradisciplinary* understanding of key features of social life. Semiotics often proclaimed its capacity to unlock the mystery of the possibility of communication. In turn, sociology made an equally ambitious and sometimes unrealistic promise to reach an understanding of the possibility and reality of the social, in terms of its mechanisms for the production of order and, simultaneously, change. Both gave for themselves a mission that was larger than life, and it is no surprise, then, that in many of their incarnations both disciplines have been perceived to have failed—and yet, sometimes, there's no success like failure.

As semiotics and sociology gave up on their "imperialistic" (Eco, 1976) attitude and aspirations, they were ready to face each other and to assess more equanimously the nature of their convergence, which was at times very implicit and subtle. The rise of interpretive social science (Rabinow and Sullivan, 1979) made the encounter very explicit, though, and "semiotic" (as an adjective) and "semiotics" (as a discipline) not only fashionable terms, but also the pillars of a research program. In many regards, what drove sociologists (some of them, in the good company of equally interdisciplinary historians, anthropologists, philosophers, and literary theorists) toward semiotics was, at the same time, the familiarity of the problems that semiotics attempted to face, and a certain family resemblance, which had deep roots in the history of sociology as a discipline. A symbolic interactionist, well versed in the sophistication of the James-Mead-Blumer lineage, could be equipped to explore the parallel, more esoteric, and sometime exasperating models developed by William James' fellow Charles Sanders Peirce, and find in them, as Norbert Wiley (2006) has argued, one of the problematic sources and classics of sociology. Functionalists of all sorts, back when they were almost hegemonic in American social science and British social anthropology, could draw on their Durkheimian premises and trace parallels with Saussure's linguistics. They could also subscribe to the attempts to formalize it even more by a polymath like Roman Jakobson—incidentally, both one of Levi-Strauss's co-authors and Talcott Parsons's close colleague—able to shape in decisive ways the latter's thinking in the early 1960s. When the "cultural turn" started to emerge, with all its attention to symbols, rituals, classifications, narratives, and texts, semiotics had already been discovered and digested, and yet—in that crucial conjuncture of the 1960s and 1970s—semiotics and its conceptual offspring offered a way out not really from systemic, abstract analysis, but from the formalism it entailed.

Yet, if this story (or set of stories) is reliable—and, under many points of view, it is—then one can wonder how many possible points of convergence semiotics and sociology had in the past, even before the cultural turn, its many threads, and the backlash against it. To the extent that reconstructing this story often involves some kind of counterfactual history (what would have happened if Peirce had been more secure in an academic position with the other pragmatists? Would semiotics at Harvard have been more integrated with sociology had Levi-Strauss accepted a position there in the early 1950s?), ifs and thens abound. And yet, one has the feeling that the many potential semiotic turns in sociology were lost, and what the discipline ended up with was an uneasy configuration, in which many contributions from semiotics and neighboring approaches (from structuralism and poststructuralism, from formal pragmatism to less formal hermeneutics) came into the picture all at once, producing a deflagration that was very hard to handle.

In many regards, each of these encounters was filtered by the then current sociological perspectives and resulted in the production of "sub-disciplinary avatars" of semiotics, images of other disciplines that are established "by sociologists for sociological consumption" (Lizardo, 2014, p. 985). Practices, methods, ideas, and approaches were reworked to fit the interests and the language of a particular intellectual community, an interesting way of practicing a largely intradisciplinary form of interdisciplinarity while being largely resistant to dialogue with the discipline from where scholars (in this case, sociologists) have imported their ideas.

It takes two to tango, though, and semiotics has often done its part willingly, accused by its own practitioners of certain imperialistic attitudes vis-à-vis other disciplines. Indeed, while there is not an avatar that could be unmistakably described as pushing toward a "semiotic" sociology (although the label itself has been sometimes proposed: see Rochberg-Halton, 1986; Heiskala, 2003, 2014, 2021), within the broad domain of semiotics we find plenty: cultural semiotics (Torop, 1999; Posner, 2003; Lorusso, 2014), social semiotics, sociosemiotics, the semiotics of culture, and the like. When it goes "social" or "cultural," however, semiotics is more interested in the analysis of social artifacts or texts than it is in the process of social life in its sociality and not just in its textuality, and only in rare instances it approaches—albeit almost asymptotically—the core questions that constitute sociology as a discipline.

Perhaps the most relevant distinction on this aspect—one crucial in the definition of the intellectual space at the crossroads between semiotics and sociology—was the one famously proposed by Roland Barthes, who raised the question of the distinction between a more semiotically informed "socio-logic," and the more traditional, science-like methods and outlook of sociology. Barthes' distinction, indeed, was an attempt at christening a discipline or a subdiscipline, and not surprisingly he did that by establishing differences and oppositions. Sociology, his strawman, was in itself a conservative discipline in epistemological as well as in broadly political terms. Ironically, he perceived sociology as a science that dealt with "content" and institutions, while his more semiological socio-logic was interested in the first instance with forms and abstractions. Echoes of this structuralist sensibility can be witnessed often in the ways sociology constructed its own avatar of semiotics, particularly as it appropriated in many ways the promise of structuralism, to define and retrieve an invariant logic that, with a theoretical twist that often equaled to walking a tightrope, came dangerously close to that all-purpose—and thus ill-defined—term on which both sociology and semiotics thrived and failed: structure. It was while chasing the dream of structure—and realizing quite soon that the effort was impractical—that sociology had its closest encounter with semiotics, particularly in one of its most abstract and formalist manifestations. As Charles Lemert (2012, p. 423) writes, "Where sociologists have taken an interest in classical semiotics, they have tended to select such binary concepts of meaning as signifier/signified, speech/language, or performance/competence."

In Lemert's understanding, sociologists have also created a hierarchy within each binary (in this case, a hierarchy centered on the relevance of the signified, of language, of competence), because it seemingly enabled them to place culture (in the form of cultural or meaning structures) at the same explanatory level of social structures, making abstraction and generalization possible and thereby having—seemingly but mistakenly—more leverage in the production of what John Levi Martin (2011) has identified as theory "in the third person." Semiotics, in turn, also went a long way toward the definition of a third-person, systematic palace, to the point that it— particularly in the tradition of structuralist semiotics—eschewed pragmatics and brought any consideration of the first person (a prominent sociosemiotic theme in the Peircean tradition, where it is supplemented by the dimension of dialogue) under the more reassuring safety net of textuality, where action could be understood as embedded in a *textualized* system of action or could be analyzed, as Paul Ricoeur (1973) famously claimed, as a "text," insofar as it was "meaningful."

Yet, where do we stand now, beyond the age of text and interpretation, and beyond the optimism that characterized semiotics' and sociology's rise to prominence? Sociology is still pursuing its integration with semiotics from the point of view of the avatar it built a while ago—codes, narratives, webs, signs, and symbols. Is the avatar sufficient to achieve interdisciplinarity or should we, on the contrary, take a decisive step toward an as yet underdeveloped theoretical and conceptual shift?

An important goal of this volume is to explore how semiotics can provide innovative analytical tools to refine sociological research and theory. We believe that productive cross-fertilizations between semiotics and sociology have much to contribute to deeper understandings of challenging questions that always seem to recur in our discipline, such as the questions of emergence, interpretation, or habituation, among others. Although some fields, for example linguistic anthropology (Mertz, 2007), have productively incorporated into their research programs semiotic models based on language's indexical-contextual features, sociology as a multidisciplinary field still needs to engage with semiotic mediation more rigorously. Much sociological research aims to explain meaning-making processes in social life (Pachucki and Breiger, 2010; Spillman, 2020), but often with limited understanding of the multilayered and subtle ways that signs—the vehicles of meaning—"signify" and are communicated among social actors or institutions.

In this regard, we believe that a sophisticated understanding of semiotic processes and mechanisms can provide sociologists with key analytical tools to better explain the constitutive nature of signification in the production of social life. For instance, as discussed later, the full significance of the Peircean indexical sign as the metapragmatic context-making nexus linking culture and practice is still undertheorized in sociology. Thus, it is vital that sociology engages with semiotics rigorously to problematize wanting structuralist-derived or symbolic models of meaning and contextualize cultural practice in wider understandings of reflexive linguistic and non-linguistic semiosis (processes that anthropologist Paul Kockelman, 2006, has aptly described as constitutive of the "semiotic stance"). The aim of this volume is precisely to open spaces to explore some of these issues and bridge gaps through rich conversations between semiotics and sociology.

Sociocultural and biological systems are—unlike inorganic systems—high informational systems with stochastic, nonlinear, and path-dependent histories (Prevosti, 1994; Krakauer, 2011). These systems require complex communications among its component parts to self-organize and adapt to their environments. But sociocultural systems are not simply a more elaborate version of biological systems and thus cannot be reduced to them. Whereas biological systems accumulate historical information across generations in genomes primarily via random variation and natural selection, human social systems accumulate historical information in intergenerational cultures primarily through the semiotics of language. Thus, a natural language—with its self-referential, open-ended capabilities and reflexive context-making mechanisms—is our species' *differentia specifica* that unleashes the next emergent leap in systems complexity. As Harrison White (1992, p. 211) put it, "polymer molecules don't tell stories about their encounters or strategize in those encounters. Human [social] molecules do, but in ways shaped by their social gel."

In this light, we contend that a sophisticated theory of human communication must be at the center of our understanding of social emergence and complexity (Sawyer, 2005). Moreover, such theory must draw on complex semiotic knowledge, given that actual human communication depends on processes of signification at multiple and interconnected metalevels. Ultimately, we claim that human semiosis is not transparent or epiphenomenal but highly constitutive of social practices and institutions. As Eco (1984, p. 45) insightfully puts it in this chapter's epigraph, humans not only generate semiosis but recognize themselves as semiosis in progress through historically changing signifying systems and communicational processes. In short, to lay solid foundations to sociocultural explanations, it is important that sociology turns to semiotic insights on the complex nature and use of signs and, more specifically, linguistic signs. In line with Duranti's (2003, p. 343) remarks on the future of anthropology, we believe that a sociology without a sophisticated grasp of language semiotics, or semiotics in general, is bound to produce "a naïve understanding of communication."

A naive understanding that takes language for granted and identifies it—and culture by extension—with crude notions of "code" or "discourse."

Following Heiskala (2014) and others, deeper semiotic insights emerge by integrating the two main traditions of semiotic studies, namely structuralist semiology (Saussurean tradition) and pragmatist semiotics (Peircean tradition). These two traditions offer foundational analytical tools to explain signification processes. On the one hand, from the Saussurean tradition, we learn that signification occurs through self-referentiality; that is, when signs "relate" to each other via rules of contrasts and differences within a syntactico-semantic system that is nonetheless open to its pragmatic consequences, from language and ritual to other cultural artifacts. On the other, from the Peircean tradition, we know that signification also occurs when some signs (indexes) reflexively "anchor" such self-referential systems in pragmatic contexts of use. These two features of signification—self-referentiality and indexicality—constitute the quintessential building blocks of meaning-making and communication in social life. They form the basis of the constitutive power of language to produce more elaborate and layered meanings, including metaphor, myth, and narrative (Taylor, 2016). We discuss these two features in turn.

## Signification as self-referential differences

Against commonsensical traditions that postulate meaning as correspondence exemplified by Saint Augustine's nomenclaturism, Ferdinand de Saussure (1959 [1916]) transposed the paradigm of linguistic reference to the study of grammar. In this view, the linguistic code no longer acquired referential sense by correspondence to pre-existent reality but by self-referential relations in a system of signs. Although the Saussurean sign is still a "standing for" relation (*aliquid stat pro aliquo*), semiotic mediation is not between the external "thing" and its "name" but within a syntactico-semantic system that articulates mental concepts (signifieds) to sound-images (signifiers). Each sign is a formal dyad that is drawn from relational sets of signifieds and signifiers where sound-images stand for concepts. In Saussure's (1959 [1916], pp. 111–112) own words, thought and understanding without such signs would be a "shapeless and indistinct mass … a vague, uncharted nebula."

Moreover, the bond articulating signifier with signified is not naturally motivated but arbitrarily established by social convention. For most words in a language, there is no inherent connection between a sound-image (for example, the sound "house") and the concept it stands for (the idea or schema of a house). This renders language unique among many other semiotic processes. In short, meaning—Saussure defines it as the sign's value—is not bestowed from the external world but carved off in patterns of signifier and signified relational orders according to oppositions and differences at play in a particular language. So, at the phonological level, for example, some languages have a grammatical opposition between signifier [s] and its absence that creates a system where only units and pluralities are habitually distinguished by speakers. Other languages can habitually distinguish among units, dyads, and pluralities by interplay of three distinct signifiers (see Duranti, 1994, for the Samoan language).

Similarly, the Boasian school of American anthropology moved from reference to self-reference—from lexicon to grammar as the source of meaning (Boas, 1911; Sapir, 1924; Whorf, 1995 [1941]). Boas, like Saussure, claimed that referential meaning could be fully grasped only within an overarching grammatical system. These scholars argued that different grammars around the world tended to produce distinctive local forms of thought. However, such linguistic relativism (often called the "Sapir–Whorf hypothesis") never claimed that language determines thought in utterly incommensurable ways. It simply postulated the weaker claim that different grammars tended to "habituate" ways of looking at reality below the threshold of speakers' awareness. This in turn created referential projections onto the world that native speakers of the language attributed to the nature of their outer experience—folk ontologies. For Whorf (1995 [1941]), this "objectification" of our outer experience—for example, form and substance distinctions, time as linear or cyclical, causality as a real noun, or humans essentialized as male—grew from the complex interplay of covert and overt grammatical categories that native speakers often took for granted but which could be reflexively uncovered with analytical effort.

Saussure understood language (*la langue*) as a sort of "collective consciousness" of signs and their rules passed across generations within a community of speakers. Language as a social fact followed its own objective laws of transformation, which no individual could modify by their speech (*parole*) alone without risking severe communication breakdown. In other words, in Saussurean linguistics, there was no room for private language. He also thought that his linguistic model could be used to study other systems of signs, such as ritual, forms of politeness, military signals, and so on. He called this field *semiology*, a science "that studies the life of signs within society" and examines "what constitutes signs, [and] what laws govern them" (Saussure, 1959 [1916], p. 16).

However, the problem with semiology as a science of semiotic systems is that Saussure never developed it beyond language. Later schools, under the umbrella term of "structuralism," adopted Saussurean linguistics as a model for their semiotic research strategies to study culture. However, significant misunderstandings led these schools to downplay Saussure's concept of language as arbitrary convention and to overemphasize its mentalistic, universalistic, or even unconscious overtones (Levi-Strauss, 1963; Barthes, 1972; Lacan, 1977 [1966]). The outcome was a problematic schism between semiotic notions of competence and performance that ultimately lost sight of the empirical relationships that link grammars to their local practices.

Moreover, Saussure's model—in addition to relations of articulation between signifiers and signifieds—includes other sets of relations of difference that signify, namely associative and syntagmatic relations. Associative relations render meaning to a sign by relating it to a set of others *in absentia* that could be used instead; for example, "his" acquires value because it can be used instead of "hers" or "yours," and so on, in the associative set of possessive pronouns. Syntagmatic relations render meaning to a sign *in presentia* of other signs in sequential or co-present patterns; for example, the order of nominal and verbal inflected relations in a sentence. A syntactico-semantic grammar emerges out of the rules and conventions that structure such syntagmatic and associative relations within a general system of signifiers and signifieds.

Unfortunately, many structuralist schools following the Saussurean model misunderstood that associative relations "signify" only when contained in closed paradigmatic sets with a finite number of elements (Barthes, 1994 [1964]), or when reduced to binary cognitive operations (Levi-Strauss, 1963). But more sophisticated readings claim that Saussure never theorized associative relations as closed or binary sets. Heiskala (2014, p. 40), for instance, interprets Saussure to explicitly characterize associative relations as "infinite and radiating in several directions from any given term in a way that produced a situationally varying network in constant flux." In fact, few semiotic sets of associative relations become closed codes in social life (traffic lights are among the few, for example), most other associative sets typically undergo relentless historical change (an aspect that Saussure himself approached in the *Course* in the sections on diachronic linguistics, but which did not enter the post-Saussurean, largely structuralist, canon).

For example, with respect to gender associative relations of the early 21st century, the open-ended nature of their signifier/signified set is illustrated by recent adoptions of more fluid units such as non-binary or queer identities and expressions, besides the traditional man and woman. In turn, new signifier sets are being reconstituted and pragmatically deployed to avoid marking grammatical gender in English, such as the use of "they" or "their" for the third-person singular. Needless to say, this associative flux historically shifts the semiotic boundaries between man and woman traditional signifieds.

Further theorizing the complexities of associative relations among semiotic processes, Eco (1984) characterized their inescapable open-endedness by introducing the analogy of the encyclopedia, as a relational net of units of meaning that is endlessly connected, followed from path to path, sometimes with dead-ends, others with turnarounds. This associative net is a form of collective knowledge that is never fully available in its totality to a community of speakers but only to local networks with partial knowledges of the net's associative relations. As discussed later, due to their radical open-endedness, associative relations become relentlessly reinterpreted by speakers via abductive inferential framings to make sense of their semiotic shifts. Moreover, to visualize such associative net, Eco also adopts the imagery of the "rhizome" from Deleuze and Guattari (cited in Eco, 1984, p. 81). In his own words:

> No one can provide a global description of the whole rhizome; not only because the rhizome is multidimensionally complicated, but also because its structure changes through the time; moreover, in a structure in which every node can be connected with every other node, there is also the possibility of contradictory inferences. (Eco, 1984, p. 82)

## Signification as reflexive indexicalities

Inasmuch as syntactico-semantic theories of self-referential meaning constitute a breakthrough with respect to simplistic correspondence theories of denotational meaning, the emphasis of the Saussurean or Boasian traditions on grammar leaves out other meaningful functions of language. For instance, language can be reflexively used to index context and segments of narrative events, talk about itself and describe its structure, report directly or indirectly other speakers' utterances, indicate shifting speakers' roles, label the mutable existence of entities through so-called "proper names," among others. Language is unique because of these reflexive capacities serving as guides for speakers to interpret and frame their own utterances.

Moreover, although language's most extraordinary semiotic property is perhaps its capacity to describe and predicate about the world—a semiosis of open-ended reference—such semantic capacity attains full operational meaning in social life only if anchored in real contexts of use (situations and circumstances, scenes and occasions). In this sense, language as the semiotic system par excellence is about meeting human communication. However, it is worth noting for our sociological purposes that what language communicates is not simply predication about the world but, most significantly, the nature and meaning of the social relationships that constitute the speech event itself. We thus turn to language's constitutive and reflexive mechanisms to examine another important feature of signification, namely how linguistic and other signs through their indexical capacities produce social context and sociality.

In this light, a turning point in our understanding of semiosis, and specifically language semiosis, occurred when pragmatist Charles S. Peirce (1931–1958) explored the logical triadic nature of signs and signification. In this model, semiotic mediation is conceptualized—in contrast to Saussure's dyadic signifier/signified—as a triadic process, including a sign ("representamen," that is, an expression) that relates an object (whatever the sign stands for, be it physical or mental object) to an interpretant (the mechanical, affective, or cognitive effect created in a mind by the sign in its standing relationship to its object). In his own words:

> A sign, or representamen, is something which stands to somebody for something in some respect or capacity. It addresses somebody, that is, it creates in the mind of that person an equivalent sign, or perhaps a more developed sign. The sign which it creates I call the interpretant of the first sign. The sign stands for something, its object. (Peirce, 1938–1951, CP 2.228)

Two important consequences follow from Peirce's definition. First, according to this model, the three components of semiosis (sign, object, interpretant) enter an iterative dynamic by which interpretants become signs, even more developed signs, to further signifying triads. Every signifying triad creates an interpretant, which then triggers another signifying triad and so on, and thus a process of unlimited semiosis theoretically proceeds ad infinitum in this model. Thus, interpretants become chains of signs to further interpretants. As Eco (1979, p. 184), paraphrasing Peirce, expressed it, "meaning is the translation of a sign into another sign." However, as discussed later, this infinite regress of unlimited semiosis becomes typically interrupted by the practical demands of everyday life, including cognitive limitations and intersubjective habits.

Second, the inclusion of the "object" in Peirce's model of semiotic mediation brings to the fore motivational aspects to the sign that are key to surpass the more mentalistic limitations of Saussure's arbitrary sign as disconnected from an external world—including overcoming the structuralist derivations that in Cartesian dualist mode severed linguistic and cultural meaning from actual practice. Moreover, it opens more refined ways of classifying signs according to their level of arbitrariness versus motivation. Thus, signs in Peirce's model can relate to their "immediate" objects by arbitrary rule (symbol), analogy or similarity (icon), or spatiotemporal contiguity (index).[1] This latter capacity of signs—indexicality—constitutes the basis for the constitutive and contextual function of language in sociocultural practice (Duranti, 2003; Mertz, 2007; Fontdevila, 2010).

---

[1] Peirce (1938–1951, CP 2.228) further argues that the sign stands for an object "not in all respects, but in reference to some sort of idea ... called the ground of the representamen." This "ground" is an elementary pre-framing cognition, part of a universe of discourse, that selects "relevant attributes" of the "dynamic object" (that is, the object in itself) to constitute the perceived "immediate object," which then triggers the semiotic mediation via the sign to the interpretant (Eco, 1994, p. 28; Cossu, 2017).

## Context and interpretation, habit and power, culture and cognition

We believe it is important for sociologists to acquire a sophisticated understanding of semiotics by integrating these two main traditions, Saussurean and Peircean. Semiotic analyses can then shed light on challenging metatheoretical problems that seem to recur in our sociological field. In this regard, we now turn to three open sociological problems that we believe can be illuminated by productive cross-fertilization across the boundaries of semiotics and sociology. These are the problems of context and interpretation, habit and power, and culture and cognition. We contend that a deeper understanding of semiotics informing a theory of human communication in social life is thus key to explaining some of these challenging problems.

### *Context-making and indexical interpretation*

Most applications of semiotics to sociology have focused on the analysis of cultural texts or artifacts, rather than the everyday life production of ongoing sociality. Hence, we propose that sociology engage with semiotic mediation rigorously—in particular, with language's contextual-indexical semiosis—to understand the production of everyday sociality in all its complexity. As indicated earlier, a close reading of Peirce's triadic model of semiotic mediation (sign, object, interpretant) can provide critical insights on how social context and meaning are produced in social life. The "object" element of the triadic model opens ways of classifying signs according to their level of arbitrariness versus motivation. By expanding the sign to include motivational aspects and not just arbitrary rule, Peirce opens the door to theorizing more elaborate sources of meaning-making in social life, from analogy (for example, metaphor) and iconicity to indexes and discourse markers. For Peirce, the elementary unit of meaning is still the sign, but "arbitrary" signs à la Saussure (what Peirce calls "symbols") are only a subset of all signs and signification processes.

In this connection, it is important to highlight the indexical capacity of certain linguistic and paralinguistic signs to signify context by spatiotemporal contiguity. Indexicality is crucial to the constitutive and context-making function of language semiosis that produces human sociality. Unlike symbols that denote, indexes are more or less grammaticalized elements that "point" to features of the social and physical world and that speakers use reflexively to lay out the contextual parameters of their interactions. From deixis (for example, this, now, here), pronouns (for example, I, you), verb tenses to entire code-switchings, registers, deference and status markers, prosodic tones, silences, and so on, indexes anchor the linguistic code in practical contexts of use. For instance, two people switching to first-name basis index (constitute) a "new context" of status proximity, or co-workers switching from slang to formal register index resumption of "professional context." Thus, indexes enable speakers to contextualize their social ties and relative footings, making semiotic processes fully operational in communicative practice (Fontdevila and White, 2013).[2] Silverstein (1976) claims that indexes anchor the syntactico-referential system of language in meaningful contexts of everyday life by providing relevant cues and redundancies to interpret communicative messages in interaction. Thus, the indexical "analysis of speech behavior—in the tradition extending from Peirce to Jakobson—allows us to describe the real linkage of language to culture, and perhaps the most important aspect of the 'meaning' of speech" (Silverstein, 1976, p. 11).[3]

Moreover, language is unique among semiotic systems because of its reflexive capacity to speak about itself. Silverstein (1976, 1993), following Jakobson's (1960) insight on the ubiquitous metalingual function, claims that language's reflexivity is primarily metapragmatic. In other words, most metalingual activities are not just about semantic understanding (glossing, translation, propositional truth claims) but about the (appropriate) pragmatic uses of language in social interaction (see Wittgenstein, 1953, for language as social tool). With variable awareness, we always use language metapragmatically, that is, reflexively, to index and constitute our social ties and contexts. For instance, to create a context of deference, rather than indexing it via a direct imperative (for example, "shut the window! it's cold in here), we metapragmatically index it via indirect speech to signify respect for the hearer's autonomy to act otherwise (for example, "it's kind of chilly, could that window be broken?"). As Sawyer (2005, p. 182) states in relation to social emergence and complexity, "speakers use the metapragmatic function of language to reflexively communicate about the emergent process and flow of the encounter or about the ground rules and the communication itself."

---

[2] Linguistic indexes are classified according to the degree in which their pragmatic use "presupposes" or "creates" the context that is being singled out (Silverstein, 1976). Many languages, like Javanese, include deference indexes that "create" status differences by stylistic and grammatical switches (Brown and Gilman, 1960, for tu/vous pronouns of address; Irvine, 1985). Others, like some Aboriginal languages, switch lexicon without changing referential content simply to index the presence within earshot of a mother-in-law or affine (Dixon, 1972).

[3] It is worth clarifying that indexes in this sociolinguistic sense depart somewhat from the indexical "secondness" sense that Peirce theorized as two events or relations "naturally" associated by contiguity (for example, smoke signaling fire). Sociolinguistic indexes are signs that do include aspects of "thirdness," in that they are embedded in semiotic conventions of use, even though they signify context by spatiotemporal contiguity rather than denotation. Moreover, certain grammaticalized indexes do contain semantico-referential traces (for example, indexical shifters "that" and "this" denote distal and proximal relations, respectively, across any context).

A semiotic tradition that offers important analytical tools to understand the reflexive and indexical metapragmatics of social life is the one that coalesced around Russian scholar Mikhail Bakhtin (Volosinov, 1973 [1929]; Bakhtin, 1981; Holquist, 1990). Drawing on Marx's early philosophy of praxis, this Russian school strongly criticized the Saussurean notion of language as an abstract system removed from social practices. Instead of the isolated "monological" utterance of a passive mind, they proposed that utterances are always organized "dialogically" embedded in an intricate social matrix. Any speaker's utterance already involves juxtaposing multiple "voices" (or points of view) drawn from different social spheres. Such *heteroglossia* is expressed in social life via utterances that are always interpenetrated by various forms of social "consciousness" in a rich dialogue (Bakhtin, 1981).[4]

Moreover, utterances anticipate the active understanding by someone and hence involve "addressivity." As Bakhtin (1986, p. 95) explains:

> both the composition and, in particular, the style of the utterance depend on those to whom the utterance is addressed, how the speaker senses and imagines his addressees, and the force of their effect on the utterance. Each speech genre in each area of speech communication has its own typical conception of the addressee, and this defines it as a genre.

Thus, it is not the sentence but rather the heteroglossic utterance that is the basic unit of communication, produced with metapragmatic understanding of others in the horizon, capable of coordinating addresser and addressee to accomplish the tasks of the social.

For this semiotic tradition, grammar and stylistics, although analytically distinct, should not be reduced to one another but "organically" combined in their study. Any grammatical choice is ultimately a stylistic act, in turn influenced by the language's repertoire of patterns that over time have assumed grammatical shape. Change in language always occurs at the boundaries between grammar and stylistics. Boundaries that are fluid and ambiguous "because of the very mode of existence of language, in which, simultaneously, some forms are undergoing grammaticalization while others are undergoing degrammaticalization" in choices of styles and genres according to the indexical metapragmatics of social context (Volosinov,

---

[4] For Bakhtin, the novel, a historically late form of literary production that incorporates a multiplicity of genres—voices—in its composition, is considered to be the quintessential expression of the modern consciousness.

1973 [1929], p. 126; see also Fontdevila and White, 2013, for institutional rhetorics through heteroglossic voicing).[5]

In short, indexical devices, stylistic or otherwise, are key to "metacommunicate" ongoing social context. Any message uttered in face-to-face encounters signals a meta-framing context by providing indexical cues (context-markers) to speakers to discern at what level of abstraction the interaction should be interpreted. Thus, for Bateson (1985 [1955], p. 188), "any message, which either explicitly or implicitly defines a frame, *ipso facto* gives the receiver instructions or aids in his attempt to understand the messages included within the frame." Some examples of indexical markers that metacommunicate and shape social context are pronouns of address to index hierarchies, linguistic register switches to index identities or tasks, irony via tone emphasis to index intended opposite meaning. This reflexive capacity to interpret metapragmatic indexicalities in shaping context is actually the capacity to understand the "meaning" of the interaction—the phenomenological question of relevance, "what is going on?" (see Gumperz, 1982, for contextualization cues; Goffman, 1974; Lucy, 1993). Meaning in sociality is thus accomplished, among other things, through indexical switches of context-markers across metacommunicative levels. And these levels are essentially heteroglossic, anchored ultimately in speakers' multiple social spheres and networks.

It is worth noting that any contextual interpretation that emerges from indexical switches is inferred, albeit incompletely, via hard phenomenological work of abductive reasoning. Introduced by Peirce to explain semiotic interpretation, abductive reasoning refers to forms of cognitive inference by which deductive rules and formal principles become reflexively linked to local features of interactive settings that are known inductively from everyday life experience (Peirce, 1931–1958; Tavory and Timmermans, 2014). Thus, effective communication in social life does not proceed just by following automatic rules of grammar codes but also by inductive knowledge of the practical meanings of a situation.

In everyday life, these contrasting levels of abstraction, deductive and inductive, become integrated and negotiated via abductive inference during the performance of speech. As Eco (1984, p. 43) insightfully stated, "we deal both with language and with every other kind of sign by implementing inferential processes … The understanding of signs is not

---

[5] The legacy of the Bakhtin school, with its emphasis on heteroglossic and stylistic indexical devices to create social meaning in context, is evident in a body of research known as "ethnopoetics" and performance-based studies (Bauman and Briggs, 1990). This research takes seriously Jakobson's insights on the pervasive poetic function of language in everyday practices to index metamessages that may be quite tangential to an utterance's actual referential content.

a mere matter of recognition (of a stable equivalence); it is a matter of *interpretation*."[6] In this Peircean abductive view, semiosis is ultimately not about relations of equivalence (p ≡ q) between expression and content—perhaps equivalence only works for decoding simple codes—but about relations of inference ("*if* p, *then* q") (Desogus, 2012).[7] In other words, speakers do not passively decode ongoing utterances against a backdrop of culturally reified contexts but reflexively use their own verbal and nonverbal interactions as indexes to infer and constitute such contexts (Duranti and Goodwin, 1992). Social context is never separate from talk. Social meaning is context-dependent, but "speaking" itself via indexicalities is what creates the context that ultimately shapes the nature of speakers' social relations. Moreover, contextual indexing occurs in real time and so "the mechanisms by which relational information is signaled are inherently ambiguous, i.e., subject to multiple interpretations … In conversation, such ambiguities are negotiated in the course of interaction" (Gumperz, 1982, p. 208).

In this light, we argue that a semiotic analysis of context-making must problematize structural models of culture as an abstract symbolic system (*langue*), and recognize that culture and language are largely contextual, indexical, and metapragmatic. As Silverstein (1976, p. 54) put it, "we need invoke 'symbolism' for a certain modality of speech alone; the vast residue of language is culture, and culture is [indexically] pragmatic." Finally, it is worth pointing out that since semiotic understanding is not just about decoding but ultimately an act of abductive interpretation, interpretive sociology has a crucial role to play in uncovering complex semiotic processes that produce sociality. Interpretive sociology with its extensive toolkit of qualitative methodologies, for example participant observation, grounded theory, in-depth interviewing, is ideally positioned to analyze the semiosis of context-making in everyday life (Timmermans and Tavory, 2012; Lamont and Swidler, 2014), as well as the way both lay agents and specialists employ semiotic, inferential capacity to produce their own premises, conclusions, and more or less sophisticated "theories" (Swedberg, 2010).

---

[6] According to Bianchi (2015, p. 116), Eco's semiotic "shift from code to encyclopedia marks the shift from a static concept of decoding to a dynamic concept of abduction." This move brings together semantics and pragmatics to avoid the impasse provoked by a view that dismisses situational meaning (for example, the dictionary) and another that claims an unlimited range of meanings (for example, Derrida's "deconstructive drift").

[7] Thus, "interpretation is always an inferential act, what changes is only the degree of automatism and the certainty of the conclusion" (Proni, 2015, p. 17).

*Habit formation and power*

As explained previously, semiosis is not simply about decoding relations of equivalence but ultimately an inferential act of interpretation. Peirce (1931–1958) realized that during the process of abductive inference, the three components of semiotic signification (sign, object, interpretant) enter an iterative dynamic by which interpretants become signs, even more elaborate signs, to further signifying triads, in an infinite regress that, while potentially endless, stops in the face of the practical demands of everyday life and thinking. For Peirce, this potential for unlimited semiosis of interpretants becomes eventually albeit contingently stabilized by the formation of a habit or "a disposition to act upon the world."[8]

In this regard, we contend that Peirce's idea of "habit" as that dispositional attitude or operative rule to act that stabilizes the possibility of endless semiotic regress—what he calls the "final interpretant"—has not been given sufficient analytical attention in sociology. Markedness theory has explored habituation processes that stabilize meaning systems and taken-for-granted signs, but often descriptively and with limited understanding of the mechanisms of power that produce "unmarked" categories.[9] Habituation has also been theorized by phenomenological sociology as the basis of institutionalization in a legitimation continuum (Berger and Luckmann, 1966). However, phenomenological analyses are still pre-semiotic, in that their constitutive notion of typification—their primitive for habituation—does not integrate complex sign systems except at a most basic level of a natural language required for socialization. This language is reduced to a transparent telementation in line with the phenomenological presupposition

---

[8] Eco (1994, pp. 34–41) claims that the fundamental difference between Peirce's "unlimited semiosis" and Derrida's "deconstructive drift" is that for Peircean semiotics there is "something" (in contrast to Derrida's "nothing") outside the text. In the Peircean view, semiosis is endlessly creative—interpretants are embedded in open-ended rhizomatic networks of multiple interpretations—but there are extra-semiotic limiting cases that anchor semiosis to the world, including indices (signs that acquire meaning by their spatiotemporal contiguity to the world) and dynamic objects (the thing in itself, physical or mental, that provides intrinsic resistances and affordances to the signifying action of perceiving the "immediate" object to be represented). Additionally, habits or dispositions to act on the world are yet another (upper) limiting case of semiosis. Habits act like "absolute objects" to a "final interpretant" provided by the intersubjective meanings of an external community, which always privileges some interpretations over others.

[9] Markedness theory originates in the Prague linguistic circle and refers to the notion that oppositions within a linguistic or semiotic paradigm are typically hierarchical in that some encoded signs are more general or specific than others; for example, "woman" is the patriarchal "marked" sign of a dual paradigmatic system in which "man" is signified as the generalized type of human, the "unmarked" taken-for-granted type (Steiner, 1982, for a review; see Waugh, 1982).

"of the existence of a consciousness which thinks prior to signs" (Heiskala, 2003, p. 280).[10]

Contrary to this pre-semiotic understanding—what Derrida calls a "metaphysics of presence"—we argue that habituation as the semiotic object of a final interpretant that disposes a social group to act in patterned ways is seldom about transparent consensus or socialization but part of historically situated contentious processes of power and domination. Thus, domination in social life typically proceeds via symbolic violence and semiotic misrecognitions that pass as "natural" habituation but through which hierarchical and power relations become inscribed in historically specific "doxas" (Bourdieu, 1977) and discursive "epistemes" (Foucault, 1994 [1966]). Or as Butler (1999, p. xix) has asked in relation to the taken-for-granted yet unequal reproduction of gender performances, "what does transparency keep obscure?"

In other words, "domination is [always] conjoined with habituation" (Fontdevila et al, 2011, p. 196). For instance, language's reflexive semiosis explained earlier—indexicality, metapragmatics, heteroglossia—should not be conceived just as context-making performative acts in isolation but as cumulative traces of radical historical discontinuities and struggles over semiotic control. These are semiotic struggles that are embedded in networks of asymmetrical power spreading across historical time and social space. Moreover, the grammaticalization of a language—always in complex flux of various genres, sublanguages, styles, and registers—is laden at all scales with struggles for identity and control. Thus, standard national grammars with their seemingly "naturalized" semantico-referential codes are also "indexes" that point to wider historical struggles and social distinctions (see Lodge, 1993, for the contentious origins of French grammar; Fontdevila and White, 2010). Similarly, the degrammaticalization shifts that we are currently witnessing among English gendered marked and unmarked forms and pronouns have more to do with indexing historical struggles of heteronormative domination and resistance than with operative "habitual" rules to carve out the world. In short, semiotic processes may become routinized as final interpretants but "by domination rather than innocent habituation" (Fontdevila, 2010, p. 601).

---

[10] The telementation metaphor stemming from the Saussurean tradition is the notion that meaning passes from the mind of a speaker to that of a listener identically without transformation. According to Heiskala (2003, p. 289), Berger and Luckmann's "telementation theory of socialization may be seen as an idea in which norms, roles, values and definitions of reality pass in socialization identically from the socializing environment to the psyche of the socialized." In this view, habituation and internalization are a transparent "identification" with significant others.

In this light, sociology as a multidisciplinary field is well positioned to examine the power and domination processes embedded in semiosis. Following recent calls for methodological and theoretical pluralism (Lamont and Swidler, 2014; Tavory and Timmermans, 2014; Simko and Olick, 2021), we believe that sociology provides a wealth of analytical tools to capture the social mechanisms and historical conditions that can stabilize chains of interpretants into habits and operative rules of social action. From ethnography and survey to comparative historical analysis, sociological methods can unmask "stable" interpretants of habits that become hegemonic doxa shaping the taken for granted of "unmarked" discursive categories, for example "unmarked" heterosexuality in colonial and modern sexual classifications (see Patil, 2018).

As historical objects of final interpretants interrupting unlimited regress, social habits "semiotically" inscribe power and domination at various degrees of emergent institutionalization, from ephemeral interactional frames to established discourses and registers (Sawyer, 2005). In this regard, sociology has much to offer to Peircean semiotics by contributing sophisticated socio-historical analyses of meaning-making in contexts of power and domination.

## Format of culture and cognition

A final problem on which we point to the potential of a renewed encounter between sociology and a semiotic attitude is the understanding of how culture works, which involves reflection on what format of culture and its operations can be viable for sociological analysis and, at large, for interpretive social theory. As a notoriously complicated term (Williams, 1976), the movement that effectively placed culture at the center of sociological reflection was at the same time a blessing and a curse. Particularly after the rejection of functionalism as an attempt to provide a grand or synthetic theory that relied on the interdependence and relative autonomy of the cultural and the social system (Parsons, 1951; Kroeber and Parsons, 1958), culture has been defined sociologically more in terms of what it is not than in terms of what is. It is not, to quote from a recent contribution (Simko and Olick, 2021), "Parsonian norms and values" as ultimate ends of action and propositions for the definition of rules of action to be instantiated in social roles. And it is not, at the same time, the means and end goal of "oversocialization" (Wrong, 1961). What it is, however, is much more difficult to argue than what is not, whether it is an "environment" of action (Alexander, 1988), a "seed or a weed" (Lemert, 2006), a "web of significance" (Geertz, 1973) or a "toolkit" (Swidler, 1986, 2001), or even more interdisciplinary labels like ritual, discourse, symbol, text, or narrative. No matter how captivating and slippery those labels are, at some point semiotics enters into the picture, in order to provide sense and order in a way that would not imply falling back into *functionalist* sense and order.

Function, in many respects, was replaced by concerns about internal order and relations, and the cultural turn really took off when the language of semiotics (if not its formalist rigor) offered social scientists some idea about how relations could be adequately described. This was no great departure from one core theme of Parsonian thinking, though, insofar as the analytic autonomy of culture from social structures was a granted assumption (see Kane, 1991), and yet it was free from the constraints of understanding culture as essential to value-commitment.

And yet, two broadly semiotic assumptions came to make things possibly more complicated, rather than resolve matters once and for all. The influence of structuralism's invitation to understand systems in terms of their paradigmatic relations, and the idea that culture was in itself semiotic, its dominant mode of organization being a network of significant symbols, converged toward the idea that culture—as a system—had to be understood according to the principle that its internal associations had to be understood. For Levi-Straussian structuralism, associations were predominantly paradigmatic in form and ultimately dependent on invariant, yet unreachable, structures of thinking. For Geertzean interpretive social science, associations took the form of organized (yet open-ended) relations that were completely inscribed (and constitutive of) the cultural system, with very little exchange with human agents and their interactions. For structuralists, culture was operationally and programmatically outside individuals (the latter being able, at best, to move at the level of the *parole*); for the radical interpretivists of the time, culture was accessed through interactions and situations (*that* cockfight, *that* cat massacre), but became swiftly removed from them in order to move deeper down from the level of discourse to the level of the text, and the relations and ontologies the text implied. In both cases, there was a move toward some stronger or weaker degree of relationalism, and in both cases—regardless of their mutual divergence—they ended up endorsing a "conflationist" point of view (Archer, 1996 [1988]) that had little room for issues of agency, practical or cognitive. Semiotics, in other words, was instrumental in reinforcing the position of "analytic autonomy," and to endorse a "disembodied" notion of culture.

In this sense, semiotics helped reinforcing, within sociology, a vision that "culture is public because meaning is" (Geertz, 1973), and the format of this meaning is largely a set of associations that take the form of binary "codes" (Alexander and Smith, 1993; Alexander, 2003) or loosely structured networks. Its format, thus, resonates with semiotic ideas of "structure" (sometimes, disposing of Saussure's original and radical associational open-endedness; for a critique of alleged misinterpretations of Saussure, see Stolz, 2021) and, more implicitly, with the legacy of Peirce's insistence on semiosis and its resulting notion of culture as a succession of interpretants (Kockelman, 2006, 2012) and an "encyclopedia" (Eco, 1984), largely understood as the whole of interpretive relations that exist within a system of signs/interpretants. Culture, both as system and as process, is in this regard the domain of interpretability, of what has been thought, is thought, and is thinkable, and yet if its operational definition is so close to a complex, potentially infinite network, what happens to the process of semiosis, which is rooted in the human agent to the point that it is constitutive of it (as Peirce reminded us, "Man is a sign")?

From this point of view, the fascinating challenge comes not from within different paths toward semiotic integration, but from the possibility of an interpretive social science that is in close contact with semiotics while taking into account some of the cognitive implications of semiotic thinking. In other words, can we build a semiotic sociology that follows the line of interpretive social theory, with its attention to cultural autonomy and its relational organization, and the demands that cognitive social science makes?

The fascinating challenge lies from the fact that it is difficult to disagree with John Levi Martin (2010, p. 229) when he argues that "if one wants to define culture as something complex, then it is not going to be inside of people," a statement that could well be endorsed by proponents of an analytic (in the Parsonian sense) notion of culture, but not by proponents of an *analytic* (in the social-mechanisms sense) idea of culture as crucial for the process of belief and action formation.

Indeed, the challenge of a semiotic sociology lies in its confrontation with cognitive social science, and the recognition that much less in culture is public as previous encounters with semiotics suggest; on the contrary, culture is as much personal (in declarative and non-declarative form, as in Lizardo, 2017) as it is public, and an objective of semiotic sociology would address this complexity, in which explicit and implicit dimensions interact (Simko and Olick, 2021). Indeed, much work on both sides of the debate has attempted to tackle the issue of the compatibility between a semiotic program and a cognitive one, and the surprising thing is that they often converge, from very different positions, on some aspects of the theory of meaning (for example, Lizardo's use of a notion of meaning as relying on a causal-historical theory of reference, which he derived from the work of Hilary Putnam, and which was earlier inscribed in Eco's analysis of semiotic ontologies, as in Eco, 2000). On the other side of the spectrum, the interface between semiotics and cognition has been addressed by proponents of a more nuanced approach to cultural autonomy, by integrating semiosis as a process *and system* into analyses of "heterogeneous semiotic networks" (Norton, 2019, 2020) and "representationalism" (Mast, 2020). In some regard, both the powerful critiques and the defenses of a role of semiotics in the advancement of interpretive sociology evoke cognition (and cognitive compatibility) not merely as a constraint for the production of an integration between semiotics and sociology, but also as a background for theorizing culture. The outcomes of theorizing are radically different, but some of the tools, some background references, and most of all the *problems* this thriving literature aims to solve, all hint to a new phase in which a reworked semiotics has to play an interesting role.

## Outline of the chapters

The contributions we present, each coming from a different perspective of the interaction between semiotics and sociology, aim at showing the directions, as well as the consequences, of such a renewed approach to semiotic sociology. Each contribution moves beyond the common—and often times shared—notion of semiotics as a discipline of signifying systems, or as a discipline that can provide a method for sociology. There is, in fact, an underlying theme that deals with the contribution that a semiotic sociology can give toward theorizing certain highly debated and sometimes equally unresolved nodes of social theory. While the semiotic outlook will be immediately recognizable in all of them, each approaches the integration between semiotics and sociology from different perspectives, both from the point of view of the former, and from the point of view of the latter discipline. The semiotic lineage, however, is always immediately recognizable and put to fruitful use.

The book starts with a presentation of the ways the loosely structural and the loosely interpretivist traditions of semiotics have found their way into sociological analysis. In Chapter 1, on the notions of the marked and the unmarked, Wayne Brekhus expands on previous work that has touched topics as diverse as sexual identity, cognition, and the production of theoretical attention. In his work, Brekhus has often focused on the convergence between cognitive sociology (following the perspective of Eviatar Zerubavel) and the methodological approach of structural linguistics, derived from Roman Jakobson's (1972) attention to the role of contradictories (and, later, antinomies) in the definition of phonetic, syntactic, and semantic categorization. What is unmarked, Brekhus argues, has often been neglected by sociologists (thus reproducing a semiotic asymmetry that extends well beyond the disciplinary boundaries of sociology), but it is essential for the reproduction of social reality. The socially specialized has a powerful counterpart in the socially generic, and the resulting asymmetry needs to be played out in full lest we miss its relationality. Using a few examples that range from inequalities to intersectionality, from risk assessment to the standpoint of the researcher, Brekhus aims at the definition of a semiotically oriented, *concept-driven sociology* that can be applied to a variety of different contexts and multiple domains of analysis.

In Chapter 2, Hans Bakker proposes to expand and refine the symbolic interactionist project by incorporating Peircean semiotics and neo-Weberian interpretation. Symbolic interactionism forgot along the way some original sources of its American pragmatist roots. To remedy this, Peirce's indirect influence on Mead and Blumer must be made central to foundational narratives of symbolic interactionism. This calls for more sophisticated understandings of meaning-making in interaction that incorporate Peirce's semiotic triadic model and classifications of signs where symbols are just one kind of signs among others. Bakker (2011) proposed a pragmatic sociology to redress what he has called the "fragmentation of sociology." Here, he expands on such concerns by introducing the project of a semiotic sociology. Thus, he lays the foundations of a metaparadigmatic model—a new synthesis for a "big tent"—that includes interactionism, interpretivism, and semiotics. He develops the model in stepwise fashion of five key arguments that build upon each other into an overall argument, including Blumer as anchor point, American symbolic interactionism, global interactionism in general, neo-Weberian *verstehende soziologie* for cross-historical comparison, and Peircean semiotics as culminating metaparadigm. In his own words, "Peircean semiotics is what pulls it all together."

Peirce's unlimited semiosis, with its succession of interpretants, opens up a space of agency, contingency, and relationality. These topics are addressed by Rein Raud in Chapter 3. In recent years, Raud's work had positioned itself effectively at the intersection of semiotics and social theory, first with his *Meaning in Action* (Raud, 2015), and then with *Being in Flux* (Raud, 2021). In his chapter here, Raud asks in what terms a semiotic view of collective agency can be built. Raud counters the established view of social processes as "things" with an idea that what matters are the relations among elements of social processes. Raud complements this relational point of view with ideas that come from "extended mind" theories. The proposal that Raud makes is ultimately anti-essentialist, and considers the individual and their agentic capacity as less a static entity than "primarily the site of a semiotic process" of meaning-making and meaning-sharing with others through communication. As a contribution that brings semiotics in close contact with relational sociology and certain contributions from critical realism, Raud opens some new reflections about both the relationality and the processuality of meaningness and its connection to individual and, most of all, collective agency.

From another perspective on relational sociology, in Chapter 4, Paul McLean and Eunkyung Song reflect on the pervasive phenomena of "side-directed behavior" in network configurations, where ego's behaviors or utterances are not aimed at alter but indirectly at third parties or audiences. For example, a student bullies a schoolmate "but more to gain status with the cool kids than to express animosity towards the afflicted schoolmate."

These side-directed configurations have implications for the analysis of social interaction at the intersection of networks and culture. McLean and Song argue that as network analysts, it is easy to miscode action when we fail to appreciate ulterior motive-based behavior directed at third parties. Side-directed behaviors are "social forms" that constitute a fundamental piece of the architecture of social networks. Yet often side-directed behaviors' shifting configurations are too subtle to be just plainly behavioral or observational, and hence we must pay closer attention to their semiotics. This involves fine-grained examination of semiotic shifts, including register switching, metapragmatics, indexical markers, multiple metacommunicative channels sustained simultaneously in ongoing interaction, among others. For McLean and Song, semiotic gestures, no matter how ephemeral, "can be deeply constitutive of social orders" because they may shift interactional frames that renegotiate ingroup and outgroup boundaries. In conversation with more formalized types of network analysis, they conclude that ultimately "ascertaining who the main participants are during SDB [side-directed behavior]—who is the primary alter and who the primary audience—is itself an interpretive exercise."

Chapters 5 and 6 explore a further distinction within semiotics, the one Charles Morris (1938) identified between syntax, semantics, and pragmatics. In Chapter 5, Todd Madigan advocates a more specific focus to the neglected dimension of cultural syntax, which has been sidelined by cultural sociology's traditional attention to the meaningfulness of symbols and performances. As he writes, the time is ripe for a focus on how sociologists examine and theorize "the rules that govern the possibilities of meaning," and Madigan calls for a conceptual distinction between a cultural semantics, cultural structure, and cultural syntax. This third level, foundational for the other two, retrieves the combinatory logic of meanings within given cultural structures, and within situations. Semiotics, in this particular case, is relevant for an understanding of how rules work, and particularly in the understanding not of paradigmatic relations but of the possibilities that open up when we reason syntagmatically.

If Madigan focuses on one of the provinces of semiotics famously identified by Charles Morris (syntax, semantics, and pragmatics), in Chapter 6, Andrea Cossu explores the contribution to cultural sociology that can come from situating one's understanding of cultural processes in the interface between semantics and pragmatics. Relying on the notion of unlimited semiosis and the format of culture as an encyclopedia, Cossu departs from basic notions of a semiotic of codes and focuses more on the semiotic operations that constitute the "cultural system" as the "web of significance" that Clifford Geertz famously wrote about. In this regard, culture is less subject to paradigmatic patterns than it is to the recursive operations that link discrete elements of the cultural system in a network of communication that is always future oriented. Starting from the perspective of memory studies, he argues that "memory" has to be understood less as what is remembered than as a crucial operation for the semiotic reproduction of cultural systems and their future imagination, which involves stability and processes of change.

In some regards, the pragmatic openness advocated in Cossu involves orientation not only to temporality, but to situations and objects. Jorge Fontdevila and Elizabeth Wissinger offer the tools to bring sophisticated semiotic thinking into close contact with empirical analysis. Within a pragmatist framework of social mechanisms, in Chapter 7, Jorge Fontdevila applies Peirce's triadic model and semiotic tools—indexicality, metapragmatics, metacommunication—to ethnographic data on HIV disclosure across migrant and local networks of gay and bisexual men. His goal is "to show how emergent properties—structural stigma, HIV disparities—of interacting complex systems become realized through semiotic mechanisms at the meso- and micro-level of social interaction." Based on rich ethnographic data, he examines indexical grammars of sexual encounters where HIV can be transmitted via polysemic (mis)interpretation. For local sexual networks, silence about disclosing HIV status often indexes condomless "bareback" subcultures of ingroup belonging. For Latino migrant men, however, silence during condomless sex may index differently—that sex partners can be trusted to disclose if they are HIV positive. Silence as the empowering response to stigma and rejection by some HIV-positive men paradoxically creates sexual contexts of HIV transmission that migrant men then encounter. Fontdevila (2020) has examined other semiotic mechanisms that partly drive emergent HIV disparities among vulnerable populations, including bisexual liminal spaces and biomeds as signifiers of unrestrained sexualities. Ultimately, multiple semiotic pathways act as performative expressions on the ground of structural stigma rooted in unequal heteronormative orders. Fontdevila concludes that ethnographic methods "are indispensable as a first point of entry to begin unpacking such semiotic complexity … [and] deliver deep insights on interpretive mechanisms that can then be used to model larger scale epidemiological processes."

Applying a feminist materialist lens in Chapter 8 on design sociology, Elizabeth Wissinger reflects on the persistent semiotic power of the old dichotomy between machine technology and human-centered craft. This dichotomy has ruled the fashion world since haute couture was born in the mid-19th century but has found recent iterations in the tensions between transhuman and posthuman embodied fashion. Transhuman designs involve computational devices worn on the body to extract and optimize bodily data, whereas posthuman designs employ organisms or biologically grown outputs to reconnect humans to their environments. Drawing on interviews and participant observation among designers of such embodied practices, Wissinger finds that transhuman and posthuman tensions are "gender inflected" and map onto a complex semiotics of gendered practices. Thus, designs are not gender neutral but shaped by implicit assumptions that become inscribed into embodied technologies. "Gadgets," "cogs," "circuits" versus "organisms," "guts," "insides" are some of the signifiers that circulate along male/female gendered lines, ultimately rooted in semiotic oppositions of hard/soft sciences, culture/nature, reason/emotion. However, contra abstract structuralist analyses of "crystalized" binary oppositions, Wissinger finds great semiotic complexity embodied in materiality and demonstrates that the "divides are not neatly aligned" and are a "messy process." She concludes that semiotic analyses bridge gaps between sociological, feminist, and fashion studies analyses to show "how signifying factors deeply affect designers' imaginations of constraints and functionalities, with outcomes as much a product of signification systems as they are of science."

The essays in this volume bring forward the many explicit and implicit strands of influence of semiotics into current interpretive sociology. Some are firmly in a pragmatist vein, while others build on the notion of the analytic autonomy of the cultural system. Some are decidedly in a poststructuralist key, while others expand the line of a cognitive sociology that, rather than marginalizing semiotics, keeps it front and center. All of them try to provide elements to answer a question that is not often asked by sociologists, even those who are better versed in interdisciplinary integration and the nuances of current semiotic theory: Is there a space for semiotics, and its many legacies, in an agenda that pushes interpretive sociology forward? As editors of this volume, we firmly believe that semiotics stands less as a seemingly old-fashioned discipline and more as a provider of problems, questions, and methods for an interpretive sociology that, in many respects, is yet to come. But the signs of it can be found here and there and connected together.

## References

Alexander, J.C. (1988) *Action and Its Environments*, New York: Columbia University Press.

Alexander, J.C. (2003) *The Meanings of Social Life*, Oxford: Oxford University Press.

Alexander, J.C. and Smith, P. (1993) "The Discourse of American Civil Society: A New Proposal for Cultural Studies," *Theory and Society*, 22(2): 151–207.

Archer, M. (1996 [1988]) *Culture and Agency*, Cambridge: Cambridge University Press.

Bakhtin, M.M. (1981) *The Dialogical Imagination: Four Essays*, ed M. Holquist, Austin, TX: University of Texas Press.

Bakhtin, M.M. (1986) *Speech Genres and Other Late Essays*, eds C. Emerson and M. Holquist, Austin, TX: University of Texas Press.

Bakker, J.I. (2011) "Pragmatic Sociology: Healing the Discipline, *Sociological Focus*, 44(3): 167–83.

Barthes, R. (1972) *Mythologies*, New York: Hill and Wang.

Barthes, R. (1994 [1964]) *Elements of Semiology*, New York: Hill and Wang.

Bateson, G. (1985 [1955]) "A Theory of Play and Fantasy," in R. Innis (ed) *Semiotics: An Introductory Anthology*, Bloomington, IN: Indiana University Press, pp. 129–44.

Bauman, R. and Briggs, C.L. (1990) "Poetics and Performance as Critical Perspectives on Language and Social Life," *Annual Review of Anthropology*, 19: 59–88.

Berger, P.L. and Luckmann, T. (1966) *The Social Construction of Reality: A Treatise in the Sociology of Knowledge*, New York: Anchor Books/Doubleday.

Bianchi, C. (2015) "Thresholds, Boundaries, Limits: Ideological Analysis in the Semiotics of Umberto Eco," *Semiotica*, 206: 109–27.

Boas, F. (1911) "Introduction," in F. Boas (ed) *Handbook of American Indian Languages*, vol. BAE-B 40, Part I, Washington, DC: Smithsonian Institution and Bureau of American Ethnology.

Bourdieu, P. (1977) *Outline of a Theory of Practice*, Cambridge: Cambridge University Press.

Brown, R. and Gilman, A. (1960) "The Pronouns of Power and Solidarity," *American Anthropologist*, 4(6): 24–9.

Butler, J. (1999) *Gender Trouble: Feminism and the Subversion of Identity*, New York: Routledge.

Cossu, A. (2017) "Signs, Webs, and Memories: Umberto Eco as a (Social) Theorist," *Thesis Eleven*, 140(1): 74–89.

Desogus, P. (2012) "The Encyclopedia in Umberto Eco's Semiotics," *Semiotica*, 192: 501–21.

Dixon, R.M.W. (1972) *The Dyirbal Language of North Queensland*, Cambridge: Cambridge University Press.

Duranti, A. (1994) *From Grammar to Politics: Linguistic Anthropology in a Western Samoan Village*, Berkeley, CA: University of California Press.

Duranti, A. (2003) "Language as Culture in U.S. Anthropology: Three Paradigms," *Current Anthropology*, 44(3): 323–47.

Duranti, A. and Goodwin, C. (1992) *Rethinking Context: Language as an Interactive Phenomenon*, Cambridge: Cambridge University Press.

Eco, U. (1976) *A Theory of Semiotics*, Bloomington, IN: Indiana University Press.

Eco, U. (1979) *The Role of the Reader: Explorations in the Semiotics of Texts*, Bloomington, IN: Indiana University Press.

Eco, U. (1984) *Semiotics and the Philosophy of Language*, Bloomington, IN: Indiana University Press.

Eco, U. (1994) *The Limits of Interpretation*, Bloomington, IN: Indiana University Press.

Eco, U. (2000) *Kant and the Platypus: Essays on Language and Cognition*, Boston, MA: Houghton Mifflin Harcourt.

Fontdevila, J. (2010) "Indexes, Power, and Netdoms: A Multidimensional Model of Language in Social Action," *Poetics*, 38(6): 587–609.

Fontdevila, J. (2020) "Epidemics as Complex Systems: Sexual Meanings and HIV among Latino Gay and Bisexual Men," in A. Patterson and I. Read (eds) *The Shapes of Epidemics and Global Disease*, Newcastle: Cambridge Scholars Publishing, pp. 132–67.

Fontdevila, J. and White, H.C. (2013) "Relational Power from Switching across Netdoms through Reflexive and Indexical Language," in F. Dépelteau and C. Powell (eds) *Applying Relational Sociology: Relations, Networks, & Society*, New York: Palgrave Macmillan, pp. 155–79.

Fontdevila, J., Opazo, M.P. and White, H.C. (2011) "Order at the Edge of Chaos: Meanings from Netdom Switchings across Functional Systems," *Sociological Theory*, 29: 179–98.

Foucault, M. (1994 [1966]) *The Order of Things: An Archeology of the Human Sciences*, New York: Vintage.

Geertz, C. (1973) *The Interpretation of Cultures*, New York: Basic Books.

Goffman, E. (1974) *Frame Analysis: An Essay on the Organization of Experience*, New York: Harper and Row.

Gumperz, J.J. (1982) *Discourse Strategies*, New York: Cambridge University Press.

Heiskala, R. (2003) *Society as Semiosis*, New York: Peter Lang.

Heiskala, R. (2014) "Toward Semiotic Sociology: A Synthesis of Semiology, Semiotics and Phenomenological Sociology," *Social Science Information*, 53(1): 35–53.

Heiskala, R. (2021) *Semiotic Sociology*, Basingstoke: Palgrave Macmillan.

Holquist, M. (1990) *Dialogism: Bakhtin and his World*, London: Routledge.

Irvine, J.T. (1985) "Status and Style in Language," *Annual Review of Anthropology*, 14: 557–81.

Jakobson, R. (1960) "Closing Statement: Linguistic and Poetics," in T.A. Sebeok (ed) *Style in Language*, Cambridge, MA: MIT Press, pp. 350–77.

Jakobson, R. (1972) "Verbal communication," *Scientific American*, 227(3): 72–81.

Kane, A. (1991) "Cultural Analysis in Historical Sociology: The Analytic and Concrete Forms of the Autonomy of Culture," *Sociological Theory*, 9(1): 53–69.

Kockelman, P. (2006) "The Semiotic Stance," *Semiotica*, 157(1/4): 233–304.

Kockelman, P. (2012) *Agent, Persons, Subject, Self*, Oxford: Oxford University Press.

Krakauer, D.C. (2011) "The Star Gazer and the Flesh Eater: Elements of a Theory of Metahistory," *Cliodynamics*, 2(1): 82–105.

Kroeber, A.L. and Parsons, T. (1958) "The Concepts of Culture and of Social System," *American Sociological Review*, 23: 582–83.

Lacan, J. (1977 [1966]) *Ecrits: A Selection*, New York: Norton.
Lamont, M. and Swidler, A. (2014) "Methodological Pluralism and the Possibilities and Limits of Interviewing," *Qualitative Sociology*, 37(2): 153–71.
Lemert, C. (2006) *Durkheim's Ghosts: Social Theory and Social Things*, Cambridge: Cambridge University Press.
Lemert, C. (2012) "Sociology's Third Problem," *Contemporary Sociology*, 41(4): 423–29.
Levi-Strauss, C. (1963) *Structural Anthropology*, New York: Basic Books.
Lizardo, O. (2014) "Beyond the Comtean Schema: The Sociology of Culture and Cognition versus Cognitive Social Science," *Sociological Forum*, 29(4): 983–89.
Lizardo, O. (2017) "Improving Cultural Analysis: Considering Personal Culture in its Declarative and Non-declarative Modes," *American Sociological Review*, 82(1): 88–115.
Lodge, R.A. (1993) *French: From Dialect to Standard*, London: Routledge.
Lorusso, A. (2014) *Cultural Semiotics: For a Cultural Perspective in Semiotics*, Basingstoke: Palgrave Macmillan.
Lucy, J.A. (1993) *Reflexive Language: Reported Speech and Metapragmatics*, Cambridge: Cambridge University Press.
Martin, J.L. (2010) "Life's a Beach but You're an Ant, and Other Unwelcome News for the Sociology of Culture," *Poetics*, 38(2): 229–44.
Martin, J.L. (2011) *The Explanation of Social Action*, Oxford: Oxford University Press.
Mast, J.L. (2020) "Representationalism and Cognitive Culturalism: Riders on Elephants on Turtles All the Way Down," *American Journal of Cultural Sociology*, 8(1): 90–123.
Mertz, E. (2007) "Semiotic Anthropology," *Annual Review of Anthropology*, 36: 337–57.
Morris, C. (1938) *Foundations of a Theory of Signs*, Chicago, IL: University of Chicago Press.
Norton, M. (2019) "Meaning on the Move: Synthesizing Cognitive and Systems Concepts of Culture," *American Journal of Cultural Sociology*, 7(1): 1–28.
Norton, M. (2020) "Cultural Sociology Meets the Cognitive Wild: Advantages of the Distributed Cognition Framework for Analyzing the Intersection of Culture and Cognition," *American Journal of Cultural Sociology*, 8(1): 45–62.
Pachucki, M.A. and Breiger, R.L. (2010) "Cultural Holes: Beyond Relationality in Social Networks and Culture," *Annual Review of Sociology*, 36: 205–224.
Parsons, T. (1951) *The Social System*, Glencoe, IL: Free Press.
Patil, V. (2018) "The Heterosexual Matrix as Imperial Effect," *Sociological Theory*, 36(1): 1–26.
Peirce, C.S. (1931–1958) *Collected Papers of Charles Peirce*, 8 vols, Cambridge, MA: Harvard University Press.
Posner, R. (2003) "Basic Tasks of Cultural Semiotics," in G. Withalm and J. Wallmannsberger (eds) *Signs of Power – Power of Signs*, Vienna: INST, pp. 56–89.

Prevosti, A. (1994) "Comparació de les Estratègies de l'Evolució Biològica i l'Evolució Cultural," *Revista d'Etnologia de Catalunya*, 5: 22–37.

Proni, G. (2015) "Umberto Eco and Charles Peirce: A Slow and Respectful Convergence," *Semiotica*, 206: 13–35.

Rabinow, P. and Sullivan, W. (1979) "The Interpretive Turn: Emergence of an Approach," in P. Rabinow and W. Sullivan (eds) *Interpretive Social Science: A Reader*, Berkeley: University of California Press, pp. 1–21.

Raud, R. (2015) *Meaning in Action*, Oxford: Polity.

Raud, R. (2021) *Being in Flux: A Post-Anthropocentric Ontology of the Self*, Oxford: Wiley.

Ricoeur, P. (1973) "The Model of the Text: Meaningful Action Considered as Text," *New Literary History*, 5(1): 91–117.

Rochberg-Halton, E. (1986) *Meaning and Modernity: Social Theory in the Pragmatic Attitude*, Chicago, IL: Chicago University Press.

Saussure, F., de (1959 [1916]) *Course in General Linguistics*, New York: The Philosophical Library.

Sapir, E. (1924) "Culture, Genuine and Spurious," *American Journal of Sociology*, 29: 401–29.

Sawyer, R.K. (2005) *Social Emergence: Societies as Complex Systems*, New York: Cambridge University Press.

Silverstein, M. (1976) "Shifters, Linguistic Categories and Cultural Description," in K. Basso and H. Selby (eds) *Meaning in Anthropology*, Albuquerque, NM: University of New Mexico Press, pp. 11–55.

Silverstein, M. (1993) "Metapragmatic Discourse and Metapragmatic Function," in J.A. Lucy (ed) *Reflexive Language: Reported Speech and Metapragmatics*, Cambridge, MA: Cambridge University Press, pp. 33–58.

Simko, C. and Olick, J.K. (2021) "What We Talk about when We Talk about Culture: A Multi-facet Approach," *American Journal of Cultural Sociology*, 9: 431–59.

Spillman, L. (2020) *What is Cultural Sociology?*, Medford, MA: Polity Press.

Steiner, P. (ed) (1982) *The Prague School: Selected Writings 1929–1946*, Austin, TX: University of Texas Press.

Stolz, D. (2021) "Becoming a Dominant Misinterpreted Source: The Case of Ferdinand de Saussure in Cultural Sociology," *Journal of Classical Sociology*, 21(1): 92–113.

Swedberg, R. (2010) *The Art of Social Theory*, Princeton, NJ: Princeton University Press.

Swidler, A. (1986) "Culture in Action: Symbols and Strategies," *American Sociological Review*, 51(2): 273–86.

Swidler, A. (2001) *Talk of Love: How Culture Matters*, Chicago, IL: University of Chicago Press.

Tavory, I. and Timmermans, S. (2014) *Abductive Analysis: Theorizing Qualitative Research*, Chicago, IL: University of Chicago Press.

Taylor, C. (2016) *The Language Animal: The Full Shape of the Human Linguistic Capacity*, Cambridge, MA: The Belknap Press of Harvard University Press.

Timmermans, S. and Tavory, I. (2012) "Theory Construction in Qualitative Research: From Grounded Theory to Abductive Analysis," *Sociological Theory*, 30(3): 167–86.

Torop, P. (1999) "Cultural Semiotics and Culture," *Sign System Studies*, 15(1): 9–23.

Volosinov, V.N. (1973 [1929]) *Marxism and the Philosophy of Language*, New York: Seminar Press.

Waugh, L. (1982) "Marked and Unmarked: A Choice between Unequals in Semiotic Structure," *Semiotica*, 38(3/4): 299–318.

White, H.C. (1992) *Identity and Control: A Structural Theory of Social Action*, Princeton, NJ: Princeton University Press.

Whorf, B.L. (1995 [1941]) "The Relation of Habitual Thought and Behavior to Language," in B. Blount (ed) *Language, Culture, and Society*, Prospect Heights, IL: Waveland Press, pp. 64–84.

Wiley, N. (2006) "Peirce and the Founding of American Sociology," *Journal of Classical Sociology*, 6(1): 23–50.

Williams, R. (1976) *Keywords: A Vocabulary of Culture and Society*, London: Fontana.

Wittgenstein, L. (1953) *Philosophical Investigations*, New York: The Macmillan Company.

Wrong, D.H. (1961) "The Oversocialized Conception of Man in Modern Sociology," *American Sociological Review*, 26(2): 183–93.

1

# Marked and Unmarked: A Semiotic Distinction for Concept-driven Interpretive Sociology

*Wayne H. Brekhus*

A unifying theme in the chapters in this volume is that semiotics offers important analytic tools for understanding the creation and reproduction of contextual meaning in social life (see Introduction). Consistent with this theme, my research program has centered on the semiotic distinction between the socially marked and the socially unmarked. I have employed these sensitizing analytic concepts to examine a range of issues, including sexual identity (Brekhus, 1996), theoretical attention in sociology (Brekhus, 1998, 2000), cognition (Brekhus, 2015; Brekhus and Ignatow, 2019), risk (Brekhus, 2018), and identity (Brekhus, 2020). Broadly speaking, I focus on identity, difference, cognition, and representation, with a particular interest in the ways that intersecting dimensions of markedness and unmarkedness shape cultural perception, worldviews, cognition, and the reproduction of social inequalities.

The semiotic distinction between the marked and the unmarked was first introduced in the 1930s by linguists Trubetzkoy and Jakobson (see Jakobson, 1972; Trubetzkoy and Jakobson, 1975, p. 162). Linguist Linda Waugh (1982), in her article "Marked and Unmarked: A Choice between Unequals in Semiotic Structure," developed the marked/unmarked distinction into a broader semiotic framework featuring semiotic pairs, such as blackness/whiteness and homosexuality/heterosexuality, across different semiotic systems (see also Zerubavel, 2018, p. 2). Following the lead of Waugh, who argued that the same logic of the actively accented (marked) and the passively unacknowledged (unmarked) that applied to linguistic contrasts also applies to social contrasts, I have helped to import these concepts into the social sciences. In my own work, inspired by Waugh's analysis, I first applied a semiotic markedness/unmarkedness analysis to sexual identity construction in the US (Brekhus, 1996), wherein I noted that some sexual behaviors and identities are marked as "deviant" and given special labels, while others remain unmarked, unaccented, and even unlabeled. Thus, for instance, "the social marking process is metaphorically illustrated in Nathaniel Hawthorne's [novel] [*The*] *Scarlet Letter* where Hester Prynne's community literally marks her with a Scarlet Letter 'A' [that] symbolizes her identity as an 'adulteress' and sets her apart from the unmarked category of 'marital loyalists,'" but Prynne's neighbors are not similarly required to mark their own identity as "marital loyalists" with an "ML" (Brekhus, 1996, p. 500). Spousal sex is unmarked and the terms "spousal sex" and "marital loyalist" are rarely even used. The marking of some sexual fetishes as specific, "deviant" psychological fetishes, such as "fat-fetishists," while leaving unmarked general cultural anthropological fetishes, such as being attracted to only thin people, illustrates the asymmetry of the marked/unmarked divide well. As blogger Virgie Tovar (2016) remarks:

> because it is totally normal to fetishize, thin, beautiful women, it is not even considered a fetish … Thin fetishism is far more rampant than fat fetishism, and yet one is invisible and the other is hyper-visible. In fact, at the core they are not different behaviors at all. Why is desire only up for interrogation when it veers off the socially charted path?

Here, Tovar makes clear that thin fetishism is just as restrictive as fat fetishism, but because the entire anthropological tribe of industrialized white Westerners shares this highly restrictive fetish, the fetish remains unmarked and unnamed.

My interest in the semiotic features of marked attention and unmarked inattention arose when I was conducting an ethnographic study exploring the sociology of identity among suburban gay men. When I told others I was writing a book based on my research among these suburban gay men, people would frequently ask if I was gay, but no one ever asked whether I was suburban (Brekhus, 2003, p. 12). I found this interesting because while gay and suburban are both identity attributes, there was an obvious asymmetry in which identity attribute people considered specialized and noteworthy and which was taken for granted as irrelevant. My interest in this question led me to further explore the bases of such asymmetries. In addition to noting the asymmetry between how people ignored "suburbanness" (a regional orientation) while acknowledging "gay" (a sexual orientation) as a potential feature of one's identity, I also discovered, while reading literature in LGBTQ studies and the sociology of gay identities, that the research literature was heavily focused on the most visible and concentrated gay male enclaves such as the Village in New York, the Castro in San Francisco, and West Hollywood in Los Angeles. Empirical work in the sociology of gay identity focused on social movement organizations, people who conspicuously performed gender as hypermasculine clones or drag queens, and gay-salient contexts in gay commercial districts of big cities. Gay culture was portrayed in popular culture and the academic literature through its most interesting statistical outliers. Where, I wondered, was the relatively unremarkable, ordinary gay man in the literature, and what were the implications for sociological theory that most theories about gay life and identity came from an unrepresentative sample of interesting extremes rather than mundane averages?

These questions motivated my semiotic imagination. In 1998, I proposed a *sociology of the unmarked*, arguing, first, that much of sociology develops greater epistemological attention to ontologically uncommon, unusual, and politically salient "marked" features of social life while often ignoring ubiquitous, mundane, and politically invisible "unmarked" features, and, second, that sociology needs to analytically mark what remains unnoticed and unremarked (Brekhus, 1998). I further took up this issue in a "mundane manifesto" (Brekhus, 2000), where I argued that we have lost sight of the theoretical significance of the unmarked. Part of why we lose sight of the mundane has to do with how cultural communities, large and small, agree on categories of social life—the "specialized deviations" and the "ordinary defaults." I therefore developed an interest in specializing in sociological theory that looks at the cultural elements of cognition and attention, and at the attentional differences that we place on marked, or remarkable, features of social reality, compared to unmarked, or mundane, features of social reality. It is this distinction between the culturally and socially marked and the culturally and socially unmarked that orients my interest in a semiotic concept-driven interpretive sociology.

In short, social marking is a process by which some part or parts of a contrast are actively highlighted as *socially specialized*, while the remaining part of the contrast is taken for granted as *socially generic* (Brekhus, 1998, 2015, p. 25). For example, transgender is marked as a socially specialized gender identity, while cisgender is unmarked. Likewise, in many white majority countries, "Black" is marked as a racially specialized category, while "white" is treated as the "generic," racially unspecialized category of humans. And, similarly, in most societies, "women are marked as sex/gender 'specialized' humans, while men are implicitly defined as the 'generic,' sex/gender 'unspecialized 'default' humans" (Brekhus, forthcoming). One can see this in the many graphic depictions of the evolutionary transition of species into modern humans, wherein the modern human is represented both linguistically and visually as "modern man" (the "generic" human) rather than "modern woman" even though statistically more members of the species *Homo sapiens* are women than men (Brekhus, forthcoming). An important semiotic aspect of social marking is that the most powerful element of the contrast is not the item that is accentuated with a marked social value, but rather the item whose social value is implicitly constructed as normative, "normal," and positive through its absence of a mark (Brekhus, 1996, p. 502; Zerubavel, 1998).

The main purpose of social marking is the construction of a *semiotic asymmetry* between the marked and the unmarked (Zerubavel, 2018, p. 10). As Zerubavel (2018, p. 10) points out, this asymmetry is manifested in the "uneven semiotization of streets that are specially marked with 'Do Not Enter' signs and ones that are *not* marked with 'Please Enter' [signs]." Similarly specialized caution signs mark specific road dangers such as "dangerous curve," "blind intersection," or "slippery when wet," but they leave the "generic" everyday road dangers unmarked rather than marked with semiotically equivalent signs such as "dangerous straightaway," "visible intersection," or "warning: crashes can occur on dry road surfaces" (see Simpson, 1996). Language plays a significant role in the uneven semiotization of social and cultural meaning. As linguists have shown in language contrasts, "the unmarked feature appears to represent the *nonspecialized* whole, while the marked appears to represent a *specialized* subset of the whole (Waugh, 1982, p. 302; Greenberg, 1966, p. 14)" (Brekhus, 1996, p. 500).

In the English language, terms like "day," for example, can refer to either the generic 24-hour period of a day or the smaller portion of the day that is not night, while "night" only references the specific subset of the day that is dark (Brekhus, forthcoming). This, in effect, makes day the default time of day and accents the night as a deviant, marked, or specialized subset of the day. Similarly, the term "man" can refer to the gendered subset of *Homo sapiens* or to the entire species, while the term "woman" refers only to the gendered subset. The effect is to make men the default standard of humanity by which women deviate. Linguistic qualifiers placed in front of terms to qualify a specific rather than generic form of the term also contribute to uneven semiotization;

> linguistic qualifiers like gay bar, single mom, domestic violence, hybrid car, and family farm, not only mark a 'specialized' type of bar, violence, car, or business, but they also implicitly define by contrast the 'generic' bar as heterosexual, the 'generic' violence as non-domestic, the 'generic' car as gas-powered, and the 'generic' farm as corporate. (Brekhus, forthcoming)

The semiotic asymmetry between the socially specialized and the socially generic is especially powerful to how we generalize. Because those items not marked are treated as default and therefore "normal," we tend to generalize from the unmarked to the general, while we generalize from the marked to the specific category. Take, for example, how social psychological studies of Westerners are generalized to conclusions about *human* social psychology even though the anthropological evidence is that Westerners are behavioral outliers rather than representative of the species as a whole (see Brekhus, 2015, pp. 2–4; Watters, 2013). On the other hand, studies of non-state societies, like the Yanomami, the !Kung, or the Nuer, are considered the realm of tribe-specific anthropology rather than generic human psychology or sociology.

I argue that a *concept-driven sociology* (Zerubavel, 2021) utilizing the semiotic concepts of the marked and the unmarked has much to offer how we do and think about sociology.

## Why markedness and unmarkedness matter for interpretive sociology

*Sociocultural cognitive defaults and the exercise of social power*

Eviatar Zerubavel (2021) emphasizes the importance of sensitizing analytic concepts for sociological methods and sociological analysis. I follow Zerubavel's concept-driven sociology approach in developing a sociology of the marked and the unmarked that is applicable to multiple arenas of social reality. The goal of concept-driven sociology is to provide disciplined attentional focus to aspects of social reality that might otherwise go unnoticed. Organizing our thinking around conceptual issues that transcend a variety of contexts is an analytic literacy that can significantly aid interpretive sociology. One of the fundamental insights that an understanding of the marked and the unmarked can provide is to better articulate the subtle exercise of social power and gain an appreciation for how cognition shapes social reproduction and the reproduction of social inequalities.

Key to the reproduction of social reality and social power are the cognitive defaults built into the unmarked side of the semiotic contrast between marked and unmarked. These defaults are powerful shapers of social reality. In my work on sociocultural defaults (see Brekhus, forthcoming), I explore cognitive defaults in cultural perception and everyday cultural practice. In contrast to the socially salient marked aspects of cultural perception, or the reflective, conscious cultural practices of members, the unnoticed elements of perception and the unconscious, habituated default practices of people are often taken for granted by analysts and members alike, but are central to the reproduction of social reality. Sociologists of cultural perception examine how marked awareness of some aspects of reality also enhances the power of the invisible and unremarked (see Zerubavel, 2018; Friedman, 2019). Sociologists of practical action similarly show how unmarked habituation and routine and the mostly unconscious embodied habits, dispositions, and skills of social actors and their automatic cognition are as important to cultural action as those aspects of declarative culture and deliberative cognition (see Bourdieu, 1990; Rawls, 2002; Vaisey, 2009; Lizardo, 2017). Whether in cultural vision or cultural practice, the power of the unfocused and unattended is significant and warrants further sociological attention. Attention to the most salient features of reality and the most deliberative conscious components of social action draws our gaze away from the most significant ways that reality is socially constructed and reproduced in embodied everyday practice (Brekhus, forthcoming).

## Markedness and unmarkedness in the reproduction of social inequalities

Using a concept-driven sociology to explore the cognitive reproduction of social inequalities, we can look at a broad range of issues and identities. An obvious application of this semiotic relationship is the ways that racial inequality is reproduced in everyday life. It is reproduced in multiple ways. First, as previously discussed, we generalize differently from the members of the marked racial category than we do from members of the unmarked racial category. Thus, for example, when social problems such as drugs, homicide, or gang membership occur in African-American communities, we generalize these as "community-specific problems." Criminologists have looked at the bases for Latino (for example, Martinez, 1996) and African-American intraracial homicide (for example, Comer, 1985) as though each is a unique, group-specific problem, but have not similarly looked for white-specific explanations for white intraracial crime. White on white crime is not semiotically coded as racialized, it is just crime. And ethnographies of racially marked communities often portray a particular African-American or Latino community as representative of the "Black" or "Latino" experience, even as the sites that ethnographers choose are often outliers chosen for their extraordinariness rather than their ordinariness. Thus many ethnographers of African-American or Black culture and interactions in the US seek out the most visible urban African-American subcultures in densely populated areas. Even studies designed to humanize their African-American subjects, by emphasizing those African-Americans living in extreme conditions, often reinforce stereotypes. Lee Rainwater's (1970) ethnography *Behind Ghetto Walls* examines how African-Americans responded to harsh social conditions at St. Louis' Pruitt-Igoe public housing projects. But even as Rainwater offered policy solutions, he still framed the issue largely in terms of damaged pathology caused by poverty and thus reinforced stereotypes about "deviant" urban African-American behavior (see Johnson, 2020, pp. 358–9).

A similar problem occurs in popular culture and media accounts. Brekhus (forthcoming, see also Brekhus 2000, pp. 92–3) provides the following extreme example of differences in generalizing from the racially marked and the racially unmarked:

As a vivid example of the ways we think very differently about the sensational aspects of the marked and the unmarked consider the following: when I was teaching a deviance course at Rutgers in the 1990s, I was struck by the book jacket to the autobiography of Monster Kody Scott—a notorious ex-LA gang member who was responsible for multiple homicides and had been shot multiple times himself. The book jacket praised the book for giving "eloquent voice to *the* black ghetto experience today [emphasis added]" (Shakur 1993). While Monster Kody Scott's race and living in a residential ghetto likely shaped his life experiences, the implication of the quote is that his experience was *representative* rather than an *extreme outlier* of the black ghetto experience. To illustrate the asymmetry in how we generalize from the sensational aspects of the marked and how we generalize from the extraordinary aspects of the unmarked, imagine a biography of Timothy McVeigh—the white middle-American terrorist who blew up the Oklahoma City federal building killing over 100 people in the 1990s being lauded as "giving eloquent voice to *the* white heartland experience in America today."

Social marking highlights the marked as distinct from the "normal" and often leads to an emphasis on the atypical and stereotypical, whereas the unmarked is passively typical and ordinary. Once we highlight a category or issue as specialized and attach to it memorable distinctive characteristics, that category or issue engages our imagination and draws added epistemological attention. But this attention often distorts reality by shining our analytic lens in only one direction. The perception that race is primarily an issue among marked racial categories leads to a lack of attention to the ways that race is an ongoing and enduring accomplishment of the unmarked racial category.

Understanding how racism is reproduced involves looking at both the extreme, marked forms of racist behavior and the mundane, unmarked, habituated ways that racial inequalities are sustained and reproduced. The enduring power of the unmarked is often reproduced through generic, universalizing language. White people who see themselves as the generic unraced standard will often assert that they don't see race, or that they don't see color, they only see the (generic) individual. These "color blind" statements hide racialized structures, and the persistence of such structures is often reproduced in color blind social policies focused on (generic) "universal" programs that benefit everyone. In the US, for example, many policies advertised as universal, such as improving schools and making home ownership more affordable, actually allowed white people to gain most of the resources from these programs (Roithmayr, 2014; Brekhus, forthcoming). Rawls and Duck (2020) argue that racism is coded into everyday interactions and social expectations through interaction orders of race but that the racial elements of these social expectations are tacit and unarticulated. Similarly, Margaret Hagerman (2018) observed that Wisconsin parents who used generic, color blind language often organized their lives, their choices of where to go, their children's school choices, and their residential choices along racial lines, but considered the very marking or mention of race itself as "racist."

Just as generic, universalizing language masks unmarked racial privilege, it also hides other kinds of privilege. Melanie Heath (2013) demonstrates how the generic language of individual responsibility in the marriage debates over same-sex marriage and the ways that "marriage advocates" contrasted "gay marriage" with (generic) "marriage" maintained specifically heterosexual marriages as the default, and therefore "natural," form and unquestioned norm (see also Brekhus, forthcoming).

A central benefit of employing the marked/unmarked semiotic conceptual distinction is to highlight the importance of cognitive defaults in the exercise of social power. Even before we apply the semiotic distinction of marked and unmarked to the populations we study, sociologists should be aware of the ways the marked and the unmarked shape the epistemic structures of our discipline and our own work. The hidden power of the unmarked has shaped the discipline of sociology and what has counted as general sociological theory. Interpretive sociologists should be aware of how their own identity shapes their research. Scholars of marginalized groups have often recognized their social standpoint as an important part of ethnographic research, but it is not only the socially marked and marginalized who come from a particular standpoint that shapes their life experiences, their perception, and their research interests.

*Unmarked power and epistemic exclusion: rethinking theory and researcher standpoint*

Sociologists' constructions of the canon of general sociological theories meriting broad, general, universal appeal and their construction of group-specific theories and observations to be relegated to *epistemological ghettos* (Brekhus, 1998) have followed similar lines of semiotic asymmetry to other unmarkedness/markedness contrasts. Julian Go (2020, p. 83) illustrates, for example, how early sociologists in the US were interested in uncovering universal, generic laws of human behavior; they wanted to find human universals rather that particulars. Noteworthy in their assumptions is that social science requires a distant "view from nowhere," and that the analyst oneself should be general, distant, rational, and inherently "objective" and that their own subjectivity and subject position should be invisible by virtue of their unmarked status. As Go (2020, p. 84) asserts, early sociology staked its claims to science on the premise that the only "impartial and rational" analysts were white Anglo-Europeans, and that "just as empire excluded nonwhites from full citizenship and democracy due to their presumed irrationality, parochiality, and hence undevelopment, so too did early sociology exclude nonwhites from being true producers of knowledge for the very same reason."

The epistemic structures of sociology have long considered general sociological theorizing as the work of white, male analysts, while other scholars are relegated to being scholars of the particular. In his *American Journal of Sociology* article in the 1940s, William Fontaine (1944) argued that while "the Negro scholar" has arrived, these African-American scholars are not passionately disinterested and are often interested in a "narrow scope of observation" related to their "particularistic" issues and "axes to grind" as African-Americans (see also Go, 2020, p. 88). The implication of Fontaine's claim was that African-American scholars could not be universal and objective, while white Anglo-American scholars were by comparison just (general) "scholars" and thus implicitly objective and unbiased by their very "non-race-specific" nature. In contrast to viewing the concerns of African-American scholars as particularistic, the particularistic concerns of white European scholars are considered generic and general. Max Weber's (2011 [1904]) *Protestant Ethic and the Spirit of Capitalism* is a part of the general sociological theory canon, even though one could view the origins of his theory as "an entire theory meant to address the parochial concerns of a handful of men in Germany in the early twentieth century" (Go, 2020, p. 93). That is, like the African-American scholars who Fontaine critiqued, Weber developed his theory out of a narrow scope of observation about particularistic issues. But while the motivations of each may have originated in specific biography-related concerns, we have long recognized the canonical value of generalizing from Weber's particularistic study to broader concerns about the force of ideas in social action and in shaping material interest. So, too, the biography-related concerns of African-American theorists present us with general theoretical canonical value to understand broad social processes, including identity construction, power relations, resistance, and the production of social inequalities. The growing 21st-century recognition of W.E.B. Dubois as a central figure in the development of sociological thought (see Zuckerman, 2004; Morris, 2015), rather than as a particularistic theorist of "African-American issues" outside the canon of general sociological theory, represents a corrective to a longstanding epistemological asymmetry between whose concerns have been considered "universal" and whose have been regarded as "particular." Go (2020, p. 93) argues that "canonization is … the universalization of the provincial" and that we should be more upfront about recognizing the benefits of starting from the particular and specific to understand the social world.

Sociologists need to contend with the implications of semiotic asymmetry between markedness and unmarkedness in how we conceive of social standpoint and how it affects our own work. Most importantly, the same kind of reflexivity that feminist scholars, minority scholars, and ethnographers of marginalized communities employ to their own identity position, masculinist scholars, racial and ethnic majority scholars, and ethnographers of unmarked communities need to employ to understand their own unmarked subjectivities.

The utility of marked and unmarked for understanding researchers' social standpoint is also a critical analytic tool for analyzing social identity and intersectionality.

## Power, privilege and identity

*Unmarked and marked identity attributes and intersectionality*

In my ethnographic research among suburban gay men, I noticed that gay men who were white, middle-class, suburban, and conventionally masculine, were often shaped as much or more by their unmarked identities as their socially salient and marked gay identity (Brekhus, 2003). This research, however, is far more likely to be classified as a study of gay identity than of middle-class identity. The combination of many unmarked attributes such as middle class and white with marked attributes such as gay allows for an intersectional understanding of identity. Interpretive sociology benefits from closely analyzing the ways that someone's social standpoint shapes their worldviews, their perceptions, their social networks, and their habits. And our social standpoints are intersectional.

Kimberlé Crenshaw (1991) introduced the term "intersectionality" to emphasize the intersecting axes of oppression that multiply marginalized individuals such as poor, Black women who are marginalized by their class, their race, and their gender face, and how these axes intersect and interact with one another. Crenshaw developed this idea in the context of critical legal studies. For Crenshaw, the idea that law responds "objectively" to generic legal defendants and litigants, rather than to defendants and litigants embodied by their raced, classed, and gendered identities, is a fiction. Legal actors make judgements and interpret actions based on race, class, and gender. Race, class, and gender also serve as categorical axes by which people interpret behavior and make judgements more generally. Although Crenshaw does not directly use the conceptual distinction of the marked and the unmarked, her analysis is very much about the semiotic asymmetry between social actors who are treated more negatively because of their marked social attributes and those who are given more benefit of the doubt because of their unmarked attributes. While the law itself is written in generic, universalizing language, the portrayal of law itself as neutral and objective because of such language masks the uneven practices in how interpretations of law are played out in actual legal decisions. Through her interest in the unequal practice of law, Crenshaw developed an intersectional standpoint theory that emphasizes the distinctive vantage point that people with multiple marginalized intersecting axes of identity observe the world through.

While intersectional theory has traditionally focused only on those aspects of identity that are marginalized, the analytic power of intersectionality can be enhanced further by taking seriously the intersecting dimensions of markedness and unmarkedness (Nash, 2008; Brekhus, 2020, pp. 104–6). Most individuals have a mix of marked and unmarked identity attributes that shape their life experiences and their worldview and it is therefore important to give epistemological weight to how people manage and navigate their unmarked privilege, as well as how they manage and navigate their marked axes of identity.

We attach greater *semiotic weight* (Mullaney, 1999; Zerubavel, 2018, p. 12) to culturally marked identities and acts, but unmarked acts and identities carry their own invisible weight (see Bonilla-Silva, 2011). Recognizing semiotic weight as a factor in understanding acts and identities provides a valuable insight for understanding the relative balance between people negotiating a combination of visibly weighted stigma and invisibly weighted privilege. One way this asymmetry has been metaphorically described is in terms of headwinds and tailwinds. In their article "The Headwinds/Tailwinds Asymmetry: An Availability Bias in Assessments of Barriers and Blessings," Davidai and Gilovich (2016) demonstrate people's availability bias in assessing the barriers they have had to overcome and the benefits that have assisted them. Overwhelmingly, people recognize and give great semiotic weight to the headwinds they have faced and ignore the tailwinds that have pushed them forward and aided their progress. Both tailwinds and headwinds shape our outcomes, but we mark and notice the headwinds, while the tailwinds that equally shape us push us along without being noticed. We cognitively attend, far more intensely, to the headwinds or barriers we encounter than the tailwinds or blessings we are afforded, and this has significant consequences for perception and the reproduction of social inequalities.

Intersectional theories have tended to emphasize the headwinds that multiply oppressed people face, but intersectional analyses focused on the partially marginalized and partially privileged and on the multiply privileged will paint a fuller picture of intersectionality and inequalities. Jennifer Nash (2008, p. 10) argues that while theorists of intersectionality have generally opposed imagining privileged, non-multiply marginalized social actors as central to their theoretical project, because of their normative commitment to recovering marginalized voices, this opposition to the intersecting dimensions of privilege limits the full potential of our interpretive analysis (see also

Brekhus, 2020, p. 105). While individuals are more likely to recognize their headwinds, our job as analysts is to recognize not only how marginality shapes lived experience, but how privilege, and the intersections of marginality and privilege, shape lived experience. Illuminating and ornamenting the unmarked allows us to perceive the default, taken-for-granted elements of habit and identity that intricately shape the world, but that remain generally hidden from immediate cognitive availability.

Braden Leap's (2017, 2019) ethnographic analysis of the ways rural white men constructed an intersectional masculinity in a small Missouri town sheds light on the analytic advantages of attending to intersectionality among people with a mix of marked and unmarked attributes. Marked by their rural status, such men frequently deployed their unmarked identities as white, masculine, heterosexual, cisgender men to assert positive self-identities and define themselves against multiply marginalized categories. While never directly mentioning their unmarked racial and class identities, these men constructed narratives that emphasized respected manliness as being tied to middle-class occupations, whiteness, and heterosexuality and they contrasted themselves with urban areas as dangerous imagined places that were less masculine and less authentic because of their concentrations of Black men, homosexuals, and urbanites. Without specifically naming or marking white, rural, maleness, they created an ideal of respectable rural masculine identity through discursive constructions of big cities as being marked, untrustworthy, deviant, and dangerously outside the generic mainstream of heartland America (Leap, 2017; see also Brekhus, 2020, pp. 115). Their views are in alignment with many white, working-class men in manufacturing and farming sectors of the US, who, having experienced the partial markedness of some loss of status, deploy nostalgia for a more parochial imagined "real America," where "native" non-recent immigrant status, whiteness, masculinity as defined by physical labor, and local "Main Street values" are valorized as more "authentically American" than the cultural cosmopolitanism of multiethnic cities, feminized labor markets, and the worldviews of cultural and global elites.

In a similar manner to Leap, Angela Stroud (2012, 2015), in her analysis of white middle-class gun owners identifying as generic "good guys with guns," shows the power of the discursively unmarked in identity constructions. There is no identifiable racial or class statement in the label "good guys with guns" but Stroud (2015, pp. 109) notes that the "good guy" identity is connected to a particular style of middle-class virtue dependent on a belief in community engagement, and that these men depict themselves as people who will stop to aid those in need but that assisting those in need only applied to "good parts of town," and that in "bad parts of town" one's guard should always be up and anyone seeking assistance is likely to be setting them up for victimhood and thus requires a good guy to reach for his gun. The power of unmarked identities, and the ways that it can lead to a decision to render aid or reach for lethal violence, shows the asymmetric nature of the unmarked/marked divide. And the real power in the unmarked is that the raced and classed and regioned nature of this distinction is hidden in the markedness process itself. What is an intensely raced and classed moral order is discursively defined as a simple case of good guys with guns acting as moral citizens.

Analysis of identity can also extend beyond the multiply marginalized to examine the ways that people who share salient marginalized attributes and less salient privileged attributes balance the semiotic weight of these distinctive attributes. Identity balance—how people balance their visibly weighty marked identities and their less visible unmarked ones—is an issue of central importance. In her ethnographic analysis of the new Black middle class, Karyn Lacy (2007) analyzes the balancing boundary work of middle-class Black people. They navigate not only their race but their social class. Lacy observes, for instance, how upscale Black residents avoided public schools (except for special magnet programs) and showed little interest in paying taxes to improve them, because of the weight of their social class identities, while Black residents in less upscale middle-class neighborhoods strongly favored improving the public schools. In balancing their identities, region, class, and the composition of the region were important components. Black residents in both majority-white middle-class suburbs and majority-Black middle-class suburbs viewed Black communities as an important site for their own constructions of Black identity, but they differed in which elements of the Black world they privileged. In the predominately Black residential subdivision, residents used their geographic community and neighborhood enclave to construct Black community and identity. Black residents of the majority-white suburb relied instead on traveling to Black social organizations—an ideological rather than geographical community—to establish their Black identities. Lacy (2007, p. 19) defines the latter strategy as "strategic assimilation," because the residents assimilate to their white suburbs in their residential life, but seek out Black-specific organizational identity enclaves in their non-residential life.

Strategic assimilation often involves adding weight to the privileging unmarked aspects of one's identity and engaging in bracketing strategies to temporarily subtract weight from one's marked aspects when assimilating into the majority culture. It also involves traveling to marked identity environments to accentuate one's connection to one's more marginalized attributes. The deployment of different identity spaces and different identity networks to add and subtract semiotic weight from parts of one's identity is a strategy by which people attempt to balance the weight of competing attributes of stigma and privilege. One way to balance identity is to mix the marked and the unmarked together, as Lacy's residents of

Black middle-class neighborhoods do when they present a combined intersectional Black middle-class identity that is distinctively Black and middle class together. Another way to balance identities is to move back and forth between different identities across time and space and, rather than intersectionally intertwine the identities together, alternate their weights on a moving scale, sometimes heavily weighting one end of the scale and at other times throwing the balance to the other end of the scale. The strategy of *identity integrating* involves balancing identities by combining marked and unmarked elements into hybrid identities such as Black, suburban, middle class, or gay, suburban, middle class (see Brekhus, 2003). The strategy of *identity commuting* entails strategically weighting identities based on the identity networks one is around; thus in suburban space one emphasizes one's generic suburbanness, while in Black organizations or gay spaces one emphasizes one's Black or gay identity (Brekhus, 2003). Identity commuting is reminiscent of code-switching in sociolinguistics, where codes/languages are deployed to index various identities according to one's shifting networks and travel across different borders and regions (see Gal 1987, 1993). Identity commuting is an embodied form of code-switching where, in addition to linguistic codes, one may alter one's visual presentational styles and nonverbal codes to index some aspects of identity and silence or submerge others. These different strategies of doing identity are significantly tied to the semiotic weight of the marked and the unmarked. Understanding identity strategies as strategies for managing semiotic weight allows us to see the connections between presentational strategies, identity performance, and the asymmetric inequalities that markedness and unmarkedness create.

Just as some identities are more cognitively attended to than others, so too are some acts visibly acknowledged and marked while others are ignored and taken for granted as mundane and unremarkable. Mullaney (1999) shows how some heavily marked acts (for example, murder, sex with a goat) draw significant moral attention and carry great mental weight, while many acts are so routine, habitual, and taken for granted that even with constant doings of them they are unlikely to be mentally foregrounded or acknowledged as important to who one is. One can repeatedly engage in the mundane and commonplace without generating attention, whereas even one non-habitual commission of a heavily marked act can earn one a permanent label (Mullaney, 1999).

Similar to acts and identities, risks and dangers also fall into those that are heavily marked and recognized, and those that are taken for granted and ignored as mundane or ordinary risks. Different identity communities composed of different social networks and varying sociocognitive worldviews also share different *cultures of attention* to what they perceptually mark and what they unmark (Brekhus, 2015).

*Perception: marked and unmarked risks and the semiotic asymmetry of cultural attention*

One way to think about risk perception is to distinguish between what disaster sociologist Lee Clarke (2006, 2008) refers to as "probabilistic" and "possibilistic thinking." Probabilistic thinking emphasizes things that are statistically likely to happen, while possibilistic thinking focuses on rare, dramatic risks that are extremely unlikely but have significant consequences if they occur. Probabilistic thinking asks what kinds of threats are likely, while possibilistic thinking asks what kinds of risks have extreme consequences. What risks one attends to and marks are organizationally and culturally shaped. Diane Vaughan (2002) shows, for instance, how air traffic controllers are socialized to be hyperattentive to and mark minor deviations that could potentially spell disaster, while NASA decision-makers, prior to the *Challenger* launch, were inattentive to routine and mundane dangers that could eventually culminate in more dramatic danger. Corporations and organizational actors often employ probabilistic thinking to dismiss the risk of nuclear power or toxic chemicals as low because the odds of something going wrong are low, while concerned citizens near environmental hazards are more interested in possibilities of what could happen than just probabilities of what is likely to happen (Brekhus, 2018). Cultures of prediction often deploy possibilistic thinking because their reward structure favors imagining the most extraordinary possibilities (Brekhus, 2018; Spain, 2018). The two cultures of risk perception vary, in that probabilistic thinking often focuses so intently on probabilities that it ignores the far end of the bell curve of possibilities, while possibilistic thinking is so focused on marking the extreme possibilities that it misses the vast space of the mundane, routine, and commonplace risks between no risk and extreme risk.

Possibilistic risk perception cultures of attention frequently highlight spectacular, charismatic possibilities at the expense of attending to the dangers of the familiar and routine (Brekhus, 2018). Shapira and Simon (2018) interviewed gun carriers who expressed the need to always carry a gun because there is always the rare possibility of facing a violent threat, carjacking, or kidnapping attempt. Reflecting the importance of thinking about the spectacular and unlikely, one argued "it's not the odds, it's the consequences." At the same time that gun carriers marked the spectacular possibility of being randomly targeted by violent criminals, they also took for granted as mundane, and as a relatively safe tool, the potentially lethal weapon itself. They gave great weight to the marked risk of violent crime, while also normalizing and cognitively unmarking as routine and not a risk the act of carrying a gun.

At the organizational level, global security analysts often mark extreme threats rather than mundane threats. In the linguistic marking of dangers, for instance, biological weapons are marked as a specialized kind of weapon in comparison to non-biological weapons, "dirty" bombs (radiological dispersal devices) are marked as a special kind of bomb compared to "generic" bombs (are there "clean bombs?"), and weapons of mass destruction (WMDs) are marked as distinct from weapons of ordinary destruction, which are not called WODs (Brekhus, 2018). Security experts' attentional concerns to specially named kinds of "novel" threats have led them to underestimate more likely, routine "conventional" threats (Brekhus, 2018; Spain, 2018). For example, while there has been tremendous concern over threats from novel biological weapons, the use of biological weapons by non-state agents has been limited without huge death tolls; in comparison, crude non-biological technologies are not extraordinary in their novelty, but such unmarked technologies continue to be the primary ways that non-state agents inflict serious damage to lives and infrastructure (Spain, 2018).

In preparing for the possible, security analysts attend to political violence's most remarkable elements, which are the destructive technologies, but in addition to the spectacular elements of terrorism, there is still much mundanity within political violence that requires greater attention to the routine, the mundane, and the unmarked features of violent movements; threat narratives emphasizing the dramatic potential of technologies often ignore the unmarked ordinariness of the people using the technology (Brekhus, 2018). By and large, the people using technologies for political violence use technologies they are familiar with and have access to and that others in their social networks are familiar with and have access to. As a result, cars and trucks, and crude car bombs and pipe bombs, while unmarked in dramatic scenarios of global threat assessment, are still the technologies that inflict the most overall accumulated damage from non-state actors (Spain, 2018). Beyond the novelty of extravagant technologies, non-state violent political actors are typically most effective in inflicting damage onto others if they are in relationships within social networks that make them feel they belong and that provide the support and the familiar technologies they can use.

The insight that the quotidian is often central extends to the novel versus the conventional more generally. Even beyond risk, novel new technologies draw more theoretical attention than mundane old ones. Colleges and universities, for example, often celebrate the latest cutting-edge technological advances and prioritize in their budgets new and novel technological frontiers in research, while often giving less priority to more mundane, established traditional infrastructures. Chambliss and Takacs (2014) demonstrate, for example, that while curricular and technological innovations may seem more exciting, what ultimately matters to college success for undergraduate students is something as simple, mundane, and lacking in novelty as committed people who establish meaningful relationships with students.

That is, rather than the latest novel innovations, what mattered the most was the less visible "technology" of fostering basic human interactions and relationships structured around shared endeavors.

Novelty and change are often analytically marked, but we must attend to the relational aspect between marked change and the more frequent and less novel "unchange" (Sabetta and Brekhus, 2018). As Lorenzo Sabetta and I have argued elsewhere, social change is frequently analytically marked through academic textbook titles such as *Sociology in a Changing World* (Kornblum and Smith, 2012) and *Cultures and Societies in a Changing World* (Griswold, 2013) (see Sabetta and Brekhus, 2018; Brekhus, forthcoming). These titles emphasize social change as a dominant force in the world and there are no comparable book titles such as *Sociology in an Enduringly Relatively Predictable Unchanging World*, which might more accurately portray a world where longstanding institutions, practices, and patterns of reproduced inequality show a relatively remarkable persistence.

## Conclusion

I have argued here that the semiotic distinction between the marked and the unmarked is important to interpretive sociology. My argument emphasizes these concepts as important to the kinds of concept-driven theoretical ideas that are transcontextual and applicable across multiple domains and levels of analysis (see Zerubavel, 2021). Among the contexts to which these ideas are applicable, we can include inequalities, researcher standpoint, identities, intersectionality, perception, and risk. For interpretive sociologists, the relational aspect of the unmarkedness/markedness contrast is especially important. Too often, the marked is analytically appreciated as distinctive in a group-specific analysis that removes it from the everyday generic features of social life (Brekhus, 1998). Because the relational aspect is often hidden by the invisible weight of the unmarked, the real power in the relationship is the semiotic power of the often unnoticed cognitive defaults. The subtle exercise of social power that occurs within the markedness/unmarkedness relational contrast is where much of the conceptual power for understanding social life and social inequalities occurs.

I used the reproduction of racial inequalities as an example of how the tacit construction of unmarkedness (in this case the construction of unmarked whiteness) creates a false genericization of the unmarked that then reproduces social inequalities. This false genericization within scholarly disciplines has led to the construction of canons of general theory that have been raced, classed, and gendered, but whose raced, classed, and gendered nature has been hidden within the power of the unmarked to appear universal and general rather than particular and specific. This requires us to rethink the place of social standpoint in the epistemic structures of interpretive sociology and understand our own combination of marked and unmarked attributes in our knowledge production and sociological theorizing. Understanding semiotic weight in the markedness/unmarkedness relationship contributes to the growing body of work on intersectionality, demonstrating that the intersections of disadvantage and privilege, barriers and blessings, are important from the headwinds and the tailwinds sides of identity composition.

The semiotic distinction between the marked and the unmarked is important to perception as well as identity. Analyzing risk perception, for example, demonstrates that sensational marked dangers often capture the imagination of people concerned with threats, but the invisible weight of unmarkedness also allows more probable, mundane risks to fly below the perceptual radar and continue to go unnoticed and unremarked. In general, novel new technologies draw more attention than more mundane established ones. This asymmetry between the novel and new and the conventional and quietly enduring is an important one for researchers to keep in mind.

Interpretive sociologists will find that orienting their work to attend to semiotic concepts like the marked and the unmarked can enrich a wide range of fields of inquiry. I have presented a few avenues in this chapter, but these are in no way exhaustive, rather they are intended to inspire the reader's own semiotic imagination to think through the ways that fundamental perceptual asymmetries in their field of study can be interrogated for theoretically rich insights into the nature and reproduction of social life.

## References

Bonilla-Silva, E. (2011) "The Invisible Weight of Whiteness: The Racial Grammar of Everyday Life in Contemporary America," *Ethnic and Racial Studies*, 35(2): 173–94.

Bourdieu, P. (1990) *The Logic of Practice*, Stanford, CA: Stanford University Press.

Brekhus, W.H. (1996) "Social Marking and the Mental Coloring of Identity: Sexual Identity Construction and Maintenance in the United States," *Sociological Forum*, 11(3): 497–522.

Brekhus, W.H. (1998) "A Sociology of the Unmarked: Redirecting our Focus," *Sociological Theory*, 16(1): 34–51.

Brekhus, W.H. (2000) "A Mundane Manifesto," *Journal of Mundane Behavior*, 1(1): 89–105.

Brekhus, W.H. (2003) *Peacocks, Chameleons, Centaurs: Gay Suburbia and the Grammar of Social Identity*, Chicago, IL: University of Chicago Press.

Brekhus, W.H. (2015) *Culture and Cognition: Patterns in the Social Construction of Reality*, Cambridge: Polity Press.

Brekhus, W.H. (2018) "Unmarked Risk and the Mundanity of Danger," Lawrence Livermore National Laboratory, Livermore, CA, August 2.

Brekhus, W.H. (2020) *The Sociology of Identity: Authenticity, Multidimensionality, and Mobility*, Cambridge: Polity Press.

Brekhus, W.H. (forthcoming) "Sociocultural Defaults at Rest and in Motion: Cognitive Sociologies of the Unmarked," in C. Lombardo and L. Sabetta (eds) *Against the Background of Social Reality: Defaults, Commonplaces and the Sociology of the Unmarked*, New York: Routledge.

Brekhus, W.H. and Ignatow, G. (2019) "Cognitive Sociology and the Cultural Mind: Debates, Directions, and Challenges," in W.H. Brekhus and G. Ignatow (eds) *The Oxford Handbook of Cognitive Sociology*, New York: Oxford University Press, pp. 1–27.

Chambliss, D.F. and Takacs, C.G. (2014) *How College Works*, Cambridge, MA: Harvard University Press.

Clarke, L. (2006) *Worst Cases: Terror and Catastrophe in the Popular Imagination*, Chicago, IL: University of Chicago Press.

Clarke, L. (2008) "Possibilistic Thinking: A New Conceptual Tool for Thinking about Extreme Events," *Social Research: An International Quarterly*, 75(3): 669–690.

Comer, J. (1985) "Black Violence and Public Policy," in L. Curtis (ed) *American Violence and Public Policy*, New Haven, CT: Yale University Press, pp. 63–86.

Crenshaw, K. (1991) "Mapping the Margins: Intersectionality, Identity Politics, and Violence against Women of Color," *Stanford Law Review*, 43(6): 1241–99.

Davidai, S. and Gilovich, T. (2016) "The Headwinds/Tailwinds Asymmetry: An Availability Bias in Assessments of Barriers and Blessings," *Journal of Personality and Social Psychology*, 111(6): 835–51.

Fontaine, W.T. (1944) '"Social Determination' in the Writings of Negro Scholars," *American Journal of Sociology*, 49(4): 302–15.

Friedman, A. (2019) "Cultural Blind Spots and Blind Fields: Collective Forms of Unawareness," in W.H. Brekhus and G. Ignatow (eds) *The Oxford Handbook of Cognitive Sociology*, New York: Oxford University Press, pp. 467–82.

Gal, S. (1987) "Codeswitching and Consciousness in the European Periphery," *American Ethnologist*, 14(4): 637–53.

Gal, S. (1993) "Diversity and Contestation in Linguistic Ideologies: German Speakers in Hungary," *Language in Society*, 22(3): 337–59.

Go, J. (2020) "Race, Empire, and Epistemic Exclusion: Or the Structures of Sociological Thought," *Sociological Theory*, 38(2): 79–100.

Greenberg, J. (1966) *Language Universals, with Special Reference to Feature Hierarchies*, The Hague: Mouton.

Griswold, W. (2013) *Cultures and Societies in a Changing World*, 4th edn, Thousand Oaks, CA: Sage Publications.

Hagerman, M.A. (2018) *White Kids: Growing Up with Privilege in a Racially Divided America*, New York: New York University Press.

Heath, M. (2013) "Sexual Misgivings: Producing Un/Marked Knowledge in Neoliberal Marriage Promotion Policies," *Sociological Quarterly*, 54(4): 561–83.

Jakobson, R. (1972) "Verbal Communication," *Scientific American*, 227(3): 72–80.

Johnson, W. (2020) *The Broken Heart of America: St. Louis and the Violent History of the United States*, New York: Basic Books.

Kornblum, W. and Smith, C.D. (2012) *Sociology in a Changing World*, 9th edn, Belmont, CA: Wadsworth.

Lacy, K.R. (2007) *Blue-chip Black: Race, Class, and Status in the New Black Middle Class*, Berkeley, CA: University of California Press.

Leap, B.T. (2017) "Survival Narratives: Constructing an Intersectional Masculinity through Stories of the Rural/Urban Divide," *Journal of Rural Studies*, 55: 12–21.

Leap, B.T. (2019) *Gone Goose: The Remaking of an American Town in the Age of Climate Change*, Philadelphia: Temple University Press.

Lizardo, O. (2017) "Improving Cultural Analysis: Considering Personal Culture in its Declarative and Nondeclarative Modes," *American Sociological Review*, 82(1): 88–115.

Martinez, R. (1996) "Latinos and Lethal Violence: The Impact of Poverty and Inequality," *Social Problems*, 43(2): 131–46.

Morris, A.D. (2015) *The Scholar Denied: W.E.B. Du Bois and the Birth of Modern Sociology*, Oakland, CA: University of California Press.

Mullaney, J.L. (1999) "Making it 'Count': Mental Weighing and Identity Attribution," *Symbolic Interaction*, 22(3): 269–83.

Nash, J.C. (2008) "Re-thinking Intersectionality," *Feminist Review*, 89(1): 1–15.

Rainwater, L. (2006) *Behind Ghetto Walls: Black Families in a Federal Slum*, New Brunswick, NJ: Transaction Publishers.

Rawls, A.W. (2002) "Editor's Introduction," in H. Garfinkel and A.W. Rawls (eds) *Ethnomethodology's Program: Working out Durkheim's Aphorism*, Lanham, MD: Rowman & Littlefield, pp. 1–64.

Rawls, A.W. and Duck, W. (2020) *Tacit Racism*, Chicago, IL: University of Chicago Press.

Roithmayr, D. (2014) *Reproducing Racism: How Everyday Choices Lock in White Advantage*, New York: New York University Press.

Sabetta, L. and Brekhus, W.H. (2018) "A Time for Unchange?: Reconsidering the Sociological Significance of Uneventfulness," Annual Meetings of the Eastern Sociological Society, Baltimore, February 22.

Shakur, S. (1993) *Monster: The Autobiography of an L.A. Gang Member*, New York: Atlantic Monthly Press.

Shapira, H. and Simon, S.J. (2018) "Learning to Need a Gun," *Qualitative Sociology*, 41(1): 1–20.

Simpson, R. (1996) "Neither Clear Nor Present: The Social Construction of Safety and Danger," *Sociological Forum*, 11(3): 549–62.

Spain, W. (2018) "Curious Incidents: Dogs That Haven't Barked," in Z.S. Davis and M. Nacht (eds) *Strategic Latency: Red, White and Blue: Managing the National and International Security Consequences of Disruptive Technologies*, Livermore, CA: Center for Global Security Research, Lawrence Livermore National Laboratory, pp. 52–70.

Stroud, A. (2012) "Good Guys with Guns: Hegemonic Masculinity and Concealed Handguns," *Gender & Society*, 26(2): 216–38.

Stroud, A. (2015) *Good Guys with Guns: The Appeal and Consequences of Concealed Carry*, Chapel Hill, NC: University of North Carolina Press.

Tovar, V. (2016) "Take the Cake: Thin Fetishism is More Common than Fat Fetishism," Ravishly.com, December 1. Available from: www.ravishly.com/2016/11/30/take-cake-thin-fetishism-more-common-fat-fetishism

Trubetzkoy, N. and Jakobson, R. (1975) *N. S. Trubetzkoy's Letters and Notes*, Paris: Mouton.

Vaisey, S. (2009) "Motivation and Justification: A Dual-process Model of Culture in Action," *American Journal of Sociology*, 114(6): 1675–715.

Vaughan, D. (2002) "Signals and Interpretive Work: The Role of Culture in a Theory of Practical Action," in K.A. Cerulo (ed) *Culture in Mind: Toward a Sociology of Culture and Cognition*, New York: Routledge, pp. 28–54.

Watters, E. (2013) Why Americans are the Weirdest People in the World, *Tampa Bay Times*, March 30. Available at: www.tampabay.com/archive/2013/03/30/why-north-americans-are-the-weirdest-people/

Waugh, L.R. (1982) "Marked and Unmarked: A Choice between Unequals in Semiotic Structure," *Semiotica*, 38: 299–318.

Weber, M. (2011 [1904]) *The Protestant Ethic and the Spirit of Capitalism*, trans. and updated by S. Kalberg, New York: Oxford University Press.

Zerubavel, E. (1998) *Social Mindscapes: An Invitation to Cognitive Sociology*, Cambridge, MA: Harvard University Press.

Zerubavel, E. (2018) *Taken for Granted: The Remarkable Power of the Unremarkable*, Princeton, NJ: Princeton University Press.

Zerubavel, E. (2021) *Generally Speaking: An Invitation to Concept-driven Sociology*, New York: Oxford University Press.

Zuckerman, P. (ed) (2004) *The Social Theory of W.E.B. Du Bois*, Thousand Oaks, CA: Pine Forge Press.

2

# Blumer, Weber, Peirce, and the Big Tent of Semiotic Sociology: Notes on Interactionism, Interpretivism, and Semiotics

*J.I. (Hans) Bakker*

## A new synthesis: incorporating Blumer, Weber, and Peirce

This chapter proposes to refine the symbolic interactionist project by incorporating Peircean semiotics and neo-Weberian interpretation. Symbolic interactionism appears to have forgotten key sources of its American pragmatist roots. Peirce's indirect influence on Mead and Blumer, for instance, is often undertheorized but should be made central to the foundational narratives of symbolic interactionism. This calls for more sophisticated understandings of meaning-making that incorporate Peirce's semiotic triadic model and classifications of signs where symbols are just one kind of signs among others. Here, I take on these matters and expand on my pragmatic sociology (Bakker, 2011a) to introduce the emergent project of a semiotic sociology. In stepwise fashion, I lay foundations of a metaparadigmatic synthesis—a "big tent"—based on five key arguments that build upon each other, including Blumer as its anchor point, American symbolic interactionism, global interactionism, neo-Weberian interpretive analysis for cross-historical comparison, and Peircean semiotics as the culminating paradigm that pulls it all together.

The Cold War is over (Menand, 2021). But new conflicts are on the horizon (Acemoglu and Robinson, 2019). Only one social science is highly respected by key elite decision-makers: neoclassical economics. The other social sciences are more fragmented. US sociology, in particular, is focused on political issues having to do with intersectionality, but it is also fragmented, lacking an overarching framework. One "fragment" that has had a lasting impact is the empirical study of the phenomena we can call "interactions" based on "symbols." Many US sociologists were intrigued by micro-level social psychological aspects of actual symbolic actions and interactions, and for a while that was for many what sociology as a discipline was all about, but the focused symbolic interactionist tradition no longer exists, except as a memory (Blumer, 1975, 1986 [1969]). It was never the paradigm that pulled all of sociology together.

Talcott Parsons attempted to establish a big tent for sociology and the social sciences in general through the Department of Social Relations (DSR) at Harvard. But the DSR is long gone (Cossu, 2021). Parsons (2012 [1951]) wrote on "social systems" and the "theory of action" (Smelser, 2012). He applied his theories to a variety of topics, including kinship and socialization, psychological relationships, and religious organization. But it was his "grand theory" that was of special value. The AGIL scheme (adaptation, goal, integration, latency) was used by many of his graduate students (Bortolini, 2021, pp. 55–7). Robert Bellah, for example, went on to develop an interpretive approach to the social sciences. However, the interpretive social science advocated by Bellah and Clifford Geertz is now not front and center. Their interpretive paradigm only gets us so far. It is a version of an interpretive metaparadigm that I argue still lacks key ingredients.

The central idea put forward here is a new *synthesis* for a potential "big tent." It is an attempt to accomplish what Parsons and later Bellah and Geertz tried to do. This synthesis involves a kind of "ramping up" or lifting up (a "sublation," an *Aufhebung*) based on a dialectical way of thinking. The chapter begins with Herbert Blumer's (1986 [1969]) conceptualization of social interactionism based on "symbols" and includes five essential paradigmatic elements. Those elements are grouped within a focused argument in which details are, of necessity, limited. The argument involves an analysis of insights from many separate interpretive networks (Bakker, 2009, 2011b). It draws from ideas found in the work of Blumer, Weber, and Peirce and builds a big tent that includes interactionism, interpretivism, and semiotics.

That is a tall order! It is a far cry from the extant reliance on a fragmented system of diverse research paradigms. Following the Cold War, the rhetoric of US social sciences eventually moved away from Talcott Parsons' approach of functional analyses of social systems (Parsons, 2012 [1951]). This paradigmatic shift involved a Geertzian version of interpretive social sciences stressing individuals' understanding of their environments. But Geertz was more of an anthropologist than a sociological theorist. His empirical work on Indonesia was good, but it did not fully illustrate what interpretive social science can offer. It stopped short of what is argued in this chapter. Despite his brilliance, he did not pursue Weberian or Peircean ideas adequately.[1]

My analysis of ideas concerning interactionism, interpretivism, and semiotics is discussed in the context of developing a broader perspective not yet common in the field of sociology in the US. Rather than focusing on the preservation of separate research paradigms, this analysis examines the ways that a common sociological "discipline" could be formed. The resulting epistemological base is an extension of a synthesis I called "pragmatic sociology" (Bakker, 2011b). I conceptualize this new metaparadigm as semiotic sociology.[2] The new metaparadigm of semiotic sociology provides a broader horizon than is common in US sociology today.

## Symbols and interactions

Let me start by discussing the ideas of "symbol" and "interaction." The word "symbol" means many things to many people. I am starting with the unexamined use of the word symbol in the general phenomena we can call actual symbolic interactions. My analysis then considers five versions of the study of "interactions based on symbols," including perspectives presented in the works of Blumer, Weber, and Peirce. As explained later, these are essentially five steps in an overall argument, or rather five complex arguments that in a general sense form a package. Thus, the five key arguments that constitute my overall argument are:

- The first argument is Blumer's view as stated in his famous book (Blumer, 1986 [1969]).
- The second argument concerns American symbolic interactionism (ASI) as developed by US contributors in the 1970s and 1980s. These sometimes build on pragmatism (Zeitlin, 2001).
- The third argument is a global view of interactionism in general (IG), a view that was developed both before and after Blumer's key contributions.
- The fourth argument is an expanded "interactionist imagination" that also incorporates interpretive social science, especially neo-Weberian *verstehende Soziologie* using ideal type models (ITMs) and comparative historical sociology (CHS).

---

[1] One difficulty is that Max Weber was often viewed through lenses made by Parsons at Harvard and Bendix at Berkeley. Those lenses still needed to be further polished. Both contributors missed crucial points.

[2] I chose not to use the phrase "semiotic sociology" in the earlier publication since many people confuse French *semiologie* with what is meant here by Peirce's global semiotics.

- The fifth argument involves including a metaparadigm with insights from neo-Peircean pragmaticism and semiotics. Peirce's triadic epistemology of symbols as a subset of signs allows us to develop a philosophically sophisticated metaparadigm or big tent.

The really big tent *can* encompass all five arguments, but rarely does. The analysis of ideas concerning interactionism, interpretivism, and semiotics are discussed here as part of my effort to arrive at a broader perspective on a framework, or big tent. A neo-Blumerian, neo-Weberian, neo-Peircean synthesis can be very heuristic. But, as time goes on, the next generation will have to work out many details of this ambitious idea. The really big tent could be referred to as the "semiotic interpretive interactionist imagination" (SIII), but this is awkward. I have previously called the central thrust of this idea "pragmatic sociology" (Bakker, 2011b), but the intention there all along was a kind of *pragmaticist* sociology that would take Charles Sanders Peirce's semiotics into account. Therefore, a more relevant and accurate designation for the purpose of linking everything into one big tent in social science could be *semiotic sociology*.

If the whole is accepted, it involves thinking more carefully than is usually done about Blumer's SI, American SI, interactionism in general (IG), Weberian ITMs to study actual symbolic interactions using the Weberian CHS approach, and semiotics. Peircean semiotics is what pulls it all together. One argument builds on the next. To visualize the big tent, think of a circus performance. The first act is fairly straight forward, perhaps a juggler. The second act involves more. Then we add other entertainers. Weber is definitely a high wire act! But we call the whole circus by one name. That convenient label could be semiotic sociology. (The phrase "big tent" is a figure of speech, of course, a kind of synecdoche, like speaking of "the Crown" when referring to far more than a physical object worn on rare occasions by the monarch.)

The big tent idea is briefly illustrated later by mention of my empirical work in Bali, Indonesia. To fully comprehend and understand Bali requires a semiotic sociology, and not just Clifford Geertz's "thick description" (Geertz, 1972, 1973; Bakker, 2015a; Cossu, 2021). Further work on semiotic sociology as part of a big tent will be heuristic if steps one to five of the argument presented here are fully understood. The overall paradigm and the logic of method will provide much for future generations to play with and will illuminate many questions in the human sciences. Grounded theory will help for theory and praxis (Bakker, 2015b, 2019).

Too often, some academics want to skip a deeper comprehension of each of the various contributions. For example, British or European thinkers may not always be fully aware of the US contributions of the 1970s and 1980s (step two) before making sweeping statements about a more global view of interactionism in general (IG). Taking all of the ideas only sketched in this chapter into account is not necessary, but a certain degree of humility is required to get it right before making sweeping generalizations about interactionism. The same is the tendency to overgeneralize about "Weber" after having only read a small portion of Weber's complex oeuvre. The idea of a metaparadigm that incorporates both neo-Peircean pragmaticism and "all of semiotics" is also a tall order. Step five of the argument will only be touched on here, but those already familiar with either Peirce's pragmaticism or semiotics in general may quickly comprehend what is being hinted at. While a certain degree of humility is required when speaking about theorists' views, it is also true that a certain degree of courage is required to sketch ideas that have not been commonly accepted in the past. Hopefully, anyone with the patience to follow all five steps of the argument will come away with a desire to read more deeply on all five topics. Then the best thing that could happen would be for this chapter to provoke some honest debate on these crucial questions. They are important in the abstract, but also can be translated into ways of reconceptualizing aspects of everyday life practices and governmental policies.

## Step one: Blumer 1969 as anchor point

Herbert Blumer wrote on what he called *Symbolic Interactionism* as both a theoretical perspective and a logic of method (not just a set of techniques or "methods" in an operationalized sense). The actual interactions that take place among human beings have also been viewed as processes of "symbolic interaction" (not capitalized) by other thinkers. Many who were not necessarily symbolic interactionists in any strict sense made contributions to the study of symbolic interaction. However, when sociologists mention Blumer, it is common to only mean what Blumer wrote in one book.

Blumer's (1986 [1969]) *Symbolic Interactionism: Perspective and Method* was read by many students in the 1970s and it put the notion of symbolic interactionism (SI) on the map in the field of sociology, but not in psychology (Converse, 1986). SI became one disciplined form of sociology (Stryker, 2003). Blumer himself was reasonably consistent in his overall assumptions and what he called his "perspective" (rather than theory or paradigm), but he sometimes diverged from some of the more strident statements in the twelve chapters of his 1969 collection of essays. The 1969 book is a bit uneven. But it became a *locus classicus* for symbolic interactionism in the same way that Garfinkel's book *Studies on Ethnomethodology* (1967) became a *locus classicus* for ethnomethodology and Herbert Marcuse's *One-Dimensional Man* (1964) became an anchor point for many young neo-Marxian activists.

Blumer is an anchor point for many sociologists. Those who did SI work regard it highly. Those who never really studied the SI perspective often refer to the book because that is all they know about the research approach. They may never even have read Zorbaugh (1983 [1929]).[3] Nevertheless, Blumer is more than just that one anchor point. Blumer's significant contribution to interactionism in general (IG) cannot be denied. Symbolic interactionism of a general sort is recognized today as a significant perspective and method (Maines, 2017; Fine and Tavory, 2019). The term "symbolic interaction" has two major components: symbols and interactions. The combining of those two terms creates something somewhat new. The older term, well known before Blumer's work, was *social* interaction. But Blumer added the word symbol. We can unpack what is meant by "symbols." In general, most researchers in the Blumerian SI tradition have emphasized the study of "interactions." They more or less ignored the ways in which the general concept of a "symbol" (or set of symbols) can be considered to be problematic. In this chapter, I touch on five interrelated topics that involve ways to broaden and deepen Blumer's useful approach to empirical research. One aspect of a broadened approach to Blumer's specific version of symbolic interaction involves focusing on the term "interaction." That has led to interactionism in general as a tent.[4] However, the concerted focus on a semiotics of "symbols" (and all signs) is what is missing in interactionism.

There were, of course, many notions of "social action" and "social interaction" in the social sciences before Blumer; but it was Blumer who underlined the way in which all aspects of social interaction can be comprehended and understood as involving symbolic meaning. He even dared to apply that to movies and the women's high fashion industry in Paris. Later he applied it to industry in the US and other topics. Some of his work from the 1930s is included in the 1969 book but other papers from the 1940s and 1950s are included as well. Only the introductory essay was written specifically for the 1969 volume. He writes:

> My conclusion in contrast to the undue length of this essay [Chapter one], is indeed brief. It can be expressed as a simple injunction: Respect the nature of the empirical world and organize a methodological stance to reflect that respect. This is what I think symbolic interactionism strives to do. (Blumer, 1986 [1969], p. 60)

That provides carte blanche for a very big tent indeed.

---

[3] Bob Prus (1996) was the first colleague to insist I had to read the classic SI ethnographers.
[4] Of course, we also need to consider "situations" and the idea of the definition of the situation (Bakker, 2007, 2011c, 2021). A "situation" occurs in real time in actual places.

## Step two: American symbolic interactionism (ASI)

There can be further discussion of the difference between the general idea of symbolic interaction and the research paradigm or framework of Blumerian symbolic interactionism. Then, as mentioned before, we also have interactionism in general (IG), which may or may not follow Blumer's original ideas, as narrowly conceived. Indeed, research now considered iconic for SI followed a general version of interactionism even before Blumer published his book (for example, Zorbaugh, 1983 [1929]). The overall "theory" of symbolic interactionism research has many subsidiary perspectives and research theories. The overall "methodology" involves many more specific methods and techniques, including grounded theory (Charmaz, 2014; Bakker, 2019).

Symbolic interaction did not stop with ideas found in Blumer's famous book. That book provided an anchor point, but many academics went full steam ahead and developed ideas they thought of as symbolic interactionist. That constitutes a somewhat bigger tent. Indeed, in terms of number of thinkers and publications, it is already very large. Blumer himself was hardly consistent or rigorous in using his own pronouncement in his 1969 book. He himself went far beyond what he wrote about the study of symbolic interactions by symbolic interactionists.

Today, we have available to us a kind of neo-Blumerian "synthesis." For example, feminist insights are already also part of the tent of interactionism as it exists today. Blumer's original formulation was not feminist. Dorothy Smith, who was influenced by symbolic interactionism, especially by the work of Shibutani (1988), has generally avoided the use of the phrase and has invented a whole new, more feminist vocabulary.[5] But I would argue she is an interactionist. Balogh (1990) has incorporated feminist insights about *agape* (love) in her nuanced analysis of Weberian ideas.

No one advocates using a string of adjectives (for example, neo-structural, radical, postmodern, existential, feminist, semiotic) to interactionism, of course, but when we discuss the big tent we imply there is room for all those variations, and more. Some of the various components are emphasized in this chapter. Neo-Marxian political economy (Bakker, 2015c) is not

---

[5] In my discussions with Dorothy Smith in Ontario and at American Sociological Association conferences, she revealed that she avoided referring to Carl Couch and Gregory Stone as well as other symbolic interactionists in her publications due to the male chauvinist ways in which they treated her at various conferences. Her British radical feminist views were unacceptable to those Midwestern American men. Other interpretive sociologists treated her differently. It is not all just a matter of "ideas" in the abstract. When we examine paradigmatic allegiances, context matters a great deal. Rock (1979) makes the difference between the UK and the US abundantly clear.

discussed, but later there is a discussion of a Marx-Weber combined approach. Determining the boundaries is a matter of ongoing negotiations and continual academic interactions. Some interactionists, for example, reject the contributions of Collins (2004) to interactionism, but others welcome his insights.[6] There is no one "pope" of symbolic interactionism. But it is fairly clear what interactionism is not. Those who reject all forms of the empirical study of interaction based on symbols cannot be deemed to be interactionists. Yet, while that seems simple enough on the surface, it nevertheless requires some further clarification.

Interactionists are interested in topics like why people enjoy certain movies or drink certain beverages. Or how consumer products are labeled using symbols. The terms of the debate in the UK are different (for example, Erikson-Goldthorpe-Portocarero [EGP] class scheme; see Tittenbrun 2015), but the issues are not only familiar to theorists but have a major bearing on social praxis. Dennis (2017) draws attention to studies on the effect of movies (Blumer, 1933) and on fashion and the fashion industry (Blumer, 1969). The comments in both of those empirical studies do not necessarily conform to some of the more stringent criticisms that Blumer made of the use of "concepts" (Blumer, 1940). He alludes to broader generalizations but he does not consider fashion in a comparative manner by also looking at the fashions that were significant in Paris in the 1930s in the working-class districts and the brothels (Brassaï, 1976).

What is clear is that Fine (1993) is quite correct to point out that interactionism is flourishing. But perhaps even he does not yet fully grasp the extent to which a neo-Blumerian synthesis can flourish even more, not only in sociology, or the discipline of interactionist sociology, but also in other fields and disciplines, even economics. The "glorious triumph of interactionism" in the general sense is assured. But a strict interpretation of only one part of Blumer's oeuvre limited to only one of his many contributions is not likely to prosper either in the US or globally. It is too clearly rooted in one time and place. Careful research on specific topics will still involve taking Blumer (1986 [1969]) seriously, but theoretical and methodological innovations, as well as new techniques for doing empirical research, will continue to shift.

---

[6] At a recent Society for the Study of Symbolic Interaction conference, Randall Collins attended, and he did so in part because a group of Danish interactionists were interested in his approach and had invited him to speak about it in Denmark. Collins distanced himself from a narrow and strictly Blumerian version of SI. That was in part because he wanted to also include theories of "social action" often associated with Parsons at a time when Parsons was the epistemological "other" for many interactionists.

## Step three: interactionism in general (IG)

Paul Rock, a writer from England, takes a much more "British" approach to the topic of interactionism writ large. He does so in a rambling book that includes a chapter on "The Roots of Symbolic Interactionism" (Rock, 1979, pp. 24–58) and another somewhat disconnected chapter on "Pragmatism and Symbolic Interactionism" (Rock, 1979, pp. 59–101). A neo-Blumerian synthesis that takes the form of interactionism in general (IG) is something that interactionists can agree on, but only if we agree that the methodological stance reflects respect for the empirical world. In that context, we need to ask what the word "world" may have meant to Blumer.

There is considerable confusion in discussions of attempts to study "interactions" based on the use of "symbols" in an empirical manner. Both of the two key terms need to be unpacked. It is not always clear what the boundaries of symbolic interactionist analysis really are. Is an "exchange" a type of "interaction"? Does a person engaged in an internal dialogue constitute a "semiotic self" (Wiley, 1994; Bakker, 2011b)? Is that semiotic self involved in an ongoing stream of consciousness series of "interactions" with one's internal "me" and "I" and "you"? Can the word "symbol" also be used to refer to "icons" and "indices" and even "arguments" or "assertions"? Could we have "iconic interactionism" and "indexical interactionism"? Is it possible to discuss "argumentative-assertional interactionism" as a subtopic of all forms of interaction? Would the relationship between a "master" and a "slave" also be a form of symbolic interaction even though Hegel (2019 [1806]) did not link up his discussion of the "phenomenology" of that interaction with any sociological studies per se? Are neo-Marxian studies of the interactions of workers or peasants with managers or plantation owners (Eidlin, 2018; Tarlau, 2019) also interactionist in some ways? These questions do not need to be resolved here, but they point to the need for a very big tent if we are going to live up to Blumer's injunction.

It is a mark of Blumer's greatness as a thinker that he formulated ideas that are still heuristic, but they can be made even more applicable if broadened and deepened in terms of both the concept of interaction and the idea of the symbol as a sign. But to some extent it is also true that Blumer was like the "emperor who has no clothes" (Low, 2013), in that he was sometimes too strident in a somewhat rigid defense of views that required further consideration (Couch, 1984). Nevertheless, it would not be heuristic to drop Blumer altogether from the pantheon of "American sociology" (Matthews, 1977). To fully understand "the empirical world" requires asking if that empirical world can be restricted to the US, and of course the answer is that it cannot be truly "generic" if it is only based on studies done in the US, or closely similar countries. Therefore, let me move on to the next step.

## Step four: Weberian interpretive sociology (ITM, CHS)

The "semiotic imagination" means different things to different people. Here the idea of semiotics will be discussed in terms of sociological thinkers well known in the field of sociology, especially in the disciplinary foci concerning Max Weber, a key contributor to the founding of *Soziologie* in Germany.

Weber's attempt to focus a more specific use of the general label and avoid a portmanteau use of the borrowed word was to modify the German word *Soziologie* by adding an adjective. That is similar to the way in which George Herbert Mead took the term "behaviorism" and also added an adjective. In both cases, the idea was not only to be more specific but also to modify key ontological and epistemological assumptions. For Mead it was "social behaviorism" and for Weber it was *verstehende Soziologie*, often translated as "interpretive sociology" or "understanding sociology." Here, I briefly discuss the idea of interaction in a more comparative and historical manner than is usually done (Bakker, 2010a, 2010b). Some indication of the type of research I am thinking of can be found in various essays on symbolic interaction (considered in general) in various cultures (primarily in the Indonesian archipelago) by Geertz (1973). By broadening the focus to many societies historically and by deepening the study of the meaning of those terms to include semiotics, we can provide a heuristic way of utilizing Blumer's insights without being hamstrung by his limitations.[7]

Max Weber (1978) wrote about "social action." But some Blumerians take that to mean he has nothing to say about social interaction. Yet, he is clearly writing about agents who interact in social settings. His approach involves social action that is interactive at micro, meso, and macro scales. He is often regarded as an important interpretive sociologist since he specifically wrote about interpretive sociology (Weber, 1968 [1922]) as *verstehende Soziologie*. However, to some extent, his focus was often on groups of social actors in more *macro-level* situations. Those macro issues have been debated by classical political economists and Marxist political economists. He is not known for *micro-level* studies of interaction, even though he does make many comments about interactions based on symbols. Weber was not a dogmatic "structuralist" and he assumed that structures are the product of

---

[7] My own research in Indonesia and India has given me a slightly different perspective than the way in which a person studying symbolic interaction exclusively in North America or in Europe might tend to have when discussing topics like making a living or maintaining family (kinship) ties. The excellent symbolic anthropological research done by Clifford Geertz (1973) is a clear example of the deeper use of the concept of the "symbol," albeit not in a Peircean manner per se. Petrilli (2013) incorporates Peircean insights in her discussion of "anthroposemiotics." Petrilli's 2015 book is a sophisticated analysis of the "science of signs" and the idea of "significs."

the interactions of groups of individual human beings. Humans act on the basis of shared values, but nevertheless also as autonomous agents.

Clifford Geertz (1973) recognized the importance of Weber's interpretive approach and utilized some of Weber's insights in his comparative historical and anthropological work on Bali, Java, and Morocco. In my own intellectual quest, a key starting point since the 1970s (and my dissertation defense) has been an attempt to better comprehend Weber's oeuvre. For example, I appreciate the heuristic value of an ideal type methodological approach (Weber, 1949 [1904–1917]). We talk about "ideal types" but sometimes fail to realize that an ideal type model (ITM) almost always consists of a set of ideal types. Weber does not just use one ideal type at a time. He often develops complex sets of ideal types. Today, some are willing to call that approach the use of ideal type models (ITMs).

For many social scientists interested in SI and a *sociological* SI approach to "social psychological" questions (as opposed to a more *psychological* approach to social psychology), the insights we find in Weber and Geertz are not directly relevant. Much more frequently SI authors and other interactionist authors will cite George Herbert Mead and Herbert Blumer as key "classical" contributors. One reason for that is that up until recent decades SI was dominated by studies of the US and most of those studies were not historical or comparative in the sense of Weberian comparative historical sociology (CHS).

Mead and Blumer, however, do *not* work directly with Weber's ideas. Mead could have since he did read German. He read German well enough to review books that (during his lifetime) were only available in German. Indeed, Mead studied in Germany and approached Wilhelm Dilthey as a possible dissertation advisor ("doctor Father"). Blumer could have since much of Weber's work was translated during Blumer's long career. Also, Blumer did make a short visit to Germany (as well as Paris, France). But neither Blumer nor his main intellectual influence, Mead, paid any attention to Weber as a sociologist relevant to the study of interaction. Blumer also never read Peirce. I will discuss this in more depth later.

To begin discussing the possibilities of an interpretive sociology that is more comparative and historical, we can ask "how should Weber's views on 'status' be considered?" What did Weber *really* mean by the term "status?" As hinted at before, it was only after decades of using the term incorrectly that I realized that Norbert Wiley (1987, p. 17) makes it clear that a shift occurred from a Marxian view that the "superstructure" was the state and the value component of institutions, to a new Marxian view that the superstructure is primarily the value component of institutions and the state has "its own [analytical] box." That is, the analysis of "the state" became dislodged from the analysis of "the superstructure" and the superstructure became linked through the work of some Frankfurt School thinkers to the idea of "culture" writ large. For me, the big surprise in what Wiley writes is the next move in the shift. It is possible to conceive of the culture in the sense of Marxian superstructure as very much like what Weber probably mostly meant by *Soziale Stünde* (social statuses). "Weber sometimes uses status more narrowly to refer to prestige, honor, and the like" (Wiley, 1987, p. 17); however, at other times, Weber emphasizes a conceptualization of status that gets away from individual prestige of noblemen (aristocratic privilege) and includes what Marxists started to call the idea of a superstructure analytically separate from the "state" per se.

Moreover, in line with comparative interpretive analysis, an important book by Blumer that has often been ignored is his *Industrialization as an Agent of Social Change* (1990). He shows no awareness in that book about Weber's theories concerning social class, status, and power. Yet they obviously are relevant to the topic of industrialization. However, there are hints in that book that Blumer went a long way toward meeting the criticisms often raised concerning his conceptual scheme and methodological position. Obviously more could be said on this important topic of class, status, and power. But my point here is that it takes some time to apply semiotic insights about the importance of "signs" in historical context.

In the British context, the discussion of what some call the "EGP class scheme" suddenly becomes clearer when one starts to realize the hidden assumptions concerning a revised European Marxist approach. Moreover, in terms of the idea of a big tent of interactionist theory and research that attempts to broaden the insights of American symbolic interactionism to also include Peirce's views on semiotics and Weber's views on interpretive sociology, we suddenly become aware that the combined Marx-Weber approach is no longer conceptualized by contemporary sociologists the way it once was. There is no necessary chasm.

## Step five: Peirce's semiotics

We can say that Blumer wrote on symbols and their importance for interaction, but without any mention of semiotics. Hence, step five of the argument is the importance of semiotics. That includes the notion that we need precise, unambiguous use of key concepts (indeed, of concepts that refer to all types of signs). We need to consider the idea of symbol more carefully, utilizing insights from semiotics. To a large extent, I focus here on Peirce's version of semiotics as a rich source of both theoretical insights and prompts for doing good research on difficult to research topics (see, for example, Anderson, 2004).

The Chicago School of sociology, in its various iterations—first, second, third—is important in this context (Low and Bowden, 2013). But even more important is seeing the study of interactions based on symbols as a powerful way to bring sociological research into a more focused theoretical and methodological perspective with regard to the use of all "signs" in all times and places. Not only is Blumer's symbolic interactionism often discussed within the context of the first Chicago School, but it is also frequently viewed as part of the legacy of the philosophical orientation known as "American pragmatism" or simply "pragmatism" (Morris, 1970; Putnam, 1981, p. 50). Charles Sanders Peirce is often considered the "father" of American pragmatism (or, pragmatisms). Thus, it is true by definition that if Blumer was in any way influenced by pragmatism, he must have been influenced by Peirce. But the influence might be somewhat obscure or even hidden, especially if Blumer himself was not directly or fully aware of Peirce's work.

In this chapter, I will not attempt to situate Blumer within the American pragmatist tradition in any thorough manner, except to point out that a general understanding of the idea of symbolic interaction preceded Blumer's articulation of a sociological research paradigm we think of as "symbolic interactionism" in a specifically Blumerian sense. Peirce, Mead, Cooley, Dewey, James, and even Royce employed the concept of individual human social actors interacting on the basis of shared significant symbols. To go even more deeply into the influence of Kant (Münch, 1981; Rock, 1979), Hegel (2019 [1806]; Rock, 1979), and Dilthey (1989; Bakker, 1999) on the various strands of American pragmatisms and sociology as a discipline would take us into a discussion involving complex philosophical themes. Such philosophical problems as ontology and epistemology have occupied many academic philosophers other than Mead. Blumer seems to have never considered in depth the impact of either philosophical or sociological phenomenology (Schutz and Luckmann, 1985).

Moreover, the idea of using the word "sign" as representing all possible forms of signification (in the generic sense) is ignored by Blumer. The general idea does not hinge on whether or not we choose to use the word "symbol" or "sign." Indeed, a thinker can be reasonably clear without necessarily being fully aware of semiotics. Just as there were many general notions of evolution in natural sciences before Darwin's 1859 book *On the Origin of the Species*, both at Edinburgh University and even in his own family (Wilson, 2017), he nevertheless made an original contribution by being very clear about the importance of natural selection.

### *An old idea in new packaging*

British sociologists often focus on different questions. But it may be that the debate concerning semiotics is useful here as an illustration of the importance of recognizing the very basic point in semiotics generally, and in any potential sociological theory that shows an awareness of the big tent idea of interactionism (including Weberian interpretive sociology), that the words (and the translations of words) really matter. A discussion of the word (sign) "status" helps to amplify what has already been said about Weber and the value of a semiotic view concerning key terms.

Thus, sometimes a conceptualization of an important question is put into a new set of clothes. The old wine is simply put into new bottles. At Bristol University, for example, Will Atkinson (2017) is doing excellent work on social class and social status, using insights about social space from Pierre Bourdieu. This is important and worthwhile. To comprehend his work, however, I had to learn what British and European (for example, Polish) sociological theorists mean by what one author calls the "EGP class scheme" (for example, Tittenbrun, 2014, 2015). That led to carefully reading a paper by an Oxford sociologist named Tak Wing Chan. Professor Chan has been working with John Goldthorpe. It turns out that the "EGP class scheme" is essentially one interpretation of Max Weber's analysis of class, status and power. Goldthorpe is well known for his work on social class using quantitative methods. Chan and Goldthorpe (2007) provide a good overview of some of that research. It resembles some of Erik Olin Wright's work, which is better known in the US. But a Polish author pointed out that it is important to know that Weber wrote using German words. Tittenbrun (2014) argues that the German-language term used by Weber (*Soziale Stünde*) should be translated into English as "social estate" or "social statuses" rather than "social groups" or "status classes."

Without again going into the remarkable arguments put forward by Norbert Wiley (1987) about the way the word "status" can mean different things, it is important to recognize that some of what Tittenbrun objects to in the so-called "EGP class schema" is part of an old debate within Marxism about Marxian academic ideas concerning infrastructure (means of production) and "superstructure." What is the superstructure exactly? For a long time, it was "everything" that is not part of the "economic base." But Marxian thinkers then shifted ground and that allowed for more resonance with key ideas found in Weber's theories (Wiley, 1987, pp. 17–18).

### *Lifting the veils as a semiotic trope*

Blumer (1986 [1969], p. 39) mentions the metaphor of "lifting the veils." He indicates that by focusing on *symbolic* interaction, we can see "what is going on." Interaction based on symbols is a key factor in all aspects of human life. Indeed, we would only be *Homo sapiens* (as animals) if it were not for the fact that the use of complex symbols is intrinsic to what it means to be human. Animals can be sophisticated, but despite studies that have indicated a far greater use of symbols among animals than was previously thought, it is nevertheless also the case that at a certain point the difference between a human being (who is both a *Homo sapiens* and a symbolic interactor) is clear. Instead of units of DNA, we have units that could be called "symbols" in the generic sense. The general idea is that a generic aspect of all human social action and social interaction is the use of symbols ("signs"). The last 100,000 years or more of being human has involved countless interactions between and among human beings involving the use of symbols. Interaction based on symbols is what make us humans, a point that George Herbert Mead sketched out philosophically and that Herbert Blumer was able to focus on sociologically. He did that in a way no philosopher (as opposed to sociologist) had previously done.

The final "sublation" (*Aufhebung*) of this argument is that a big tent that we could call "semiotic sociology" has to involve a use of some aspects of semiotics. There is no room to fully develop all that needs to be said about semiotics in general and Peirce's specific version of semiotics in particular. But that would be useful in a book-length version of this five-step argument.

## Conclusion

There has been and will continue to be a range of opinions expressed about Blumer's thinking. This chapter has attempted to indicate some of the ways in which a "tent," now called the "interpretive imagination," or, more precisely, the neo-Blumerian symbolic interpretivist synthesis, might be expanded even further than it already has been.

A possible general label for the metaparadigmatic "big tent" that I am advocating here could be "the semiotic interpretive interactionist imagination" (SIII). The metaparadigm of SIII is a deepening and broadening of the ideas well known to many academics interested in the SSSI. In addition to SI (symbolic interactionism) per se, I am advocating adding a general interactionism (IG) that could implicitly (or preferably more explicitly) also include interpretive sociology and semiotics. Of course, a simpler way to express that generalizing and synthesizing conceptualization could be to simply call it "semiotic sociology." Some academics will not fully grasp the broad sweep of the general notion. There are at least two versions of semiotic sociology already in the works. As it is, many people who are experts on Weberian theory do not (yet) contribute directly to either semiotics or interactionism. What is being discussed here is a bit of a long shot. Yet it is also a contribution to sociological theory to make the problem of a lack of a big tent clearer. Many thinkers are so focused on their own "interpretive network" (often in their own national setting, further restricted by language) that if we can accomplish the goal of making the general idea of a semiotic sociology (that is, an SIII metaparadigm) clearer, then there will also be a lot for future generations to work on in terms of further versions of a semiotic sociology.

Therefore, I come not to bury Blumer, but to praise him. The highest praise one can give of any academic scholar is to indicate that the person's thinking has stimulated many people. A kind of neo-Blumerian interactionism is alive and well in the metaparadigm of interactionism. That is already a "tent" of sorts. What is absolutely clear to all interactionists is that SI is not functionalism. The papers published in the journal *Symbolic Interaction* are certainly not likely to be based on stereotypical, naive versions of positivist, functionalist or structuralist paradigmatic assumptions. In the future, the general idea of interactionism can broaden and deepen even further. That may involve including more of the ideas associated with Weber and Peirce.

In the 21st century, it will be important to consider many aspects of "Being-in-a-Meaningful-World" (Fine and Tavory, 2019). It would take a book-length treatment to flush out all the arguments hinted at in this sketch and to fully acknowledge the ideas of thinkers like West (1989) and Halton (1995) on American pragmatism, much less pragmatism worldwide. Brief comments could have been made about Kant, Hegel, Dilthey, Simmel, Royce, Peirce, Mead, James, Park, Faris, and others who preceded Blumer's SI. It is also possible to expand the argument about interactionism, grounded theory, Weberian interpretivism, and Peircean semiotics. Koshul (2014) has linked Peirce's pragmaticism and Weber's methodological views in an innovative way.

All that was to make it clear that a very big tent we could still merely call "symbolic interactionism," but that it might be more appropriate to call "semiotic sociology," is quite possible. But that it is only if we take Blumer's seminal insights and run with them. Maines (2017) has certainly been arguing that for some time. But the interactionist imagination is even bigger than some contemporary interactionists may fully grasp. If we broaden and deepen Mead's social behaviorism (Puddephatt, 2013) and Blumer's articulation of a methodology (Blumer, 1986 [1969]), then a neo-Blumerian interactionist synthesis may serve as a fundamental basis for a more "disciplined" sociology rather than an amorphous field with many "sections" and research theories lacking any overall unity. We have to go even further.

Some interactionists may be drawn, for example, to Habermas' use of Mead's insights to construct a neo-Marxian/neo-Weberian critical theory (Habermas, 1987). Although it requires reading between the lines, writers in the liberal version of neo-Weberian theory (Barker, 2018) or the neo-Marxian tradition (Acemoglu and Robinson, 2019) are also not immediately opposed to pragmatist interactionist insights. There may also be more interest in Peirce (1998) and attempts to link Peirce more clearly to the social sciences (Petrelli, 2013, 2015; Koshul, 2014). A clear indication of the evolution of interactionism is the importance to ever more sophisticated discussions of grounded theory (Bakker, 2019), an offshoot that Blumer did not articulate as clearly as subsequent thinkers (Charmaz, 2014). It is not all just a matter of fieldwork done on the basis of intuitive approaches like those a journalist might use in even the best investigative reporting. David

Heise and his colleagues (see MacKinnon 1994; Lively and Heise, 2004; Heise, 2007) have pointed in an interactionist direction that is valuable and affect control theory can now also be included in the expanded big tent of interactionism. Another possibility is that even aspects of "critical realism" could be reconciled with interpretivism by a focus on the dialectical and even secular "transcendental" iterations of the mature versions of critical realism (Gorski, 2013).

This topic is even more exciting than I had assumed when I first set out to learn a bit more about Blumer and possibly suggest some ways to clear up some of the confusion. I also set out in the first rough draft to provide a few insights drawn from Weber and Peirce. I now perceive those insights in a way that I myself had not comprehended fully before. As I worked on various drafts of this chapter, the gaps in the study of interaction (in the generic, global, and historical sense) that is based on symbols (again, in the most general sense as "signs") became clearer to me. It would be an improvement over the reification of "structures" and their "functions". Thinkers in the sociocultural and political-economic *Wissenschaften* disagree on many things, but the ontological and epistemological value of a neo-Blumerian symbolic interactionist synthetic big tent approach (that is, semiotic sociology writ large) is perhaps a way out of the labyrinth of conflicting theories and methodologies. We need to disambiguate all the words that we take for granted, words like "symbol" and "culture" and "interpretation." We need semiotics to really understand one another, both in the sense of empathy at the personal level in everyday life and in the full academic sense of *Verstehen* as an aspect of Weberian comparative historical sociology.

Let me conclude with an anecdote. I looked at some of the work done at the University of Bristol. When I told my son about my writing of this chapter, he said: "I was in Bristol." I was surprised. But then I asked: "Did you DJ there?" It turns out he had! We wrote a paper together. It is on the "Club DJ" and it was my first publication in the journal *Symbolic Interaction* (Bakker and Bakker, 2006). My most recent interactionist, interpretive, comparative historical sociological paper in symbolic interaction is on Bali, Indonesia (Bakker, 2015a). I could not have done that analysis simply on the basis of traditional symbolic interactionism. Elements of interactionism, interpretivism, and semiotics were involved. I thought about my son having actually been to Bristol. I have been to Cambridge and Oxford. I went to a European symbolic interactionist (EU-SSSI) conference in Lancaster. Is that relevant here? Yes, it is.

This chapter is the culmination of a fifty-year process of attempting to comprehend the field of study known as "sociology." My work on Bali and statements about Geertz's failure to fully incorporate a semiotic sociological approach are not made lightly. The challenges that still confront the

*Geisteswissenschaften* are exciting. Hopefully, this broad vision of a big tent (or a metaparadigm) will be a useful step along the way toward a better, more valuable social science not restricted to the interpretive sociology put forward by people as brilliant as Geertz, Bellah and many others in a generation just before mine. It is up to the next generation to stand on the shoulders of those giants as well as thousands of thinkers like me who keep trying to approach academia as an exciting adventure.

**References**

Acemoglu, D. and Robinson, J.A. (2019) *The Narrow Corridor: States, Societies, and the Fate of Liberty*, New York: Penguin.

Anderson, D. (2004) "Peirce's Commonsense Marriage of Religion and Science," in C. Misak (ed) *The Cambridge Companion to Peirce*, Cambridge: Cambridge University Press, pp. 175–92.

Atkinson, W.J. (2017) *Class in the New Millennium: The Structure, Homologies and Experience of the British Social Space*, London: Routledge.

Bakker, J.I.H. (1999) "Wilhelm Dilthey: Classical Sociological Theorist," *Quarterly Journal of Ideology: A Critique of Conventional Wisdom*, 22(1/2): 43–82.

Bakker, J.I.H. (2007) "Definition of the Situation," *The Blackwell Encyclopedia of Sociology,* vol. III, ed G. Ritzer, Malden, MA: Blackwell, pp. 991–2.

Bakker, J.I.H. (2009) "Peirce, Pragmaticism, and Public Sociology: Translating an Interpretation into Praxis," in H. Dahms (ed) *Nature, Knowledge and Negation: Current Perspectives in Social Theory*, vol. 26, Bingley: Emerald Group Publishing, pp. 229–57.

Bakker, J.I.H. (2010a) "Interpretivism," in *The Encyclopedia of Case Study Research*, vol. 1, A.J. Mills, G. Durepos and E. Wiebe (eds) Los Angeles, CA: Sage, pp. 486–93.

Bakker, J.I.H. (2010b) "Deference versus Democracy in Traditional and Modern Bureaucracy; Refinements of Max Weber's Ideal Type Model," in B. Zaheer and J.M. Bryant (eds) *Society, History, and the Global Human Condition*, Plymouth: Lexington Books, pp. 105–28.

Bakker, J.I.H. (2011a) "Pragmatic Sociology: Healing the Discipline," *Sociological Focus*, 44(3): 167–83.

Bakker, J.I.H. (2011b) "'The 'Semiotic Self:' From Peirce and Mead to Wiley and Singer," *The American Sociologist*, 42(2/3): 187–206.

Bakker, J.I.H. (2015a) "Deeper Play: Geertz's 'Thick Description' and a Balinese Temple Ritual (the Odalan)," *Studies in Symbolic Interaction*, 44: 79–116.

Bakker, J.I.H. (2015b) "Thick Description, Nomological Laws and Ideal Types: Which Methodology Helps Most with Praxis?," in H. Dahms (ed) *Globalization, Critique, and Social Theory: Diagnoses and Challenges*, Bingley: Emerald Group Publishing, pp. 267–92.

Bakker, J.I.H. (2015c) "Introduction: The Methodology of a New Political Economy" and "Conclusion: The New Political Economy Perspective," in J.I.H. Bakker (ed) *The Methodology of Political Economy: Studying the Global Rural-Urban Matrix*, Lanham, MD: Lexington Books, pp. 1–29 and 211–55.

Bakker, J.I.H. (2019) "Grounded Theory and Grounded Theory 'Methodology'," *Sociological Focus*, 52(2): 91–106.

Bakker, J.I.H. (2021) "Gandhi, Hegel and Freedom: *Aufhebungen*, Pragmatism and Ideal Type Models," in A.K. Giri (ed) *Pragmatism, Spirituality and Society*, Singapore: Palgrave Macmillan, pp. 263–84.

Bakker, J.I.H. and Bakker, T.R.A. (2006) "The Club DJ: A Semiotic and Interactionist Analysis," *Symbolic Interaction*, 40(1): 71–82.

Balogh, R.W. (1990) *Love or Greatness: Max Weber and Masculinist Thinking, a Feminist Inquiry*, London: Unwin Hyman.

Barker, C. (2018) "Educating Liberty: Democracy and Aristocracy," in J.S. Mills (ed) *Political Thought*, Rochester, NY: University of Rochester.

Blumer, H. (1933) *Movies and Conduct*, New York: Macmillan.

Blumer, H. (1940) "The Problem of the Concept in Social Psychology," *American Journal of Sociology*, 45(5): 707–19.

Blumer, H. (1969) "Fashion: From Class Differentiation to Collective Selection," *The Sociological Quarterly*, 10(3): 275–91.

Blumer, H. (1975) "Exchange on Turner 'Parsons as a Symbolic Interactionist'," *Sociological Inquiry*, 45(1): 59–68.

Blumer, H. (1986 [1969]) *Symbolic Interactionism: Perspective and Method*, Berkeley, CA: University of California Press.

Blumer, H. (1990) *Industrialization as an Agent of Social Change: A Critical Analysis*, D.R. Maines and T.J. Morrione (eds) New York: Aldine de Gruyter.

Bortolini, M. (2021) *A Joyfully Serious Man: The Life of Robert Bellah*, Princeton, NJ: Princeton University Press.

Brassaï, G.H. (1976) *The Secret Paris of the 30's*, trans. R. Miller, London: Pantheon Books.

Chan, T.W. and Goldthorpe, J.H. (2007) "Class and Status: The Conceptual Distinction and its Empirical Relevance," *American Sociological Review*, 72: 512–32.

Charmaz, K. (2014) *Constructing Grounded Theory*, 2nd edn, Los Angeles, CA: Sage.

Collins, R. (2004) *Interaction Ritual Chains*, Princeton, NJ: Princeton University Press.

Converse, P.E. (1986) "Generalization and the Social Psychology of 'Other Worlds'," in D.W. Fiske and R.A. Shweder (eds) *Metatheory in Social Science: Pluralisms and Subjectivities*, Chicago, IL: University of Chicago Press, pp. 42–60.

Cossu, A. (2021) "Clifford Geertz, Intellectual Autonomy, and Interpretive Social Science," *American Journal of Cultural Sociology*, 9: 347–75.

Couch, C. (1984) "Symbolic Interaction and Generic Sociological Principles," *Symbolic Interaction*, 7(1): 1–13.

Dennis, A. (2017) "Herbert Blumer – From Critique to Perspective," in M.H. Jacobsen (ed) *The Interactionist Imagination: Studying Meaning, Situation and Micro-Social Order*, London: Palgrave, pp. 145–67.

Dilthey, W. (1989) *Introduction to the Human Sciences: Selected Works*, vol. I, (eds) R. Makkreel and F. Rodi, Princeton, NJ: Princeton University Press.

Eidlin, B. (2018) *Labor and the Class Idea in the United States and Canada*, Cambridge: Cambridge University Press.

Fine, G.A. (1993) "The Sad Demise, Mysterious Disappearance, and Glorious Triumph of Symbolic Interactionism," *Annual Review of Sociology*, 19(1): 61–87.

Fine, G.A. and Tavory, I. (2019) "Interactionism in the Twenty-first Century: A Letter on Being-in-a-Meaningful-World," *Symbolic Interaction*, 42(3): 457–67.

Garfinkel, H. (1967) *Studies in Ethnomethodology*, Englewood Cliffs, NJ: Prentice-Hall.

Geertz, C. (1972) "Deep Play: Notes on the Balinese Cockfight," *Daedalus*, 101(1): 1–38.

Geertz, C. (1973) *The Interpretation of Cultures*, New York: Basic Books.

Gorski, P.S. (2013) "What is Critical Realism? And Why Should You Care?," *Contemporary Sociology*, 42(5): 658–69.

Habermas, J. (1987) *The Theory of Communicative Action*, vol. 2: *Lifeworld and System: A Critique of Functionalist Reason*, Boston, MA: Beacon Press.

Halton, G. (1995) *Bereft of Reason: On the Decline of Social Thought and Prospects for its Renewal*, Chicago, IL: University of Chicago Press.

Hegel, G.W.F. (2019 [1806]) *The Phenomenology of Spirit*, trans. T. Pinkard, Cambridge: Cambridge University Press.

Heise, D. (2007) *Expressive Order: Confirming Sentiments in Social Actions*. New York: Springer.

Koshul, B.B. (2014) *Max Weber and Charles Peirce: At the Crossroads of Science, Philosophy, and Culture*, Lanham, MD: Lexington Books.

Lively, K. and Heise, D. (2004) "Sociological Realms of Emotional Experience," *American Journal of Sociology*, 109(5): 1109–36.

Low, J. (2013) "The Emperor has No Clothes: Waning Idealism and the Professionalization of Sociologists," in J. Low and G. Bowden (eds) *The Chicago School Diaspora: Epistemology and Substance,* London: McGill-Queen's University Press, pp. 357–65.

Low, J. and Bowden, G. (eds) (2013) *The Chicago School Diaspora: Epistemology and Substance*, London: McGill-Queen's University Press.

Maines, D. (2017) *The Faultline of Consciousness: A View of Interactionism in Sociology*, New York: Routledge.

Marcuse, H. (1964) *One-Dimensional Man*, Boston, MA: Beacon Press.

Matthews, F.H. (1977) *The Quest for an American Sociology: Robert E. Park and the Chicago School*, Montreal: McGill-Queen's University Press.

MacKinnon, N. (1994) *Symbolic Interactionism as Affect Control*, Albany, New York: State University of New York Press.

Menand, L. (2021) *The Free World: Art and Thought in the Cold War*, New York: Farrar, Straus and Giroux.

Morris, C.W. (1970) *The Pragmatic Movement in American Philosophy*, New York: G. Braziller.

Munch, R. (1981) "Talcott Parsons and the Theory of Action I: The Kantian Core," *American Journal of Sociology*, 86(4): 771–826.

Parsons, T. (2012 [1951]) *The Social System*, New York: Free Press.

Peirce, C.S. (1998) *The Essential Peirce: Selected Philosophical Writings: Volume 2 (1893–1913)*, ed the Peirce Edition Project, Bloomington, IN: Indiana University Press.

Petrilli, S. (2013) *The Self as a Sign, the World, and the Other*, New Brunswick, NJ: Transaction Publishers.

Petrilli, S. (2015) *Victoria Welby and the Science of Signs: Significs, Semiotics, Philosophy of Language*, New Brunswick, NJ: Transaction Publishers.

Prus, R. (1996) *Symbolic Interaction and Ethnographic Research: Intersubjectivity and the Study of Human Lived Experience*, Albany, NY: SUNY Press.

Puddephatt, A.J. (2013) "Finding G. H. Mead's Social Ontology in his Engagement with Key Intellectual Influences," in J. Low and G. Bowden (eds) *The Chicago School Diaspora: Epistemology and Substance*, London: McGill-Queen's University Press, pp. 93–109.

Putnam, H. (1981) *Reason, Truth and History*, Cambridge: Cambridge University Press.

Rock, P. (1979) *The Making of Symbolic Interactionism*, London: Macmillan.

Schutz, A. and Luckmann, T. (1985) *The Structures of the Life-World*, Evanston, IL: Northwestern University Press.

Shibutani, T. (1988) "Herbert Blumer's Contributions to Twentieth Century Sociology," *Symbolic Interaction*, 11(1): 23–31.

Smelser, N. (2012) "Foreword," in T. Parsons, *The Social System* (reissued), New Orleans, LA: Quid Pro Publishers.

Stryker, S. (2003) "Whither Symbolic Interactionism? Reflections on a Personal Odyssey," *Symbolic Interaction*, 26(1): 95–109.

Tarlau, R. (2019) *Occupying Schools, Occupying Land: How the Landless Workers Movement Transformed Brazilian Education*, New York: Oxford University Press.

Tittenbrun, J. (2014) *Concepts of Capital: The Commodification of Social Life*, New Brunswick, NJ: Transaction Publishers.

Tittenbrun, J. (2015) "The EGP Class Scheme: In Search of a Theory," *International Letters of Social and Humanistic Sciences*, 44: 29–44.

Weber, M. (1949 [1904–1917]) *The Methodology of the Social Sciences*, trans. and ed E.A. Shils and H.A. Finch, Glencoe, IL: Free Press.

Weber, M. (1968 [1922]) *Economy and Society*, (eds) G. Roth and C. Wittich, Berkeley, CA: University of California Press.

Weber, M. (1978) "The Nature of Social Action," (ed) W.G. Runciman, trans. E. Matthews, *Max Weber: Selections in Translation*, Cambridge: Cambridge University Press, pp. 7–32.

West, C. (1989) *The American Evasion of Philosophy: A Genealogy of Pragmatism*, Madison, WI: The University of Wisconsin Press.

Wiley, N. (ed) (1987) *The Marx-Weber Debate*, Newbury Park, CA: Sage Publications.

Wiley, N. (1994) *The Semiotic Self*, Chicago, IL: University of Chicago Press.

Wilson, A.N. (2017) *Charles Darwin: Victorian Mythmaker*, London: John Murray.

Zeitlin, I.M. (2001) "Classical Principles of Social Psychology: The American Pragmatist School," in I.M. Zeitlin, *Ideology and the Development of Sociological Theory,* 7th edn, Upper Saddle River, NJ: Prentice-Hall, pp. 399–440.

Zorbaugh, H.W. (1983 [1929]) *The Gold Coast and Slum: A Sociological Study of Chicago's Near North Side*, Chicago, IL: University of Chicago Press.

3

# Collective Agency: A Semiotic View

*Rein Raud*

Quite a few influential accounts of group agency (Searle, 1992; List and Pettit, 2011; Tuomela, 2013; Bratman, 2014; Gilbert, 2014) share the view that agency can only be attributed to real individual subjects, while groups can only metaphorically be considered as agents, because only individuals have the capability to really act. This view relies on an unproblematizing conception of the individual subject as a singular, self-identical, and continuous entity among other such entities of various kinds. On the other hand, it is customary to think of meanings as shared, supraindividual items that do not paradigmatically exist solely in the consciousness of one individual, but appear in their interaction. This leaves the semiotic aspect of any kind of action with a curious structural hiatus; on the one hand, the action belongs to the individual, on the other, however, any meaning that is involved in it does not. The goal of the present chapter is to have a closer look at this conceptual knot.

Let me state at the outset that I do not believe the problem can be efficiently solved in the framework of the received view of what agency is, nor in the terms of the object-centered ontology on which this view relies. The standard account of agency could be summarized as something like this: an individual mind regularly entertains a variety of identifiable mental states, such as beliefs, thoughts, ideas, and intents. In interaction with its environment, it is capable of forming particular intents to carry out particular actions. When circumstances allow, the individual whose mind it is will undertake the said action as a result of the intent that has been formed (Schlosser, 2019). Mental states behave in this scheme as distinct "things" of their own right: they can be entertained and formed by different people at different times and still be, for all purposes, identical to themselves. The mind, in turn, is seen ambiguously as both the master entity that "has" these states and the container that "holds" them. In sum, this standard account treats the whole domain where events take place as an empty space populated with different kinds of "things," some agentic, others not, some abstract (such as mental states), others not.

It is this account that I intend to dispute, first, by suggesting, along the lines suggested by relational sociologists (Donati, 2010; Crossley, 2011; Dépelteau, 2013; Powell, 2013; Donati and Archer, 2015), that the primary constituents of social processes are not things, but relations between them, and, second, by developing the insights of "extended mind" theories (Clark and Chalmers, 1998; Haugeland, 1998; Wheeler, 2010; Malafouris, 2013), according to which an individual mind, understood as the mental activity encapsulated in a particular body, is also not the locus where agentic decisions are normally taken and realized. In other words, I will contest how the received view reifies a large number of the elements needed to explain the idea of agency into self-identical object-like things, although these could be more adequately described as processes or constituents of processes. Accordingly, I will also reject its axiomatic taken for grantedness of the atomic individuals, primarily defined by their bodily limits, with mental activity usually reduced to supervenient states of their physical brains.

The problems of the received view thus begin on the level of ontology, which I will address first. After a quick look at the processes of emergence of social entities, I will move on to the problem of how to view the individual agent in process-ontological terms and, arguing that language is one of the key components to create and uphold the social fabric, to the idea that what I call "discursive consolidation" is the prerequisite of any viable agentic decision. I will conclude with a theory of the collectivity of the subject, which I will place into the context of recent debate.

## Social entities

It seems to be customary to think about social entities by default as things, as languages usually designate them with nouns that carry an aura of selfsameness with them. It should, however, be intuitively clear that most terms designating social categories in fact refer to events, practices (that is, at least minimally consciously repeatable and structured sequences of events), or elements thereof. This is perhaps more obvious for social entities such as rituals, trials, and competitions, but the same applies to seemingly less context-bound social entities as well. Thus, even when a material object has been explicitly created for the purpose of being used as a social entity (such as bills of money issued by a central bank), it is only in reference to certain practices (of exchange, credit, and so on) that the social character of these entities can be apprehended. In other words, when we talk about social entities, we are not referring to things, but rather to *reified segments of processes*, which are extracted from the flux of experienced reality during acts of signification (see Raud, 2016, pp. 38–42, for a more detailed discussion). This reification serves the legitimate and useful purpose of facilitating the production of shareable descriptions and narratives about these processes. Similar to meanings in the Wittgensteinian sense of the word, which do not exist apart from their use, social entities only become what they are in the process of practice, and ontological considerations about them should therefore take into account both their embeddedness and their dynamism.

Socio-ontological accounts about how social reality emerges (Searle, 1996, 2008; Thomasson, 2003, 2019; Ásta, 2018) indeed address this problem. One of the often-met solutions they propose is a division of social reality into two levels, by arguing that "social facts" constitute a special layer over and above the brute reality of "natural facts." Thus, certain objects can remain objectively the same, but perform the role of regular coins at one moment and collectibles at another, and the same person may be dressed up as a judge at one moment and as Santa Claus at another. On this view, entities are anchored in their primary, physical being and acquire a secondary, social role on the basis of collectively performed meaning-bestowing operations. Segments of brute reality are *turned* into segments of social reality. The task of social ontology is to specify the precise nature of the operations by which this happens, and to describe the patterns these operations follow. Obviously, certain physical constraints of the brute reality limit the usability of particular entities for particular social functions (it is not very practical to use huge rocks or ubiquitous sand as money), but otherwise the choice of natural objects for social roles can be relatively arbitrary.

Against this view, I would like to suggest that the separation of "brute" and "social" levels of reality is itself arbitrary. The social is possible precisely because reality, itself, is not brute, at least not from the point of view of the individuals making up a particular sociocultural configuration. Relying on the view of "situated knowledge," suggested by Donna Haraway (1991, pp. 188–90) as the only objectivity that is actually available to us, and the idea of "disclosure" formulated by Joseph Rouse (2002, p. 131), I would prefer to approach perceived natural reality as already endowed with certain relational qualities. In brute terms, the words "cold" and "warm," "heavy" and "light," "large" and "narrow," or even "pleasure" or "pain" do not have any meaning, and yet reality is disclosed to individuals primarily in ways that are more aptly described by such vocabulary. Desire, fear, abjection, and other emotive responses to the world color reality for the mind from the very beginning, and when language starts to be used for dissecting it, certain cultural attitudes are spontaneously acquired together with it. We therefore co-produce our natural environment—in the form in which it appears to us—just as we do with our social setting, that is, by endowing it with significance, and conversely by structuring the significance it has for us.[1] Even though we tend to forget this in the process, conceptual entities such as kinds, numbers, geometrical shapes, and other such generalizations only figure in descriptions of and narratives about reality, and are not to be found, as such, in reality itself.

On this view, the difference between natural and social kinds does not lie in the procedure by which such kinds enter the picture, but in what they are generalizations about — phenomena that are primarily social and can therefore, in principle, be changed through social procedures, and phenomena that are not and cannot. Note that this view only concerns generalizations and does not advance a view of things themselves being products of mental operations. Note, also, that in spite of their inevitable bias, it is perfectly legitimate to operate with such categories until information comes to light that casts doubt on the propriety of their further use.

This view has certain similarities with the so-called "easy" ontology outlined by Amie Thomasson (2014, p. 86), which rejects overall criteria for existence and stipulates that a kind[2] exists if and only if the application conditions associated with the term referring to that kind in a particular context[3] are fulfilled. By "application conditions," Thomasson (2014, p. 89) means "certain basic rules of use that are among those that are meaning-constituting for the term," they "should be thought of as semantic rules analogous to grammatical rules" (2014, p. 92), "rules for when it is and is not proper to use a term, which speakers master in acquiring competence with applying and refusing a new term in various situations" (2014, p. 93). Although this makes it clear that "existence" is, on this view, ascertained by and through language, Thomasson nonetheless makes the distinction between what is generally believed to exist and what "really" exists, emphasizing that

---

[1] As Michel Serres (2011, p. 74) puts it: "Knowledges and cultures leave us the imprints of references through which what we believe are givens appear ... structures through which we do not see, feel, or understand the real but rather appropriate it under the name of science, technique, thought."

[2] It should perhaps be noted here that the idea of "kinds" is cognitively useful only if a kind is defined not on the basis of one, but at least two, or preferably more, distinguishing features. The idea of "race," for example, does not imply that people of a certain skin color form a certain category that is distinct from others by nothing else than this marker, but also makes claims about their intellectual, athletic, artistic, and other inclinations or medical liabilities.

[3] Thomasson uses the word "world" for this, in the sense analytical philosophers often ascribe to that term, that is, as any of the possible worlds that might have evolved if things that did not happen necessarily would have happened otherwise. Changing this to (empirical, sociocultural) "context" makes the claim stronger, but, as it will be seen, not contrary to Thomasson's theory.

"'application conditions' should not be understood as conditions under which it would be warranted or generally accepted to apply the relevant term," but as "conditions under which it (really) would be proper to apply the term" (2014, pp. 93–4). The idea is, evidently, not that there would be situations in which certain things really, mind-independently, belong to certain kinds, to which a term could be properly applied, but that it is possible for people to be unaware or misinformed about certain situations, so that they would not be inclined to use a term, but if they were properly informed about the circumstances, they would not hesitate to do so.

I do not think the dismissal of this requirement of real applicability would hurt Thomasson's theory, but it may be that she is reluctant to sever the link between the existence of "kinds" and actually, mind-independently obtaining circumstances. In contrast, Ásta (Sveinsdottir)[4] (2018) has proposed a rather radical theory of social kinds that she calls "conferralism," which specifically rejects the idea that something "really" belongs to a social kind if that status has not been specifically (although not necessarily explicitly) assigned to it. Ásta uses examples from sports, claiming that it is correct to say about a certain sequence of movements that they constitute an "offside," "strike" or "out" in football, baseball and tennis respectively only if the referee judges them to be so, and not in a mind-independent reality. The membership in a social kind thus has to be conferred and is not possessed naturally. Ásta (2018, p. 11) does make a distinction between "detected" and "undetected properties" of the movement, admitting that the referee can make a mistake about what really happened, but this does not change the status of the movement in its social context. A famous episode from sports history confirms this: in 1986, Diego Maradona scored a decisive goal against England in the football World Cup using his left hand, but the referee did not notice it, and Maradona's team went on to become the champion. The breach of rules was later made explicit, but this did not change the results of the game and the competition (BBC Sport, 2014). Ásta (2018, pp. 21–4) further distinguishes between institutional and communal social properties, the first being conferred by an authority, the other by someone with standing, institutional properties being less dependent and more likely to elicit endorsement.

But if we take Ásta's theory seriously, we need to note its much broader and more serious implications by moving, for example, from the sphere of sports to the sphere of law. If a series of events only acquires its legal status by conferral, then we cannot say that a crime has been committed until

---

[4] I will be using here the forename as the form of reference preferred by the author herself, but it should be noted that her patronymic is being treated as a surname by many bibliographies and databases.

a judgement saying so has been passed in a court. On the one hand, this agrees well with the idea of the presumption of innocence, but, on the other hand, exonerates the people who have not been caught, no matter what they have done. This might persuade some people to agree with Thomasson rather than Ásta on the issue, but there is a way around this, namely through distinguishing between knowingly committed crimes, which would confer the status of crime to the actions by the participants themselves, in an act of self-conferral.[5] In such a case, culpability would originate in the act of knowingly committing a crime, and not in the action "really" being a crime—we may even imagine a situation where someone thinks she will be committing a crime, while what she does is actually legal in her circumstances.

Another question to be addressed about Thomasson's idea of applicability conditions is that of different, incompatible semantic systems and their relation with "real" circumstances. Already Hjelmslev (1959, p. 104) has pointed out that terms with the same overall meaning do not refer to precisely the same concepts in different languages: taking the words referring to "tree/wood" as an example: the French *bois, arbre, forêt*, the German *Baum, Holz, Wald*, the Italian *albero, bosco, foresta* and *legno*, and the Danish *træ* and *skov* all have partially overlapping but not matching semantic fields, thus the applicability conditions of these terms in any particular instance depend on the language used more than what the words are pointing to. If we add to these differences the socially and culturally added layers (such as regular metaphoric connections) that condition the use of particular words in their habitual linguistic setting, the differences will become even greater. We should therefore take "real conditions" at least with the caveat that it refers to mind-independently legitimate applicability of rules that are themselves not mind-independent, as it is empirically obvious that the semantic fields of dictionary equivalents rarely coincide fully even across closely related languages, not to speak of distant and unrelated ones.

Yet another point of divergence between Thomasson's view of kinds/categories and the view advanced here is the apparently static nature of Thomasson's kinds. These curiously seem to stand outside time, although it seems doubtful that the empirical applicability conditions of any term can stay the same over long periods of time. However, once we acknowledge the sociocultural nature of terms we use to generalize and to assign phenomena to categories, we might as well accept the temporary and changing character of these terms. Thomasson (2014, p. 94) does acknowledge that in passing,

---

[5] Ásta (2018, p. 24) briefly mentions the possibility of self-conferral, but she means by it the act of someone with authority or standing conferring a status to their actions that is public, such as an usurper crowning herself as a monarch.

but without allowing for a too significant role of such changes. Nonetheless, scientific discoveries and social cataclysms quite often have a much more decisive impact on the language we use and the applicability conditions of a certain term may change relatively quickly.

It is therefore fair to say that factors other than correspondence with reality may be decisive in determining how the rules for applicability conditions change in actual empirical social reality. Elsewhere, I have presented a more detailed account of the way in which innovative meanings are launched as bids to increase the cognitive adequacy of a sociocultural group, and gradually enter circulation (Raud, 2016, pp. 45–7); here it will have to suffice to say that although the accuracy of the narratives about and descriptions of the world and the social process is certainly one of the factors that might contribute to the triumph of innovative meanings over residual ones, it is not at all a necessary condition of success—on the contrary, simple theories engaging the desires and fears of a critical amount of people may lead them to view certain phenomena in certain terms, which in turn may lead to the proliferation of such toxic discourses as xenophobia or conspiracy theories.

However, if we treat the intrinsically diverse domain of social entities as consisting of practices and practice-derived reifications, we soon note that not only the concepts, but also the general "grammar" according to which the social world is structured, or the principles governing its organization, are already produced in meaning-producing action rather than naturally given. This means that there has to be an agentic and signifying element at work in the very core of social entities, something that the theory of Ásta also tacitly implies. It to this element that we turn next.

## Agents: individual/collective

In the discussions of individual versus collective agency, we see that in recent literature, views on this issue differ rather widely. On one extreme, there is the complete denial of collective agency, the position called "methodological individualism" or "eliminativism" (Bratman, 2014; Gilbert, 2014; Ludwig, 2016), which claims that phrases like "the board has decided" or "the opinion of the government" are always used metaphorically, because decisions can be made and opinions entertained only by single individuals. Collectives, on this view, are simply groups of individuals, whose interaction determines the position of the collective. On the other extreme, there are theorists such as Tollefsen (2015), who claim that it is possible to attribute to groups even certain cognitive qualities, which the individuals in those groups do not have, but only come to partake of through and during their joint action. On this view, the defining properties of groups are emergent, that is, they cannot be reduced to any of the properties that single members of the group have, but only emerge in their interaction. Nonetheless, even theorists who admit group selves, in the way Tollefsen does, do not consider that groups actually entertain processes that can be considered on the same terms as psychological phenomena, that is, they go on to hold that there are no collective "mental states."

One of my aims here is to defend a position that goes beyond this view, claiming that there is no fundamental difference between collective and individual subjective process, and therefore collective agency not only exists, but should be analyzed similarly to the way we treat individual agency.

The grounds for this claim lie in an understanding of the individual as a dynamic semiotic being, an open, not a closed system, following the extended and enactive mind theories put forward by cognitive science and philosophy over past decades. This argument, too, fits more neatly into a process-ontological framework, as it extends to the individual selves the view that entities are not continuous and selfsame, but embedded in frameworks of constantly changing relations to their others. Some of these changes can be very slow and therefore seem insignificant, or so quick as to be imperceptible, but these qualities of change are tied to our perceptive and conceptual apparatus rather than to those phenomena themselves—just as we notice the symptoms of a viral disease, but not the actual virus. On this view, the idea of society as consisting of single individuals and determined by the relations between them is an abstraction, convenient as a heuristic tool for some purposes, but nonetheless a simplification that glosses over a multitude of significant factors, including the signs and meanings that emerge in and often change the course of the social process as well as the nonhuman and hybrid "things" that participate in it, as convincingly argued by Bruno Latour (1993). Even though some classic (structuralist) semiotic approaches, too, advocate the elimination of "noise" for the distillation of the "message," from the present perspective this inevitably leads to significant distortions. What can seem to be "noise" from one perspective may serve as "message" from another, as deconstructive and feminist criticism has long ago made clear.

From this perspective, methodological individualism/eliminativism does not really make sense, because it relies on the presupposition that an individual is self-identical and pre-existent in regard to the social relations it engages in, rather than shaped by them, as philosophical accounts of selfhood acknowledge since at least George Herbert Mead (1972, pp. 155ff.). Moreover, the eliminativist perspective is not only erroneous in its conceptualization of social reality, but also directly harmful for social sciences, such as economics, where the presupposition of single rational individuals as the components of society makes it difficult to assess the actual nature of economic processes, as many contemporary economists have pointed out (Ackerman, 2002; Söderbaum, 2008, pp. 121ff; Lawson, 2017).

What I therefore suggest is that the individual should not be considered as a selfsame static entity with clear and defined interests, but more properly an internally contradictory and dynamic agent, who is herself in a constant process of change. From a certain perspective, we could even view the individual as primarily the site of a *semiotic process*, the word "semiotic" here used in a wide sense to refer to the constant production of new meaning of various kinds, from integrated responses to sense stimuli to conscious verbalizations of thoughts to stored memories, which are again nothing but subjective, often distorted and dynamically altered representations of past situations or articulations. All these interact with each other, placing the subject in an unbalanced situation, where multiple competing inputs of different types combine to form a complex field in which new meanings constantly emerge. These meanings need not form a coherent, flawless semiotic layout without any contradictions involved, although a certain degree of integration is necessary for a field of meanings to be able to process and assess new input. But people are not conscious machines, and, for that matter, even intelligent machines break down under controversial and incompatible orders. The functionality of human beings and societies is, I argue, precisely dependent and enhanced by the internally contradictory process of the human mind, which is constantly torn into different directions and action scripts not necessarily compatible with each other. Thus, instead of thinking of the human mind as a "thing" with an internal, self-identical structure, it would be rather more appropriate to picture it as a fluctuating field, with different points vying for the status of the central decision-making focus, and none of them succeeding permanently.

One significant aspect of that field is what I would like to call "linguistic self-awareness," or the part of the mind-process in which emotions, bodily sensations, memories, information, abstract ideas, and so on converge into a verbally articulated discourse that also substantiates the putative speaker-position implied by the first-person pronoun.[6] This is not to say that consciousness as such would be divisible into a multitude of distinct layers or autonomous segments. Arguments have been put forward both for and against the view that consciousness is unitary (see Brook and Raymont, 2017, and Robbins, 2017, for an overview of the discussion), so for reasons of space I will not go into the details of the argument here, but I take it to be legitimate to hold that consciousness/self-awareness as such is an incompletely

---

[6] It should be noted that the Cartesian immediacy of the first-person pronoun is a feature of Indo-European languages that many other languages do not share, but instead use complex systems of self-reference that depend on the character of the situation and the social status of the speaker. See Kim (2021) for a recent discussion of Korean linguistic practices of self-reference that support the idea of collective selfhood.

integrated whole heuristically divisible into elements, some of which (such as the "bodily" aspect) could dominate the whole field at some moments (for example, intense pleasure or pain), but recede into the background at others (for example, absorption into reading or listening to music). Similarly, we can point to "sensory/reflexive" consciousness sorting out the surroundings, "memorial" consciousness evoking traces of past moments, "imaginary/speculative" consciousness constructing pre-impressions of situations that are not actually there, and so on—models abound. However, instead of imagining these as "building blocks" or "modules" of a complex apparatus, I would argue that the field of self, a cross-section of the semiotic process at a given moment, may take on different configurations of tensions between various aspects and functions, which intrude in each other's movements and strive to dominate one another, situation permitting. Among these, linguistic self-awareness has an important role in ordering the internal process because of its capabilities to link particular, ongoing memories not just to fleeting images of memories or pictures produced by the imagination, but also to socially shared meanings encoded in words and labels.

Obviously, linguistic communication plays a decisive role in the production and continuous rearrangement of intersubjective relations, which is why I suggest we review Raimo Tuomela's influential account of group action with a closer look on the verbal processes involved. Unlike some other analytical theorists of subjectivity (Bratman, 2014; Gilbert, 2014), Tuomela admits that collective agency is grounded in a difference in the exercised mode of thinking of the individuals involved. The gist of Tuomela's (2013, pp. 27–8) approach is the distinction between "I-mode" and "we-mode," different ways to coordinate thinking and action, of which the first is directed toward the achievement of personal, the other toward collective goals. People engaged in "we-mode" are joined by their commitment to a "group ethos," or "certain constitutive goals, beliefs, standards, norms" that are "identity-determining." Tuomela's intent is to disassociate the dominating interests of the individual from the notion of personal agency and to explain the resulting split in terms of these two "modes" of reasoning and behavior. Moreover, in Tuomela's scheme, individuals are presented as static and well ordered in their mental states and motivations, which may help to facilitate analytical rigor, but distances the theory from actual social practice, as his critics have also pointed out (Priest, 2014, p. 296). Switching between "I-mode" and "we-mode" is thus just a skill that is part of this predominantly rational and in any case well-oiled mental apparatus. Nonetheless, Tuomela takes reflexivity and group-internal discussion into account and thus his theory is somewhat less susceptible to Margaret Archer's (2013, pp. 147–51) otherwise well-pointed critique of analytical "plural subject" theories on the grounds that these seem to exist in a timeless vacuum, are formed for the execution of a particular action, and never engage in either constructive or antagonistic discussion of what they do, quite unlike what is witnessed in empirical reality.

Nonetheless, Archer's critique fully applies to Tuomela's concept of "ethos," which is postulated fairly unproblematically. I find it not simply surprising, but downright mind-boggling that Tuomela never considers it possible, first, that different members of a group honestly entertain different versions of their identity-determining beliefs, standards, and norms and, second, that members of the group may be committed to some but not all of the elements of the "ethos" (as they understand them) and that their commitment may also be half-hearted, so that they, for example, follow certain rules at some moments, but ignore them at others, depending on the particularities of the situation, or their moods and inclinations. It seems altogether much more realistic to imagine the "we-mode" and "I-mode" not as two alternative modes of behavior that can be switched on and off, but as the two ends of a gradient, ideal types between which different degrees of collectivistically inclined and individualistically inclined patterns of behavior can be situated.

In actual social practice, people indeed often think, say, and do things that do not correlate with each other at all. I would like to argue that, the importance of ideas and actions notwithstanding, it is the level of communication between group members that provides us with the best access to the process of collective agent formation. Making presuppositions about what goes on in individual mental processes—and whether these processes overlap—is tempting, but still based on communicated evidence, and making generalizations about collective agency on the basis of collectively performed acts is misleading because of the distinction between a deliberative group and a marching army. This is not, by any means, to say that collective agency is primarily dependent on linguistic self-awareness, but simply that if we want to establish a shared ground for the collective subject, something like Tuomela's "ethos," it is the linguistic self-awareness of the group that we should be primarily looking at. Of course, verbal communication is certainly not the only practice needed to create and maintain a collective subject[7] (for example, we can imagine a relationship developing between two people without a shared language who meet at recurring dance parties in a multicultural environment), but it is clearly the most efficient one and is most likely inevitable for enduring and multifaceted interpersonal commitments to develop.

---

[7] Tuomela (2013, p. 124) also makes the distinction between verbal, or "explicit" commitments and "implicit" agreements to the elements of the ethos, but the latter are nonetheless, according to him, typically formalized by mimicry or gestures, which does not make a lot of difference from the semiotic point of view.

In other words, a "we" is not constituted so much by norms and goals as by the sharing of narratives about and descriptions of the world as well as the self-perception of the members of the groups in it. The rest of a social framework, including norms and goals, as well as the limits within which these can be disputed, is based on the basic settings of a jointly endorsed discourse.

## Language and the social fabric

John Searle has correctly pointed out that the Western tradition of social philosophy has taken language for granted, and, in particular, social contract theorists have assumed that people "in the state of nature" were already endowed with language when they decided to enter into a contractual relationship with each other and form a group. In reality, Searle (2008, p. 444) writes, "language is an extension of prelinguistic forms of intentionality." However, much of his own account of how the development of language out of prelinguistic consciousness took place remains speculative, and strong assertions such as the claim that prelinguistic humans already have to "operate with a rather hefty set of traditional philosophical categories (for example, Aristotelian and Kantian)" (2008, p. 446) are presented without any evidence. But Searle (2008, p. 444) is certainly correct in saying that the assumption of a fully fledged linguistic awareness prior to the emergence of social relations is unwarranted. For our present purposes, the question of when and how the shift from prelinguistic to linguistic communication took place is not very important; however, the main thing is to point out that language and social organization have developed simultaneously, mutually enhancing each other, and clearly constituted a significant evolutionary advantage to the groups that had them over those that did not (see Fontdevila et al, 2011; Lewens, 2015, pp. 44ff. for a more detailed discussion). And not just that: I would hold that the sense of atomic selfhood, with which Searle has credited prelinguistic primates, is itself also the result of a long, cultural development; it does not precede, but follows the development of social relations between human beings and is thus, in a way, not a prerequisite, but a product of evolving linguistic skills and also culturally variative.

Beside the exchange of information, the preservation of cultural memory, and the verbal practice of power, one of the functions of language has always been to uphold the social fabric. The entire society constantly has to maintain, but also to update its foundational views of the world. Therefore, social communication does not merely share factual information, instructions or opinions, but also works as the re-enactment of individual commitments to those shared principles on which joint activities are based, similar to how romantic relationships are upheld by constant assurances of mutual affection. Ideas, moreover, do not acquire their force by being articulated. They become powerful by being repeated. We therefore need to distinguish between, on the one hand, the formulation of certain ideas or claims about reality or their adjustments and interpretations, and, on the other hand, the ritualistic reiteration of all such formulations, original or otherwise, that turn them into discourses, which are able to encapsulate the procedures and norms that members of the society need to abide by if they want to be accepted by their peers.

I use the word "discourse" here in the particular sense of a collectively endorsed or enforced norm of speaking about certain things in a certain way, and in any particular society being culturally competent normally implies the ability to use different discourses in different situations. For example, there is an economic discourse that sees people as "employers/employees," a political discourse that sees them as "citizens/non-citizens" or "voters," and a military discourse that sees them as "personnel"; a house may be "home" or "real estate," and so on. A map of discourses that are considered as legitimate, or even most appropriate, in certain situations that occur in a society is able to tell us a lot about that society. For example, in some societies, healthcare is considered to be a task of the society as a whole, which should be upheld by all for the benefit of those in need, while in others it is governed by the economic discourse, which treats it as a "service" to be paid for by its recipients.

Societies and particular institutions are quite conservative in that they do not change immediately whenever a new discourse about their functioning is proclaimed, but only when it is broadly endorsed and perceived to be cognitively adequate, that is, able to deliver workable (not necessarily true) answers to socially relevant questions. In this respect, philosophical, legal, political, and other discourses act precisely like cultural phenomena always do: first, certain individuals put forward claims about how things are, next, these turn into bids for the increase of collective capacity to understand and act, and, finally, whenever such bids are endorsed by what represents the symbolic authority in that particular sociocultural situation, they enter broader circulation. Some of these discourses only survive for a short period and fade out, while others crystallize into the very fabric of beliefs that holds that particular society together.

These discourses are not static or immune to change. They may have more stable elements, especially when certain conservative institutions rely on them, but the ability to deal with the changing world is dependent on their ability to adapt to the circumstances. Furthermore, it is important to note that such discourses are causally efficacious, that is, influence the opinions and behavior of people, only inasmuch they are being practiced. For the present context, one of the most important aspects of this practice is what I would like to call *discursive consolidation*, an effort to formulate how a certain collective sees itself at a particular moment, in a particular situation, facing a particular challenge. This can occur in various ways: through acts of power, when an authoritarian leader uses the collective "we" to designate both themselves and their subjects; as a result of negotiations between agents with different micro-goals who nonetheless recognize certain joint macro-aims; and, finally, in an Arendtian manner, when the common sentiment is articulated by someone and endorsed by the rest of their group. Regardless of how it has come about, however, the aim of discursive consolidation is to create a shared linguistic awareness, which, as suggested above, is the prerequisite of a collective subject even on the most basic level, but much more so when we are dealing with larger entities such as corporations, political parties. or nations.[8]

What I mean by discursive consolidation is perhaps best exemplified by a venerable genre with a long history, which, in the West, can be traced back to ancient Greece and Rome: the public speech. Orations, such as Cicero's diatribe against Catiline, Saint-Just's speech on the fate of king Louis XVI, and Martin Luther King Jr.'s "I have a dream" speech, continue to be read not just for their historical significance, but also for their literary quality and the ideas they articulate. And yet, perhaps more and more characteristically in modern democracies, whenever we hear a politician speak, we are not waiting so much for absolutely unexpected and completely new ideas, but the choices from among the available discourses for addressing certain topics, and, of course, the choices of the topics themselves.[9] Less a composer than the conductor of a discursive orchestra, a politician signifies by reiterating certain claims, reassuring the audience of certain commitments, proclaiming allegiance to certain values selected from the whole range of the sociocultural repertoire, and doing all that by enacting a relationship with the listeners, which implies a choice of vocabulary, style, demeanor, and so on. It is not even important whether the politician believes these phrases herself, as Jeffrey Alexander (2011, pp. 53ff.) has made clear, because the success of the performance depends on whether it is able to convince its audience.

The politician's speech is a particular and also an extreme case of discursive consolidation, in that it is almost entirely devoid of active dialogicality—only the speaker can speak, while the reaction of the audience is restricted to a

---

[8] Benedict Anderson (2006) has famously defined "imagined communities," that is, collectives where individual members do not know all other members of the group while sharing with them the feeling of belonging to it, by an informational space, pointing out the role of newspapers in nation-building.

[9] See Steven Lukes (2005, pp. 20ff.), relying on Peter Bachrach and Morton Baratz, elaborating on how the design of the discursive field constitutes an exercise of power.

spectrum of endorsement and rejection, applause and booing.[10] In the social process, agentic articulations in genres such as speech, decree or verdict mark certain thresholds, endpoints of a longer discursive development, moments of transition and reorganization. This is because such a degree of discursive consolidation is the prerequisite of collective action as well as the implementation of changes that affect the life trajectories of a vast number of people. Neither is successfully manageable without manipulating a critical mass of those involved or affected into (at least passive) consent. Of course, this discursive agreement may leave it open for the individual or even small groups to disagree with the majority opinion, but, if efficient, it coerces and co-opts the network of lower level decision-making points into positions where they necessarily have to adopt the hegemonic discursive choices endorsed by the authority if they want to succeed in what they do. For example, when we look at the process, over the past several decades, of subjugating academic knowledge to politico-economic control by promoting a view of education as a service that needs to be adjusted to the expectations of the client, and judging research as a means to increase corporate profit, we can see that this has been largely achieved by shifting decision-making power to individuals willing to speak about the academic field in the terms of the neoliberal political discourse—and when the discourse had gained wider currency, appearing almost commonsensical, it became much easier to implement devastating academic policies in practice.

Although the above view is based on the modern political model of elected authority, I think it is to some extent applicable also for non-modern or non-democratic societies, where the legitimacy of the ruling speaker-positions is guaranteed by religious or ideological discourses that are upheld by powerful institutions such as a church or a party, which have options to use legitimate violence at their disposal. The two main differences between such societies and modern democracies are that, first, in modern societies the debates and arguments are mostly carried out in the open, while in non-modern and non-democratic systems they may be conducted in veiled language for fear of reprisals, which, in turn, may make such debates impenetrable for the uninitiated. Second, democratic societies allow for various forms of public participation in these debates, while in non-democratic systems they are restricted to covert or elite (or covert elite) groups. Neither side of these oppositions is more than an ideal type, however, as totalitarian and populist-authoritarian governments are keen to present themselves as enacting the will of the "people," with appropriate performances staged to that end, and in

---

[10] It has to be added though that the role of the audience is significant in the formation of the circumstances in which the politician speaks, as demonstrated, among others, by Jeffrey Alexander's theory of refusion (2011; Alexander et al, 2006).

democratic societies, too, powerful lobby groups use astroturf organizations and other political technologies to keep the decision-making process under their control. Moreover, by the downplaying of expert opinions as "elite," truly elitist interest groups may be able to manipulate popular opinion into backing their causes, as happened, for example, during the debates in the UK leading to Brexit.

For the present purposes, these cases show that extreme discursive consolidation is only achieved as a result of an extensive sociocultural process that involves the articulation, endorsement, circulation, and political choice to apply certain discourses from the position of power. I am calling this "extreme" in two senses, neither of which is alarmist: on the one hand, the consolidation is extreme precisely in the minimization of the dialogicality involved in the use of the discourse, and, on the other, it represents one extreme, one pole on an axis that has on its other end an imaginary opposite, a complete social cacophony of not necessarily coherently articulated opinions, incompatible action scripts and contradictory value judgements. In social practice, extreme discursive consolidation, which is sincerely endorsed by a qualified majority of a society is very, very rare and might occur at a decisive turning point of the historical process, such as mobilization for a war effort. In a functional society, the other extreme of discursive cacophony is impossible, and even nearing that state is symptomatic of an approaching breakdown.

In actual situations, therefore, what we can speak of are *degrees* of discursive consolidation, positions on a gradient that indicate the level of success of the political performance in Jeffrey Alexander's terms. Another issue to address is that of the *stages* of the process leading up to discursive consolidation, which, I argue, typically involve more dialogicality while they round up a certain domain of agendas and opinions as well as extradiscursive input into formulations that will later be uttered from the speaker-position of power. It is obvious that discursive formulation of political positions is not itself the locus of decisive change, but normally the endpoint of a long deliberative process that, in order to be successful, must have made the effort to co-opt as much of the relevant "field" as would suffice to carry the articulated visions out. In other words, a politician's speech should not be treated primarily as an utterance of individual will, but as an instance of channeling a longer collective process into a clearly definable turning point.

## The collective subject

I would like to argue that various practices of discursive consolidation are always at work in the production of a subject, be it individual or collective. Diaries, to-do lists, notes on the refrigerator, and other forms of self-communication are necessary for holding the individual process together, performing the same role that history-writing, newspapers, and public notices have in the social sphere. And although we do not necessarily articulate our decisions internally in verbal form or are even always able to produce coherent narratives about them retrospectively,[11] I think it is fair to say that decisions taken and choices made by an individual result from the consolidation of her subjective field, aligning the elements active on it (including the representations of all relevantly significant others) into a configuration wherein the decision or choice seems to be the most valid alternative among others. The same happens when the collective subject acts, although here the process of consolidation is perhaps more explicitly discursive, even though in smaller and more closely integrated groups, such as married couples or sports teams, non-discursive aspects of subject consolidation are often just as relevant.

The agentic subject is thus always situated at the intersection of various heterogeneous processes and is emergent over them in the sense that its capacities cannot be reduced to the characteristics of these processes by themselves. This applies in equal manner both to the individual subject, whose choices and decisions are made as a result of settling the tensions between impulses coming from the body, the memory, the principles, the outside, and to the collective subject, which emerges over a number of individual subjects who mediate the stream of their own internal polylogue to the shared discursive space. Just as in the individual the various and contradictory aspects of the person—desires, principles, habits, moods, and so on—engage each other during the process of deliberation, each vying for control, a collective subject presents a similar field in which the different aspirations of the members of the group tackle each other. In other words, a group can be as smart as its smartest member and as dumb as its dumbest, as bold as its boldest member and as conservative as its most conservative one, depending on who, in the internal deliberations, happens to gain the upper hand at the decisive moment. The physical fact that the collective subject relies on several individuals instead of just one is irrelevant in view of the fact that, during the internal polylogue, these individuals form a united circuit, a consolidated discursive arrangement that is similar enough to the internal deliberative space of an individual subject and thus merits the label of a collective subject. Just as an archipelago can be a country, a group of people can form what for all practical purposes functions as a person. And this is by no means limited to the rational and articulated linguistic space that the participants of such a collective subject share with each other: irrational motivations, such as the need to prove

---

[11] This is not to dismiss theories of narrative selfhood put forward, among others, by Paul Ricoeur and Charles Taylor. On the contrary, I fully agree with the idea that one of the predominant ways to produce self-continuity is the integration of experiences and memories into a narrative that makes sense to the individual, or the collective.

oneself or the desire to compete with another member of the group, or to form alliances against a third one, and so on, may lead to the formation of efficient ad hoc links and aversions that may have a powerful influence on the dynamic of the group not unlike the effect of unconscious drives on the behavior of a rational individual.

In one of the best hitherto proposed models of collective subjectivity, Kay Mathiesen (2005) proposes three criteria of what it takes for a group to satisfy this label: plurality, which implies that the stream of consciousness is not shared, but diverse; awareness, or the requirement that the members of the group actually feel themselves to be parts of a collective subject; and collectivity, or "a 'we-experience' where we are not just perceiving things from our own perspective, but are also aware of the other's perspective and experiences at the same time" (2005, p. 246). Mathiesen (2005, p. 236) calls this simultaneous validation of multiple perspectives "co-subjectivity," and argues that this is one of the prerequisites of any social process to take place.[12] Unlike Tuomela, for whom "we-mode" and "I-mode" are distinct orientations of behavior, Mathiesen thus very appropriately conjoins the two perspectives into a whole that is integrated, but not unitary. This is what I would also like to suggest, adding an instability of balance between the two, or several, perspectives, and allowing for internal tension also in the primary perspective of the individual, in whom multiple motivations may be in conflict.

This latter addition leads, however, to a point of disagreement I have with Mathiesen's model: she rejects the "emergent" nature of the collective subject, claiming that this implies a lack of awareness about the nature of the group in its individual members. To this, I have two objections: first, it seems to me quite possible that a member of a group is aware of the group's emergent characteristics and is committed to that group precisely because she finds these desirable; second, that no one, individual agents included, is ever completely aware of the full range of the effects of their behavior or potential, and therefore it is completely possible to be aware of one's involvement in a collective subject and some of its effects, but to remain ignorant of others.

This development of Mathiesen's model is also compatible with the theories of "extended mind" applied to collective subjects. Andy Clark and David Chalmers (1998) have claimed that there is no fundamental difference between a person they call Inga, who has a good memory and stores all necessary information in her brain, and someone called Otto, suffering from

---

[12] The discovery of so-called "mirror neurons," or physiological mechanisms that reproduce in the organism reactions to somebody else's experience, indeed suggests that this capacity may be, so to say, hardwired to the human organism.

Alzheimer's, who writes everything down in his notebook that he carries around with him at all times. From this, Clark and Chalmers conclude that it is justified to view the mind as something not simply encapsulated in the cranium, but distributed around the particular person's peripherals and accessible environment. I, too, would say the notes on the margins of the books I have read are a part of my broader memory system, as I too often do not recall what exactly were my objections to or developments of the ideas in them without looking the relevant volume up. An interesting twist has been given to the extended mind theory by Deborah Tollefsen (2015, pp. 70–7), who brings Olaf, the absent-minded husband of Inga, into the picture. Unlike Otto, Olaf does not need a notebook, but relies on the excellent memory of Inga instead. When Otto needs to go to a place that he does not remember the address of, he finds it in his notebook, while Olaf simply asks Inga and gets the right answer. "Inga and Olaf form a coupled system," Tollefsen (2015, p. 75) argues, "because the interaction between them is *functionally equivalent* to that found in biological memory." We could thus well say that Inga and Olaf form a collective subject (quite possibly Inga relies on Olaf's ideas as well, from time to time), in that a linkage exists between their mental processes, and in both processes the other is present at most times as a gateway to resources (which include the other's peripheral systems) that can be tapped into. It goes without saying that the linkage operates verbally, at least most of the time, and presupposes a shared linguistic awareness as well as a degree of discursive consolidation that allows the coupled individuals to maintain coherently compatible pictures of their worlds.[13]

## Conclusion

What I hope to have shown is that the discrepancy between considering only individuals to be "real" agents on the one hand and acknowledging the role of shared meanings in the decision-making process on the other boils down to the level of axiomatics, where process ontology shows much more explanatory potential than the traditional, object-centered view. Social entities, this view reveals, are reified segments of practices rather than self-subsistent entities describable in essential terms. This view also enhances our perception of selfhood, regarded as an intersection of various processual streams, a field, rather than a self-identical and persistent entity. Moreover, considering agentic decisions and choices to emerge not from a unitary

---

[13] It should nonetheless be noted here that Margaret Archer (2013, p. 156) has persuasively argued for the possibility of different participants in a coupled system to have conflicting interpretations of their joint process even while engaging in it in similar ways.

center of mental control, but in the process of constant self-reorganization of the individual as a field of tensions between inputs of different kinds, we can also see that there is a fundamental similarity between an individual person and a group, the members of which can form coupled systems in which each of them mediates their own internal process into a shared space. (Less has been said here about the nonhuman elements of that space, which is not to deny their importance.) Such spaces can be small and large, and also overlapping, and normally they rely on a shared linguistic awareness brought about by processes of discursive consolidation, the reiteration of certain views and principles, as well as semiotic linkages that are arbitrary in themselves, but become naturalized in this process.

To sum it up: all subjects can effectively be seen as collective, and what we call individuals simply form a particular, but not necessarily paradigmatic case. It is certainly possible, and often also useful, to narrow down the focus to the individual level in order to analyze certain phenomena, but this should not cheat us into dismissing the broader view.

## References

Ackerman, F. (2002) "Flaws in the Foundation: Consumer Behavior and General Equilibrium Theory," in E. Fullbrook (ed) *Intersubjectivity in Economics: Agents and Structures*, London: Routledge, pp. 56–70.

Alexander, J.C. (2011) *Performance and Power*, Cambridge: Polity Press.

Alexander, J.C., Giesen, B. and Mast, J.L. (eds) (2006) *Social Performance: Symbolic Action, Cultural Pragmatics, and Ritual*, Cambridge: Cambridge University Press.

Anderson, B. (2006) *Imagined Communities: Reflections on the Origin and Spread of Nationalism*, London: Verso.

Archer, M.S. (2013) "Collective Reflexivity: A Relational Case for It," in C.J. Powell and F. Dépelteau (eds) *Conceptualizing Relational Sociology: Ontological and Theoretical Issues*, New York: Palgrave Macmillan, pp. 145–61.

Ásta (2018) *Categories We Live By: The Construction of Sex, Gender, Race, and Other Social Categories*, Oxford: Oxford University Press.

BBC Sport (2014) "World Cup Moments: The 'Hand of God'," *BBC Sport*, March 22. Available at www.bbc.co.uk/sport/av/football/26696506

Bratman, M. (2014) *Shared Agency: A Planning Theory of Acting Together*, Oxford: Oxford University Press.

Brook, A. and Raymont, P. (2017) "The Unity of Consciousness," in E.N. Zalta (ed) *The Stanford Encyclopedia of Philosophy*, Metaphysics Research Lab, Stanford University.

Clark, A. and Chalmers, D.J. (1998) "The Extended Mind," *Analysis*, 58(1): 7–19.

Crossley, N. (2011) *Towards Relational Sociology*, London: Routledge.

Dépelteau, F. (2013) "What Is the Direction of the 'Relational Turn'?," in C.J. Powell and F. Dépelteau (eds) *Conceptualizing Relational Sociology: Ontological and Theoretical Issues*, New York: Palgrave Macmillan, pp. 163–85.

Donati, P. (2010) *Relational Sociology: A New Paradigm for the Social Sciences*, London: Routledge.

Donati, P. and Archer, M.S. (2015) *The Relational Subject*, Cambridge: Cambridge University Press.

Fontdevila, J., Opazo, M. and White, H.C. (2011) "Order at the Edge of Chaos: Meanings from Netdom Switchings across Functional Systems," *Sociological Theory*, 29(3): 178–98.

Gilbert, M. (2014) *Joint Commitment: How We Make the Social World*, Oxford: Oxford University Press.

Haraway, D.J. (1991) *Simians, Cyborgs, and Women: The Reinvention of Nature*, New York: Routledge.

Haugeland, J. (1998) *Having Thought: Essays in the Metaphysics of Mind*, Cambridge, MA: Harvard University Press.

Hjelmslev, L. (1959) *Essais Linguistiques*, Copenhagen: Nordisk sprog- og kulturforlag.

Kim, Hye Young (2021) *We as Self: Ouri, Intersubjectivity, and Presubjectivity*, Lanham: Lexington Books.

Latour, B. (1993) *We Have Never Been Modern*, Cambridge, MA: Harvard University Press.

Lawson, T. (2017) "What Is Wrong with Modern Economics, and Why Does It Stay Wrong?," *Journal of Australian Political Economy*, 80: 26–42.

Lewens, T. (2015) *Cultural Evolution: Conceptual Challenges*, Oxford: Oxford University Press.

List, C. and Pettit, P. (2011) *Group Agency: The Possibility, Design, and Status of Corporate Agents*, Oxford: Oxford University Press.

Ludwig, K. (2016) *From Individual to Plural Agency*, Oxford: Oxford University Press.

Lukes, S. (2005) *Power: A Radical View*, New York: Palgrave Macmillan.

Malafouris, L. (2013) *How Things Shape the Mind*, Cambridge, MA: MIT Press.

Mathiesen, K. (2005) "Collective Consciousness," in D.W. Smith and A.L. Thomasson (eds) *Phenomenology and Philosophy of Mind*, Oxford: Clarendon Press, pp. 235–52.

Mead, G.H. (1972) *Mind, Self & Society*, Chicago, IL: University of Chicago Press.

Powell, C.J. (2013) "Radical Relationism: A Proposal," in C.J. Powell and F. Dépelteau (eds) *Conceptualizing Relational Sociology: Ontological and Theoretical Issues*, New York: Palgrave Macmillan, pp. 187–207.

Priest, M. (2014) "Social Ontology: Collective Intentionality and Group Agents," *Ethics*, 125(1): 293–98.

Raud, R. (2016) *Meaning in Action: Outline of an Integral Theory of Culture*, Cambridge: Polity Press.

Robbins, P. (2017) "Modularity of Mind," in E.N. Zalta (ed) *The Stanford Encyclopedia of Philosophy*, Metaphysics Research Lab, Stanford University.

Rouse, J. (2002) *How Scientific Practices Matter: Reclaiming Philosophical Naturalism*, Chicago, IL: University of Chicago Press.

Schlosser, M. (2019) "Agency," in E.N. Zalta (ed) *The Stanford Encyclopedia of Philosophy*, Metaphysics Research Lab, Stanford University.

Searle, J.R. (1992) *The Rediscovery of the Mind*, Cambridge, MA: MIT Press.

Searle, J.R. (1996) *The Construction of Social Reality*, Harmondsworth: Penguin Books.

Searle, J.R. (2008) "Language and Social Ontology," *Theory and Society*, 37(5): 443–59.

Serres, M. (2011) *Malfeasance: Appropriation through Pollution?*, Stanford, CA: Stanford University Press.

Söderbaum, P. (2008) "Economics as Ideology," in E. Fullbrook (ed) *Pluralist Economics*, London: Zed Books, pp. 117–27.

Thomasson, A. (2003) "Foundation for a Social Ontology," *ProtoSociology*, 18: 269–90.

Thomasson, A. (2014) *Ontology Made Easy*, Oxford: Oxford University Press.

Thomasson, A. (2019) "The Ontology of Social Groups," *Synthese*, 196(12): 4829–45.

Tollefsen, D.P. (2015) *Groups as Agents*, Cambridge: Polity Press.

Tuomela, R. (2013) *Social Ontology: Collective Intentionality and Group Agents*, Oxford: Oxford University Press.

Wheeler, M. (2010) "In Defense of Extended Functionalism," in R. Menary (ed) *The Extended Mind*, Cambridge, MA: MIT Press, pp. 245–70.

4

# Theorizing Side-directed Behavior

*Paul McLean and Eunkyung Song*

China's Military Provokes Its Neighbors, but the Message Is for the United States.[1]

Much action within social networks occurs ostensibly as a dyadic behavioral gesture or verbal utterance or response directed to a particular alter. And that is how we often code behavior within networks. Yet, in many instances, integral to a behavior or utterance's meaning and relational objectives is the presence of an audience. Indeed, the behavior or gesture may be more urgently targeted at the audience than the ostensible principal alter. A student insults a teacher, but more to entertain classmates and signal friendship clique membership than to express enmity toward the teacher per se. Another student bullies a schoolmate, but more to gain status with the cool kids than to express animosity toward the afflicted schoolmate. An email between colleagues includes a cc to the department manager—arguably the alter of primary concern, despite not being explicitly addressed. A patron supplies a favor to another man's client, more as a signal of respect to the other patron than to build a relation with the fortuitously served client. A participant on social media responds, ostensibly, to the immediately preceding post,[2] but the actual target may be the initiator of the thread, another respondent, or

---

[1] The epigraph is a headline from an article in *The New York Times* (Myers, 2020). We use it here because it succinctly articulates the truism that side-directed behavior is a typical, almost definitive feature of strategic gamesmanship in international relations.

[2] Or they may be compelled to respond to the immediately preceding post, by the architecture of the platform.

potentially someone outside the thread entirely. Or, as in the epigraph we cite at the outset, one superpower sends a signal to another via local actions against neighbors who are mostly exchangeable tokens in a geopolitical game.[3] This is how strategic diplomacy works.

These are examples of "side-directed behavior," Frans de Waal's (1982, pp. 37–40) term[4] to describe a common pattern in chimpanzee social networks, in which, for example, competition among males for leadership of the colony is carried out in the context of observing females. We have two main arguments to put forward in this chapter. First, we misunderstand and quite likely miscode action within networks when we fail to appreciate, and fail to code as a potentially distinct type of tie, ulterior motive-based behavior directed fundamentally towards co-present audiences and other third parties.[5] Consequently, we may habitually analyze networks whose construction is distinctly misrepresentative of social reality. Second, we emphasize the need for closer attention to the semiotics of these situations, which are more complex than what is often dealt with in the literature on sociolinguistics.

We begin by fleshing out some examples of side-directed behavior (SDB) using existing empirical literature to suggest that it is quite common in social interaction. We see this effort as consistent with a recent trend in network theory to upend mistaken and/or simplistic assumptions about what networks are and how they are built, by attending to the phenomenology of network processes.[6] Next, we draw on some existing concepts and frameworks within social network analysis and relational sociology more broadly to further characterize this type of behavior and these kinds of situations or events, and to situate the phenomenon within existing sociological concerns. Some of the conceptual apparatus for thinking about such situations already exists, and yet SDB has not been an explicit object of theoretical attention.

---

[3] In many of the cases here, the most significant recipient of the sender's message is another individual, but we can imagine collective recipients, too. For example, dog whistles in political speeches can communicate a sinister message to a shadow audience, while the putative recipients may be unaware of the subtext. Similarly, activists assailing politicians may be addressing potential recruits more than the politicians themselves. In this chapter, we stick mostly with smallish networks made up of non-collective actors.

[4] Earlier in the book, de Waal refers to "triadic awareness" (p. 20; also p. 182) as an element of chimpanzee social interaction.

[5] This judgement grows directly out of the first author's experiences coding network data from historical documents.

[6] Two examples come readily to mind. Martin (2009) shows that some network aggregation processes we often take to be lawlike do not actually apply in real-world networks. Small (2017), like Bearman and Parigi (2004) and others before him, questions fundamental assumptions concerning core discussion networks and what happens in them, via a deep dive into the relational experiences of a set of students new to graduate school.

Third, we draw out some implications of SDB for how we think about and analyze social interaction at the intersection of networks and culture (McLean, 2017; Song, 2019). As noted above, we briefly consider two kinds of theoretical and practical issues, one primarily structural, the other primarily semiotic (or we might say, cognitive, or discursive, or cultural). The first concerns how we conceptualize, code, depict, and analyze network structure in light of SDB, while the second concerns how we explore, describe, and assess mechanisms of communication and shared (or deliberately unshared) understandings within networks in light of SDB. Ultimately, we would like to see SDB situations treated as a distinct class of social interaction, with an appropriate toolkit of methods and concepts. This chapter is a prelude to that goal.

## Some empirical evidence

We define "side-directed behavior" (SDB) as actions taken in a social network ostensibly directed toward a particular alter but actually more meaningfully directed towards a third party. The type of tie obtaining between ego and alter may or may not be the same as that existing between ego and third party, such that analyzing SDB may often require that we pay attention to multiple network ecologies: that is, how do ties across networks impinge on, overlap with, and intersect with each other? We also wish to draw a distinction between SDB strictly defined, and the more general idea that the interaction within any given dyad is often affected by the presence of other network participants close by, a core tenet of network thinking going back decades but also seemingly continuously rediscovered (for example, Battison et al, 2020).[7] SDB is not about structural constraints on behavior writ large, but deployment of the network ecology for strategic ends.

### *De Waal on chimpanzee politics*

We take inspiration from de Waal's (1982) ethology of chimpanzee behavior for our initial understanding of SDB. Specifically, we proceed from his attention to small group situations in which "communication takes place simultaneously in two directions" (1982, p. 40). Often, "it involves females

---

[7] The effect of third actors on dyadic interaction can be modeled, especially within single type of tie networks. The difference with SDB is that it calls into question who is part of the fundamental dyad. For one articulation of how dyadic relations depend fundamentally on third parties, see Martin (2009, Ch. 4), who provides an excellent account of how dominance orders within animal groups are pliant and changeable according to which individuals are co-present.

who recruit a male to attack another female." The female interacts with the male, making a fuss over him, while pointing in a distinctive way at her female rival. Thus the male functions as a "pawn" in the interaction between the females, yet integrally to the very construction of their relationship at that moment. Similar scenarios crop up later. At one point, the young male Luit challenges the dominance of the older male Yeroen; Yeroen immediately runs to a group of younger, mostly female chimpanzees and "embraces them all in turn" (1982, p. 93), not as a gesture of affection toward them but as an attempted display *to Luit* of his own political strength. In numerous instances, dominant males intervene in skirmishes to support the weaker party, the goal seemingly to show the stronger contender that the leader will allow no pretenders to usurp his own power (for example, p. 124).[8] Such situations indicate complex political dynamics at play in the chimpanzee colony. These dynamics require awareness by each member of the relationships existing among the other members, and they entail efforts at solidifying or improving one's own position by means of gestures in the presence of audiences. Social structure here is more than a pecking order (Chase, 1980), more than the outcome of a sequence of dyadic matches, because who dominates whom is essentially a function of whom else is present at any particular point in time. That context in turn enables or constrains, or even *motivates*, action at the ostensibly dyadic level—action that is, in fact, triadic in its composition.

However much chimpanzees may astound us with their social knowledge, absent speech, their toolbox for sustaining communication simultaneously with multiple audiences using multiple registers is limited. We must expand the study of SDB to more richly symbolic behavior in human networks, including a consideration of the variability of the relevance of different audiences, according to different possible framings of situations.

## *McFarland on classroom dynamics*

McFarland's (2001, 2004) work on student defiance in high school classrooms is a nice place to start. His general, networks-centric claim is that "the *informal organization* of the classroom determines which students have the greatest political opportunities, or rights to discourse, that enable them to use the available social opportunities that task structures define" (McFarland, 2001, p. 618). Less abstractly, students in classrooms comprised of like-minded peers and friends are more likely to be supported, and buffered from punishment,

---

[8] Fine (1987) observed a similar phenomenon in Little League baseball, where team leaders enact and solidify leadership by mocking strong adversaries while defending vulnerable ones.

should they be inclined to express defiance. Indeed, it seems likely they are encouraged toward defiance by such peers often (p. 658).[9]

So far, this means only that the action of an individual student (A) toward the teacher (B) is affected (that is, disrupted from what it otherwise might be) by the presence of other students (C), especially if they are A's friends and have previously been disruptive themselves. But it may go beyond that "influence" effect to something more. Tellingly, McFarland (2001, p. 618) acknowledges that "there are cases where the teacher is not even aware of the defiance, but the students are." Now we are getting toward the heart of SDB: a defiant student's action ostensibly directed toward the teacher, but actually directed at peers as a kind of insider joke. Indeed, some defiance works best when it goes undetected by the teacher, or where it is ambiguous, thus shielding the student from punishment while building camaraderie with peers. Peer group formation or reinforcement is the goal, achieved by means of interaction with an outsider (in this case, an authority figure). Note that communication is taking place on multiple channels here. The student simultaneously sustains two distinct lines of communication with distinct alters: one verbal (likely drawing at least superficially on a conventional and legitimate cultural script normally deployed between student and teacher), the other tonal or nonverbal (to "key" the exchange [Goffman 1974, Ch. 3] with the teacher in a humorous or ironic mode with the goal of entertaining fellow students).

McFarland further describes situations of this sort in his companion work (2004) on problematic classroom encounters. Here, "jokes build solidarity among those 'in the know'" (pp. 1263–4). For example, some girls in a particular classroom would lure the teacher into a private conversation, behave flirtatiously toward him, then exchange giggles and knowing looks with their friends (p. 1265). Or, in another instance (p. 1268), a student "personally attacks her teacher in order to get a laugh out of her peers," asking: "Do you live with your Mom?" Resituating the agency somewhat, McFarland describes another situation in which a student complains to the teacher about not understanding her assignment, but rather than respond to her directly, the teacher shows support for the students who are getting the work right, thereby signaling to Jocelyn that her lack of understanding

---

[9] Adding to the coding challenge we discuss below, McFarland notes that the same student might be compliant in one classroom and defiant in another, as a function not only of her dyadic relationship with the teacher, but also as a function of the course material, the class composition, and more. He labels such complex interleavings of personalities, networks, and cultural material, "situations," which seems descriptively accurate, and amenable to rich qualitative description, but perhaps not so tractable to comparative analysis because of the number of moving parts. See Diehl and McFarland (2010) for more conceptual development.

is her own fault (p. 1273). Subsequently, "the conflict becomes covert as teacher and student play the audience to their sides once again" (p. 1274). Their actions ostensibly directed toward each other are actually directed at the audience of students present. Now the educational mission has been fundamentally compromised, but the sophistication of the cultural agency within small group dynamics remains intact.

## Bullying dynamics in schools

Consider next some of the networks-based research on aggressive behavior in middle and high schools (Faris and Felmlee, 2011; Fujimoto et al, 2017; Callejas and Shepherd, 2020). Citing Faris and Felmlee's work, Fujimoto et al (2017, p. 102) write that aggressive behavior is a negative relational process of "'instrumental targeting,' whereby aggressors, motivated by status attainment, tactically choose targets with relatively high levels of peer status, which will yield higher social rewards in the eyes of their peer observers, instead of choosing marginal ones." Note that aggression here is partly based on some property of the person attacked (their high status), and perhaps some characteristic of the aggressor's and the victim's dyadic relationship; but the crucial motivation for attacking a particular alter may lie in the value of attacking someone *perceived to have high status by peers*. Put succinctly, the function of the aggression is to achieve or strengthen ingroup membership. The specifics of *who* is attacked may be incidental to that signal sent to members of the ingroup.[10] Callejas and Shepherd (2020, p. 321) offer a suggestive argument in the same vein. Rather than interpreting conflict dyadically, as an expression of an aggressor's attempted dominance over specific others, they propose "an alternative mechanism by which conflict might shape social status: through signaling participation in the social scene of the school." Conflict then becomes functional to achievement of ingroup belonging, such that the behavior is fundamentally directed towards the in-crowd (or members of it) as audience. Of course, the dyadic target for conflict must still be carefully chosen: beating up a vulnerable kid confers little status, and past a certain threshold the value of indiscriminate conflict seems to decline. But it is misleading, they hypothesize, to treat dyadic conflict independent of the audience toward whom it is primarily directed as ingratiating performance.

---

[10] The triadic ramifications of dyadic conflict are also suggested by Faris (2012, pp. 1212–13): "a perpetrator who insults or harasses a peer may have also indirectly established a superior position vis-à-vis not just the victim, but others who had thought themselves the status equals of the victim."

*Workplace dynamics*

Turning to a different setting, consider David Gibson's research (2005) on the structure of talk at organizational meetings. Gibson exhaustively documents what he calls "participation shifts" (turn-takings) at a large number of meetings he attended and coded. Person A speaks to B, and B responds to A; or person A speaks to the group and person X takes it upon themselves to respond to A's general remark. These are especially common interaction patterns within meetings-based organizational networks. The former dyadic coupling seems determined by the conversational norm of reciprocation. In the latter case, X may be more likely to speak up if she enjoys some prior relationship with A that empowers her to speak. That is, both conversational norms and network structural effects impinge on action. But Gibson does not rule out more complicated turn-takings, for example of the SDB variety, in which a participant may ostensibly address the group, or someone previously spoken to, while simultaneously signaling their connection to a particular alter—say person A, their boss. For example, A speaks to B, admonishing him; X then piggybacks on the boss's comment, similarly speaking to B and admonishing him. The explicit target of the admonition is B; but strategically, the target of X's utterance is A, from whom X seeks approval. "Subordinates were especially apt to address their superiors or the group after their superiors spoke or were addressed, and were particularly *un*likely to direct the floor *away* from superiors" (Gibson, 2005, p. 1583). "Being a dutiful subordinate" may therefore "entail amplifying a superior's remark to the group" (p. 1588). Curiously, Gibson rigorously restricted himself to coding overtly pair-wise interaction moments;[11] and yet, in our view, some of what goes on in the meeting is not so easily understood as a sequence of dyadic engagements—even with the coding device of treating "the group" as a unitary potential target of address.

*Digital communication*

Notwithstanding the variety of forms of digital communication and the disparate affordances built into different digital platforms, online communication can be viewed as a form of interaction in which messages are commonly directed simultaneously to multiple diverse audiences. This may take the form of individual comments interpreted differently by different audiences, but it can also be observed in the ambiguity of addressee in responses within complex

---

[11] Elsewhere, in his work on the Kennedy cabinet's Cuban missile crisis discussions, Gibson (2012, p. 40) acknowledges that in a meeting, "having more than one person to address" means "the number of actions a given utterance can perform is multiplied," as each participant may be indirectly addressed by comments explicitly addressed to co-present others. But he does not treat this insight extensively.

threads of initial posts, replies, replies to replies, and, in general, complicated action-reaction strands. Indeed, we argue that online communication can be coded as reaction networks (for example, who leaves comments to whom, and prompted by whom), with the complexity of sustaining multiple lines of communication at once potentially amenable to computational text analysis. And yet, which recipient is "primary" may remain undetermined until the reactions themselves arise; the "proof" of the structure is in the reactions.[12]

## Developing a theoretical framework

There are evidently many specific, real-world situations in which side-directed behavior takes place. Social action is triadic, not merely in the sense that action within dyads *is affected by* the presence of third parties (that is, behavior is shifted from what otherwise might occur, as in an argument between co-workers that gets muted in the presence of another employee), or that there are triadic (or larger structural) *implications* of dyadic behavior (for example, two people getting married closes off the chances of other people marrying one of them instead). Rather, more strictly, behavior ostensibly directed toward one alter may be more significantly and more consequentially targeted at another, whether that third party is an audience physically present or someone important in ego's cognitive map (Krackhardt, 1987) of their social network.

The question then arises whether, given its regularity and recurrence, we can conceive of SDB as a kind of *social form*, with distinct properties and implications that are identifiable, applicable, and even quantifiable across cases. This is challenging, because in many real-world settings, it will be difficult to establish which dyadic relations are most important and which are less so in any possible triadic configuration.[13] Worse, it could even be difficult to establish definitively the relevant members of the triad, and whether the different types of dyadic tie that constitute the triad can or should be coded in equal importance with each other in the same network "space."

This seeming tension between fluid indeterminacy and formal structure brings to mind Emily Erikson's (2013) exegesis of what she sees as competing theoretical tendencies or foci within network analysis, with one branch characterized as relationalism and the other as formalism. In Erikson's view (p. 219), "relationalism rejects essentialism and a priori categories and insists

---

[12] See Fuhse (2015) for a similar line of thought.
[13] Jorge Fontdevila informs us (personal communication) that various ethnographies have shown that people juggle complex kinship relations and alliances in their dyadic dealings, and that these mental imaginings of network positions inform their action with respect to co-present others. So the "third" might be not an individual but a social group or, as he put it more capaciously, a "social shape."

upon the intersubjectivity of experience and meaning as well as the importance of the content of interactions and their historical setting." Accordingly, it is rooted in the pragmatic perspective developed by Dewey and Mead and further articulated by Emirbayer and Mische (1998). While individuals always exist and evolve within structures of relations, "the dynamism of those structures requires actors to imaginatively construct the nature of their situation" (Erikson, 2013, p. 223). For example (and possibly alluding to Gibson's research), Erikson (2013, p. 234) proposes: "in negotiations within a boardroom, actors must decide whether they are responding to the other individuals in the room, individuals they represent who are outside of the room, or perhaps their mother's expectations for the kind of person they would become as adults." She characterizes this situation as temporally and contextually open-ended, requiring that the focal actor "creatively determine and negotiate an otherwise unfixed social context" (p. 234).

In contrast with relationalism, Erikson (2013, p. 219) argues that "formalism is based on a structuralist interpretation of the theoretical works of Georg Simmel," in which researchers deploy "a priori categories of relational types and patterns that operate independently of cultural content or historical setting." While we take Erikson's point that there is some tension between the bottom-up, flexible, and situated open-endedness of relationalism and the top-down, rigorous, universalist, typological approach of some formalisms, we aspire to synthesize relational and formal approaches. In fact, we would argue that SDB sits astride Erikson's distinction. It depends on nuanced interpretive and discursive dynamics, yet certain regularities exist in when and where it happens and by what means. We can look to Goffman for analogues: think of his efforts to identify regularities in interaction dynamics, say the definable properties of situations in which "audience segregation" is deployed (Goffman, 1959, 1967), or the cataloguing of "tie-signs" enacted as normative displays of dyadic relations in public places (Goffman, 1971, Ch. 5). Can we pick out the network correlates of such situations? In some ways, SDB is too radically indeterminate to fit into even the relational paradigm Erikson (2013, p. 228) describes, as it will be difficult to comprehend it fully via an analysis of "behavioral data."[14] Key elements of SDB are semiotic rather than overtly behavioral.[15] Nevertheless, some of the semiotic gestures

---

[14] Erikson refers to and draws a distinction from Martin (2009, p. 11), who argues that observable interactions are "too particular and disparate for structural analysis," and consequently a coherent account of the aggregation of social structure into durable large-scale forms of organization must be based on "relationships," such as friendships that perdure even between moments of actual interaction. This is a crucial topic for debate.

[15] More precisely, while behavioral clues are sometimes available for both participants and observers to understand "what is going on here," essential to the definition of SDB settings is the signaling of *meaning(s)* to multiple parties.

deployed in SDB may be amenable to analysis, along the lines of the strategies and techniques identified by sociolinguists and discourse analysts in the study of speech (for example, Gumperz, 1982). We take this up later.

## Simmel on triads and secrecy

Let's turn back to Simmel briefly, because he addressed *both* the nuances of interaction, and its patterned regularity (and constraints) in the shape of distinct *forms*. While there are interesting traces of the triadic composition of competition in *Conflict and the Web of Group Affiliations* (Simmel, 1955), more concerted attention arises with his discussion of triads (Simmel, 1950, pp. 145–69). Among the three versions of the triad presented, in the *tertius gaudens* form SDB may well be present, and in the *divide et impera* form it is almost definitional to the action. In the former scenario,[16] person A receives unexpected benefits from a contest between B and C. For example, a child receives treats in turn from each of his squabbling parents, each intent on outdoing the other to be the preferred parent. Undoubtedly, gaining the love of the child in the dyadic relationship is primary, but the full value of the favor is lost if it is not both superior to the favor granted by the rival parent, and somehow or other *signaled to* the rival parent. In *divide et impera* scenarios, favor or approval directed by the controlling actor or party toward one subordinate is often effective precisely to the extent competing subordinates are made aware of having been deprived of a reward themselves. "The third person creates a jealousy between them" (Simmel, 1950, p. 165), most artfully achieved by maintaining distance "between himself and the action which he starts" (p. 166). Frequently, this art is expressed by means of a close alternation in support for the contending actors. The heart of the control effort is allowing the disadvantaged party to know they are disadvantaged by signaling the reward given to the preferred one.

Also of possible interest is Simmel's writing on secrecy, which he sees as a constitutive feature of the social world: "Out of the counterplay of these two interests, in concealing and revealing, spring nuances and fates of human interaction that permeate it in its entirety" (1950, p. 334). From this dialectic, suspicion, for example, may arise, which can be catalytic for certain SDB situations. Furthermore, secrecy is one means of drawing both inclusive and/or exclusive social group boundaries, based on the unequal distribution

---

[16] Simmel distinguishes between a *tertius* who is permitted to take action ("get action" in Harrison White's (2008) terminology) by virtue of the fact that "the remaining two hold each other in check, and he can make a gain which one of the two would otherwise deny him" (1950, p. 154), from the situation where the *tertius* enjoys "benefits and promotions which a party bestows upon him, only in order to offend its adversary" (1950, p. 155). The latter form is more relevant to our argument.

of knowledge, including knowledge of how to interpret the current social situation. The subtly insolent student communicates secretly with classmates while the teacher is kept in the dark; the loyal employee would like to signal her loyalty to the boss without appearing overly sycophantic to co-workers. Secrecy, or something like secrecy, is important in SDB situations because they often involve subtle manipulations of communication. Actors exhibit ability to send disparate messages to different alters, and thus to maintain two (or more) lines of communication at once. Further, they can convey at a metalevel to certain alters that multiple lines of communication are in fact being sustained, resulting in a complex lamination of different frames of interaction on top of each other (Goffman, 1974).

## White on switchings

Since our treatment of SDB suggests that it includes both structural and semiotic elements which should be considered synthetically, we must visit the theoretical program established by Harrison White in his 1992 book, *Identity and Control,* and further developed after the revised version appeared in 2008. In White's overall argument, actors aim to manage uncertainty in their emergent ties with others. They do this by working out scripts, simple procedures, or provisional accounts of their action and each other's actions. These "identities" (the provisional accounts) provide the basis for "going on" in a predictable manner, thereby achieving cognitive "control" of the situation. A lot of interaction amounts to just one somewhat amorphous thing after another, a flow of encounters that don't result in lasting relations or durable structures. But in the move between situations, we engage in "switchings:" changes of script or protocol or identity that demarcate the boundaries of one situation and establish the terms of engagement used in it (Fontdevila and White, 2013). Switchings collectively mark out domains of social space within which certain network structures tend to develop and reproduce.

As switchings grow in our experience, we also develop metalevel skills and vocabulary for entering and exiting relations, crucial symbolic equipment for navigating through social space. Consequently, whereas we might imagine social life is made up of networks or domains between which we periodically switch, it might be more accurate to regard switching as *defining* the topology of social space: defining which network domains are relevant to which others at particular points of inflection. One may hypothesize that there is a lot of interesting action—meaning-laden activity, signaling, careful behavior management, cascading of implications across social domains—at these switches.

And, of course, we are suggesting that SDB often capitalizes on and exploits these switching opportunities. Code-switching in sociolinguistics research focuses on bilingual encounters; but the two languages spoken could be everyday communication and an insider argot, with switches between them designed to keep some participants in the dark. We can imagine some parties to an interaction being moved in and out of the dark over the course of a single interaction episode, based on skillful language deployment and careful indexing of talk. On the structural side, whereas quantitative network analysis tends to isolate different types of social ties or encounters from each other, often ignoring the action in switchings by taking established singular meaning for granted, White (2008) suggests we make these generative moments, or pivot points, central to our sociology.

Furthermore, as Fontdevila (2018, p. 234) notes, White considered the fixation on dyadic ties "reductionist." White emphasizes how "navigating social life entails reflexive juggling of expectation sets across multiple contingencies of shifting network configurations, including ties' relentless couplings and decouplings" (Fontdevila, 2018, p. 234). And so the "interactions between direct or co-present ties" that constitute social life "are rarely conducted in true dyadic isolation but always reflexively monitored and anchored in patterns and perceptions of each other's indirect relations" (p. 234). One can imagine how third parties (for example, clients, the bullied, polite classmates) can get roped into dyadic relationships capriciously or contingently, finding themselves drawn into fluid and emergent networks created out of energies originating elsewhere, and largely focused elsewhere. Communication and leverage in typical interaction settings are often achieved via the capacity for ambiguity and "ambage."[17]

White follows linguists and discourse analysts (for example, Duranti and Goodwin, 1992; Gumperz, 1982) in stressing the importance of communication in network construction. So much communication is indexical in nature; that is, it is composed of many indicators of one's own location, the location of others, and the location of objects and events in actors' environments. These communicative tools for signaling the situating of action are just as important as substantive symbolic content.[18] SDB situations seem specially to abound in the subtleties of indexicality, so that who is being

---

[17] Fontdevila (2018, p. 241) defines ambage as "social uncertainty," or we might say, the capacity of a social structure to be navigated along many possible paths. White himself was somewhat opaque on the term. Fontdevila offers the example of "using direct ties to influence indirect ties" (p. 241) as an instance of ambage, which surely has a flavor of SDB to it.

[18] So, for example, a flag has rich symbolic content, but whether it is "our flag," "your flag," "that flag over there," "white people's flag," "the goddam flag," and so on, is all about positioning the meaning of the flag in relation to social actors and social spaces. See McLean (2007) for an extended treatment of how these deictic modifiers matter from a social relational standpoint.

referenced, who is being addressed, how to assess the purity of the goals of the actor, and more, are up for grabs and not to be taken for granted. In sum, within White's general scheme, SDB might be seen as one instance of the anchoring of ostensibly dyadic interaction, continuously, in the perceptions and expectations of other actors co-present in that interaction—whether physically or cognitively, tangibly or merely spectrally.

## How to proceed

In this final section, we introduce some suggestions about possible equipment to use for honing in on a more systematic treatment of SDB situations. These "situations" may arise all over the social landscape, but following the examples we used above, we propose that we are most likely to find SDB in moderately to highly bounded social settings, and frequently formal organizational ones, even as SDB likely capitalizes on informal networks inside those formal organizations and manipulates them. Concomitantly, we could explore how the norms or quasi-institutionalized rules of particular social systems tend logically and/or urgently to the engagement of third parties in dyadic interactions. Examples that come to mind include political clientage systems (Eisenstadt and Roniger, 1984), feud-based societies and organizations encouraging the escalation of violence (Gould, 2003; Papachristos, 2009), courtroom settings in which dyadic interaction is routinely performed highly strategically before juries or judges (O'Barr, 1982; Sarat and Felstiner, 1995; Jacquemet, 1996), and online settings with specific structures of affordances that encourage third-party tagging (Song, 2019). These won't be the only places it can happen, but best to look first in those settings where it is most likely to appear as a recurrent and decisive feature of interaction.

### Networks

What *network* tools exist, and what network tools require revision, to study SDB structurally? First, we need to attend carefully to triads and think in a "triadic" way, including systematic attention to triad structures that spill across or operate at the "switchpoints" between types of tie. Second, we should consider the importance of enmity and conflict, that is, negative ties, in networks. Third, we need to pay greater attention to temporality. As it stands now, network analysis often treats one type of tie at a time and employs coarse-grained approaches to temporal change. Too often, triads have to occur within a single type of tie to draw our attention and be seen as commensurable.[19] And when network analysts entertain interactions

---

[19] Going beyond the specific scope of this chapter, the way multiple networks impinge on behavior at the micro-level has to be more fully examined. For example, social movement

between or cascades across multiple networks (Padgett and McLean, 2006), they usually do so at the whole network level rather than the micro-level.

Regarding triads, conducting a triad census is a routine part of many network analyses: looking for overall patterns among ties at the triadic level so as to characterize the network's general structural "character." Hypothetically, we could look for the 021D triad configuration in a network as a partial expression of how an actor might gesture toward two distinct actors at once. But with SDB, the implications of observing such a structure are substantively quite distinct from the characteristics typically sought in such microstructures, such as brokerage (Burt, 1992) or dominance (Chase, 1980).[20] So we need to be attentive in a fuller (and different, that is, not merely structural) way to discerning what is going on in these "two-gestures-at-once" situations. One structural advancement might be to map triad-based ties simultaneously with group boundaries, along the lines of Gould and Fernandez's (1989) typology of forms of brokerage. SDB gestures are often designed to signal boundaries of group inclusion or exclusion and to imply that some ties are effectively more "solidaristic" than others.

Recently, network analysts have shown renewed interest in balance theory and negative ties. Harrigan et al (2020) suggest the value of studying negative ties in settings very much like those we discussed earlier: friendship and bullying at school, positive and negative gossip in the workplace, and voting strategies in parliaments or courts. Leskovec et al (2010) propose their importance for analyzing interaction on social media. Negative ties are arguably pervasive, although commonly neglected, notwithstanding the disproportionately large consequences of their existence. It is reasonable to propose that negative ties (animosity) will be catalytic in network triads where jealousy or competition is present, where status-seeking or the achievement of dominance is pronounced (Leskovec et al, 2010), or where attacks may be made on third parties to garner favor with significant alters (Boda and Néray, 2015). Consider also triadic situations in which the presence of a specific despised person in a workplace (let's call him Bob), who is the "continual object of negative office gossip" (Harrigan et al, 2020, p. 4),

---

scholars (Hsiao and Yang, 2018; Song, 2019) are aware that both online and offline networks matter for mobilizing participants. But we often don't know how they work together, even as there is good reason to believe that mobilization is accomplished via complex contagion (Centola and Macy, 2007) with *combined* effects *across* networks, not only reinforcement within one network at a time. Absent a consideration of multiple network interleavings, analyses of structures like Twitter networks quickly become untethered from the complex relationality of the real world.

[20] This point resonates with the general claim that network structures are not strictly determinative of substantive network meaning, a caveat disregarded in many exponential random graph model-based network analyses.

may be instrumental for group solidarity among the rest of the staff, such that actions ostensibly directed toward Bob are more significantly directed at accomplishing approval from like-minded co-workers. Furthermore, workplace norms and regulations often suppress direct animosity, precipitating necessarily more subtle forms of communication, including meta signals to others co-present that "I don't quite mean what I actually said" when I addressed Bob directly.[21]

Third, let's consider temporality. Traditional network analysis conventionally flattens or eliminates temporality for the purposes of depicting structure as a kind of enduring tableau. That is unfortunate for analyzing inherently dynamic processes. There is an evident urgency in recent research in network analysis (for example, Kitts and Quintane, 2020)—and in fact, in work going back two decades (for example, Snijders, 2001; Moody et al, 2005)—to incorporate temporality (or more accurately, temporal change) into network datasets and visualization. That said, SDB depends heavily on timing at a granular level, not in the form of panel data. Either two lines of interaction are simultaneously sustained via individual utterances that are ambiguous, signaling different meanings to different audiences at the same time, or a close sequence of utterances or gestures unfolds that metapragmatically shifts what is the figure and what is the ground as different alters are sequentially addressed. Butts (2008) offers an approach to time-stamp network data as a series of "relational events." Could we not treat utterances as such relational events? Each "tie" would be an utterance or gesture, simultaneously instantiating a social relationship and offering meta-commentary on which ties matter and who is within or outside a particular network domain, perhaps shuffling specific actors in and out of the local network of shared meaning. Think of an employee interacting with her team but periodically interspersing praise or showing deference toward the team manager. Mapping this temporally and "spatially" could reveal the ongoing management and accomplishment of relationships within network structure through the layered and/or sequential unfolding of gestures.

For a study of resistance in schools or business meetings dynamics, keeping track of time-stamps could be exhausting (although it's pretty much what McFarland, 2001 and Gibson, 2005 did). But, in other cases, the obstacles might not be as great. The time-stamped quality of a lot of social media

---

[21] An anonymous reviewer of this chapter notes that SDB takes quasi-institutional form in debates in the US governed by Robert's Rules of Order. The rules stipulate that comments be directed to the chair, not antagonistically to fellow members of the assembly. The intended effect may be to mute or domesticate overt dyadic conflict—one thinks of Elias's (1994 [1939]) work on etiquette and the civilizing process here—but unintended consequences may include intensifying strategic side-directed *double entendre* speech and amplifying manipulation of the audience.

data, plus the directionality inscribed into a lot of social media content by virtue of the fact that it unfolds as a thread or branching set of threads over time, means we can at least hypothetically track patterns of responses to previous posts, and (again, hypothetically) identify multiple proximate targets of individual posts.[22]

*Semiotics*

Arguably, things are in better shape on the semiotics front, although our networks background may make us more sensitive to the shortcomings on our own side of the ledger. Bauman and Briggs (1990), among many others, have reminded us of the need to examine the artful use of language in social contexts as it is connected to questions of power. "Entextualization" (p. 79), as they describe it, denotes a process whereby talk becomes an object of reflection and analysis not only to researchers, but to those embedded in episodes of it. Brown and Levinson (1987) identify different forms of politeness, some of which may be deployed as techniques of circumlocution designed to manage and re-represent social relations. Deictic expressions (Hanks, 1992) can be crucial for judgements and for drawing boundaries of inclusion and exclusion within conversation: "You are doing a good job *over there*, Jason" includes a deictic expression possibly meant to draw a comparison or contrast with what others are doing *here*. Gumperz (1982) offers keen insights for analyzing how people use various forms of meta-discourse, embedding signals of intentionality or the broader context of meaning in what they say. Abundant work on code-switching reveals that (bilingual) speakers' utterances are often layered with at least two linguistic codes that are semantically and semiotically distinguishable. When a student asks her teacher a question in the classroom by using words that are marked only among students, her question also depends on code-switching, signaling to researchers an instance of SDB.

Although there are a multitude of semiotic concepts such as these to utilize for examining SDB, it nevertheless seems to us that such tools have almost always been used to analyze dyadic interaction rather than triadic. An early exception (but not especially rich example) is Goffman's (1971, p. 212) treatment of "pointed displays" of ties in public settings, such as "showing off one's date" or making evident one's connection to a prestigious business associate, or talking on the telephone with one person in the presence of a third (pp. 220ff.). In the latter scenario, one may be compelled to signal different things to the two alters: engagement, perhaps, to the person on the phone; impatience, perhaps, to the physically co-present third. One

---

[22] For one effort in this direction, see Song (2019, Ch. 5).

may "treat the party on the phone as if no bystander were present, while collusively using gestures to bring the bystander into the act" (p. 222). Either of these "lines" of communication may be genuine or feigned—conceivably alternately so in the course of a single conversation.[23]

Perhaps the most systematic and fruitful attention to triadic interaction in sociolinguistics appears in research on courtroom dynamics (for example, Cotterill, 2003; Ehrlich, 2010). Lawyers use presuppositional statements as a way of trying to get a witness to commit to a particular representation of reality, which actually has the primary goal of portraying the witness's credibility (or lack thereof) to the jury. Cross-examination questions taking the form of accusations frame hypotheses as truths for the purpose of incrimination. Doubtless there is much more. As Ehrlich notes (2010, p. 372):

> on a very superficial level, trials involve dialogue, the examination and cross-examination of witnesses by lawyers, and monologue, the opening and closing arguments of lawyers. However, given that these modes of speech are produced for the benefit of adjudicators—judges and/or juries—trial talk is more accurately characterized as multiparty in its structure.

This area of research could be especially formative for making more explicit and complete the analytical toolkit for a more systematic treatment of SDB.

## Conclusion

In this chapter we have sought to illuminate side-directed behavior as a recurrent form of three-way (or N-way) social interaction, to illustrate its presence across a number of commonly observed social networks-rooted settings, and to offer some suggestions for analyzing it empirically in something resembling a systematic way. SDB is a potent mechanism for marking switches among network domains, and for using activity and gesture in one to strategically inform constructions of meaning and forge relationships in another, making it a worthy object of analytical focus.

Significant methodological, epistemological, and ontological challenges remain for moving our agenda forward. We don't always know how to code SDB, we sometimes can't be sure we are observing it, and we don't always know who the relevant parties are. The two authors of this chapter were initially attracted to network analysis by the promise of concreteness: here

---

[23] Goffman (1971) extrapolates from the phone situation to cases with co-ethnics who share a language to the exclusion of a third, thus conjuring the vast topic of code-switching in sociolinguistics.

was a method that didn't rely from the outset on abstract collective actors, but achieved a take on social structure and social dynamics via tangible patterns of interaction. But, in its pursuit of concreteness and fixity in relations over time, network analysis can be deliberately inattentive to consequential non-actions or (mere) gestures, as if they had less ontological weight than observable behaviors, whereas we are arguing here, of course, that those gestures can be deeply constitutive of social orders. It takes considerable skill—both as a participant and an outside observer—to notice these momentous but evanescent gestures-cum-"ties" and "code" them correctly. After all, a wink vanishes into thin air if not noticed, and in turn correctly semiotically processed, by exactly the right recipient(s). One might even question whether it is defensible to try to measure such relational gestures in some cases, compared to the durable "relationships" network theorists often privilege (Martin, 2009, Ch. 1). Furthermore, ascertaining who the main participants are during SDB—who is the primary alter and who the primary audience—is itself an interpretive exercise. Explicit reference to C in communication from A to B might be the simplest kind of clue that SDB is occurring, but by no means is it a sufficient condition of its occurrence. Even if we can identify and code SDB in particular interaction episodes, ramping up to see the structural consequences of these micro-level switches will pose a more difficult challenge.

Let us return momentarily to consider the potential value of computational text analysis for SDB detection, picking up on a theme introduced earlier. Because such data contain traceable, complex patterns of relations via time-stamped posts, likes, dislikes, replies, replies to replies, and broadcast-oriented messages, minimally the data—and the data structure—exist to identify in the aggregate patterns in how people might sustain two or more lines of communication at once. But could we train an algorithm, along the lines of sentiment analysis (Fuhse et al, 2020), to recognize those traces of directed conversation and/or analytically definable gestures that betoken strategic manipulation of networked relationships? We should not minimize the difficulties here. For the sake of parsimony and rigor, most natural language processing protocols suggest (or require) deleting words that cannot connote a certain and firm meaning without being linked to other words—notably, definite and indefinite articles, personal pronouns, indicative pronouns, negatives, and verb tenses. All of these are specifically the elements that discourse analysts see as crucial to establishing and signaling social meaning! Without some better capacity to incorporate these directional and boundary-drawing syntactical elements into natural language processing, it's not clear that such computational approaches can deliver the goods quite yet.

SDB is an intriguing but vexing concept, because while we can offer illustrations of it readily enough, and it feels like a readily recognizable building block in constructing the social order, it combines deceptively complex (multiple network) social structure with remarkably subtle and ambiguous semiotic practices, both of which make scaling up beyond the study of small group dynamics quite challenging. Nevertheless, we hope this chapter helps as a first step toward developing a clearer understanding of this intriguing social "form," and points the way toward a more rigorous empirical investigation of it and its conceivably profound effects on social structure and social outcomes.

**References**

Battison, F., Cencetti, G., Iacopini, I., Latora, V., Lucas, M. et al. (2020) "Networks beyond Pairwise Interactions: Structure and Dynamics," Working paper. Available at https://arxiv.org/pdf/2006.01764.pdf.

Bauman, R. and Briggs, C. (1990) "Poetics and Performance as Critical Perspectives on Language and Social Life," *Annual Review of Anthropology*, 19: 59–88.

Bearman, P.S. and Parigi, P. (2004) "Cloning Headless Frogs and Other Important Matters: Conversation Topics and Network Structure," *Social Forces*, 83(2): 535–57.

Boda, Z. and Néray, B. (2015) "Inter-ethnic Friendship and Negative Ties in Secondary School," *Social Networks*, 43: 57–72.

Brown, P. and Levinson, S.C. (1987) *Politeness: Some Universals in Language Usage*, Cambridge: Cambridge University Press.

Burt, R.S. (1992) *Structural Holes*, Chicago, IL: University of Chicago Press.

Butts, C.T. (2008) "A Relational Event Framework for Social Action," *Sociological Methodology*, 38(1): 155–200.

Callejas, L.M. and Shepherd, H. (2020) "Conflict as a Social Status Mobility Mechanism in Schools: A Network Approach," *Social Psychology Quarterly*, 83: 319–41.

Centola, D. and Macy, M. (2007) "Complex Contagions and the Weakness of Long Ties," *American Journal of Sociology*, 113(3): 702–34.

Chase, I. (1980) "Social Process and Hierarchy Formation in Small Groups: A Comparative Perspective," *American Sociological Review*, 45(6): 905–24.

Cotterill, J. (2003) *Language and Power in Court: A Linguistic Analysis of the O.J. Simpson Trial*, Basingstoke: Palgrave Macmillan.

De Waal, F. (1982) *Chimpanzee Politics: Power and Sex Among Apes*, New York: Harper & Row.

Diehl, D. and McFarland, D. (2010) "Toward a Historical Sociology of Social Situations," *American Journal of Sociology*, 115(6): 1713–52.

Duranti, A. and Goodwin, C. (eds) (1992) *Rethinking Context: Language as an Interactive Phenomenon*, Cambridge: Cambridge University Press.

Ehrlich, S. (2010) "Courtroom Discourse," in R. Wodak, B. Johnstone, and P. Kerswill (eds) *The Sage Handbook of Sociolinguistics*, London: Sage, pp. 361–74.

Eisenstadt, S.N. and Roniger, L. (1984) *Patrons, Clients, and Friends: Interpersonal Relations and the Structure of Trust in Society*, Cambridge: Cambridge University Press.

Elias, N. (1994 [1939]) *The Civilizing Process*, Cambridge: Blackwell.

Emirbayer, M. and Mische, A. (1998) "What is Agency?," *American Journal of Sociology*, 103(4): 962–1023.

Erikson, E. (2013) "Formalist and Relationalist Theory in Social Network Analysis," *Sociological Theory*, 31(3): 219–42.

Faris, R. (2012) "Aggression, Exclusivity, and Status Attainment in Interpersonal Networks," *Social Forces*, 90(4): 1207–35.

Faris, R. and Felmlee, D. (2011) "Status Struggles: Network Centrality and Gender Segregation in Same- and Cross-Gender Aggression," *American Sociological Review*, 76(1): 48–73.

Fine, G.A. (1987) *With the Boys: Little League Baseball and Preadolescent Culture*, Chicago, IL: University of Chicago Press.

Fontdevila, J. (2018) "Switchings Among Netdoms: The Relational Sociology of Harrison White," in F. Dépelteau (ed) *The Palgrave Handbook of Relational Sociology*, London: Palgrave Macmillan, pp. 231–69.

Fontdevila, J. and White, H.C. (2013) "Relational Power from Switching across Netdoms through Reflexive and Indexical Language," in C. Powell and F. Dépelteau (eds) *Applying Relational Sociology: Relations, Networks, and Society*, New York: Palgrave Macmillan, pp. 155–79.

Fuhse, J. (2015) "Networks from Communication," *European Journal of Social Theory*, 18(1): 39–59.

Fuhse, J., Stuhler, O., Riebling, J. and Martin, J.L. (2020) "Relating Social and Symbolic Relations in Quantitative Text Analysis: A Study of Parliamentary Discourse in the Weimar Republic," *Poetics*, 78: 101363.

Fujimoto, K., Snijders, T.A.B. and Valente, T.W. (2017) "Popularity Breeds Contempt: The Evolution of Reputational Dislike Relations and Friendships in High School," *Social Networks*, 48: 100–9.

Gibson, D.R. (2005) "Taking Turns and Talking Ties: Networks and Conversational Interaction," *American Journal of Sociology*, 110(6): 1561–97.

Gibson, D.R. (2012) *Talk at the Brink: Deliberation and Decision during the Cuban Missile Crisis*, Princeton, NJ: Princeton University Press.

Goffman, E. (1959) *The Presentation of Self in Everyday Life*, New York: Anchor Books.

Goffman, E. (1967) *Interaction Ritual: Essays on Face-to-Face Behavior*, New York: Pantheon.

Goffman, E. (1971) *Relations in Public: Microstudies of the Public Order*, New York: Basic Books.

Goffman, E. (1974) *Frame Analysis: An Essay on the Organization of Experience*, New York: Harper & Row.

Gould, R.V. (2003) *Collision of Wills: How Ambiguity About Social Rank Breeds Conflict*, Chicago, IL: University of Chicago Press.

Gould, R.V. and Fernandez, R. (1989) "Structures of Mediation: A Formal Approach to Brokerage in Transaction Networks," *Sociological Methodology*, 19: 89–126.

Gumperz, J.J. (1982) *Discourse Strategies*, New York: Cambridge University Press.

Hanks, W. (1992) "The Indexical Ground of Deictic Reference," in A. Duranti and C. Goodwin (eds) *Rethinking Context: Language as an Interactive Phenomenon*, Cambridge: Cambridge University Press, pp. 43–76.

Harrigan, N.M., Labianca, G.J. and Agneessens, F. (2020) "Negative Ties and Signed Graphs Research: Stimulating Research on Dissociative Forces in Social Networks," *Social Networks*, 60: 1–10.

Hsiao, Y. and Yang, Y. (2018) "Activists on the Cloud? An Empirical Test on Commitment for Online and Offline Protest Participants," *Information, Communication & Society*, 21(7): 996–1013.

Jacquemet, M. (1996) *Credibility in Court: Communicative Practices in the Camorra Trials*, Cambridge: Cambridge University Press.

Kitts, J.A. and Quintane, E. (2020) "Rethinking Social Networks in the Era of Computational Social Science," in R. Light and J. Moody (eds) *The Oxford Handbook of Social Network Analysis*, Oxford: Oxford University Press, pp. 71–97.

Krackhardt, D. (1987) "Cognitive Social Structures," *Social Networks*, 9(2): 109–34.

Leskovec, J., Huttenlocher, D. and Kleinberg, J. (2010) "Signed Networks in Social Media," *Proceedings of the SIGCHI Conference on Human Factors in Computing Systems*, New York: Machinery, pp. 1361–70.

McFarland, D.A. (2001) "Student Resistance: How the Formal and Informal Organization of Classrooms Facilitate Everyday Forms of Student Defiance," *American Journal of Sociology*, 107(3): 612–78.

McFarland, D.A. (2004) "Resistance as a Social Drama: A Study of Change-Oriented Encounters," *American Journal of Sociology*, 109(6): 1249–1318.

McLean, P.D. (2007) *The Art of the Network: Strategic Interaction and Patronage in Renaissance Florence*, Durham, NC: Duke University Press.

McLean, P.D. (2017) *Culture in Networks*, Malden, MA: Polity Press.

Martin, J.L. (2009) *Social Structures*, Princeton, NJ: Princeton University Press.

Moody, J., McFarland, D.A. and Bender-deMoll, S. (2005) "Dynamic Network Visualization," *American Journal of Sociology*, 110(4): 1206–41.

Myers, S.L. (2020) "China's Military Provokes Its Neighbors, but the Message Is for the United States," *The New York Times*, June 26. Available from www.nytimes.com/2020/06/26/china-military-india-taiwan.html.

O'Barr, W. (1982) *Linguistic Evidence: Language, Power, and Strategy in the Courtroom*, New York: Academic Press.

Padgett, J.F. and McLean, P.D. (2006) "Elite Transformation and Organizational Invention in Renaissance Florence," *American Journal of Sociology*, 111(5): 1463–568.

Papachristos, A.V. (2009) "Murder by Structure: Dominance Relations and the Social Structure of Gang Homicide," *American Journal of Sociology*, 115(1): 74–128.

Sarat, A. and Felstiner, W.L.F. (1995) *Divorce Lawyers and their Clients: Power and Meaning in the Legal Process*, New York: Oxford University Press.

Simmel, G. (1950) *The Sociology of Georg Simmel*, trans. and ed K.H. Wolff, New York: Free Press.

Simmel, G. (1955) *Conflict and the Web of Group Affiliations*, trans. K.H. Wolff and R. Bendix, New York: Free Press.

Small, M.L. (2017) *Someone to Talk To*, New York: Oxford University Press.

Snijders, T.A.B. (2001) "The Statistical Evaluation of Social Network Dynamics," *Sociological Methodology*, 31: 361–95.

Song, E. (2019) Power from the Fingertips: Writing Alone and Working Together in Digital Media in Korea, Ph.D. dissertation, Department of Sociology, Rutgers University.

White, H. (2008) *Identity and Control: How Social Formations Emerge*, Princeton, NJ: Princeton University Press.

5

# Cultural Syntax and the Rules of Meaning-making: A New Paradigm for the Interpretation of Culture

*Todd Madigan*

## Introduction

Ever since its emergence from the sea foam of anthropology's cultural turn,[1] cultural sociology has been focused almost entirely on *meaning* and *structure*. But should it be? Should cultural sociology lavish the entirety of its intellectual affection on this pair of favored children? That is the question this chapter takes up, a question that is sure to sound surly to the ears of the initiated. After all, "For the cultural sociologist, meaning drives the entirety of social life" (Alexander et al, 2012, p. 9) and without "structure society cannot survive" (Alexander, 2003, p. 4). But however impertinent it might be to ask this question—and however heterodox it is to answer it in the negative—the point is certainly not to suggest that cultural sociology shouldn't concern itself with meaning and structure. Of course it should.

Rather, the point of this question is to direct our attention toward a sin of omission, to what the blinkered focus on meaning and structure has caused those working in this corner of the discipline to miss. My contention here

---

[1] See Cossu (2021) for a more nuanced account of what I gloss as "sea foam," that is, the confluence of theoretical currents within the social sciences that led to the development of cultural sociology.

is that in their profligate devotion to these two aspects of social life, cultural sociologists working under the auspices of cultural autonomy, as well as interpretive social scientists more broadly, have largely neglected to examine and theorize the rules governing the possibilities of meaning, what I will take up and champion as *cultural syntax*.[2]

In the present chapter, I develop the contours of a new paradigm based on the distinction between three hierarchically related levels of cultural analysis. Two of these levels are articulated by Paul Ricoeur (1976) in his theorizing on interpretation and meaning. In Ricoeur's classic construction, the lower stratum belongs to the science of semiotics and can be thought of as analytically analogous to the *word*, whereas the higher stratum belongs to semantics and can be thought of as analytically analogous to the *sentence*. The two levels are closely related, but wholly autonomous. Ricoeur puts it this way:

> there is no way of passing from the level of the word as a lexical sign to the sentence by mere extension of the same methodology to a more complex entity. The sentence is not a larger or more complex word, it is a new entity. It may be decomposed into words, but the words are something other than short sentences. A sentence is a whole irreducible to the sum of its parts. It is made up of words, but it is not a derivative function of its words. A sentence is made up of signs, but is not itself a sign. (Ricoeur, 1976, p. 7)

While Ricoeur's model has certainly proven fruitful in the analysis of culture, it also illustrates the blind spot I have already pointed out above in the case of cultural sociology. However, a modified version of this paradigm produces a theoretical model with the capacity to correct this defect and illuminate otherwise unrecognized features of the social world, ultimately yielding greater descriptive and explanatory power. Retaining the linguistic scaffolding built by Ricoeur, I propose a reconfigured tripartite construction: at the subordinate level of the *word*, analysis focuses on semantics (that is, the meaning of the words), whereas at the superordinate level—the level of the *sentence*—analysis focuses on structures that correspond to types of sentences (for example, declarative, interrogative, imperative, and

---

[2] To be clear at the outset, I do not argue that these rules are universal or otherwise invariable. There is, in fact, continuous historical change and subcultural variation regarding what constitutes the rules governing meaning-making for any social group. What's more, some of these rules are more strictly enforced than others and are subject to fluctuation based on the social positions of the actors (see Fontdevila, 2010, for a discussion of how social power affects grammatical rules).

exclamatory).[3] In addition, I propose a crucial intermediate level: that of *syntax*, that is, the rules governing the combining of words.[4]

In this new paradigm for the analysis of culture, *cultural semantics* identifies and examines the meanings that imbue the social world (for example, the meaning of condoms, electric chairs, or hurricanes), *cultural structure* identifies and examines the patterns that emerge from certain arrangements of meanings (for example, the structures of social performances, narratives, or discourses of democracy), and *cultural syntax* identifies and examines the rules that dictate which meanings can combine with which other meanings within a given cultural structure (for example, which meaningful incidents must not be included in a particular narrative or which captions must not accompany certain meaningful images).

Cultural sociologists have worked wonders in terms of mapping the topography of the social world, yet there are features still to be discovered. Entire mountain ranges and unfathomable oceans assuredly exist within the unexplored regions of culture, features that should we approach them would restrict and redirect our movement. In the world of culture, we cannot simply go where we will; there are limits to what can be meant. Semiotician Jerzy Pelc (1982, p. 2) alludes to this in the following: "in a certain situation, anything can be used as a sign. Then it has meaning." The tantalizing suggestion that it is *only* in certain situations that a specific thing can be used as a sign points to the fact that nothing can be made to mean just anything under any and all conditions. But why not? The answer I offer is that meanings are limited in the ways in which they can combine within cultural structures; they are limited by the rules of cultural syntax. While cultural sociologists Jeffrey Alexander and Philip Smith (2003a, p. 26) suggest that meaning and structure "can be made into fine bedfellows," I argue that there is room in that bed for one more.

Before I elaborate a fuller description of the theory of cultural syntax and its rules of meaning-making, I want to obviate an objection that is bound to arise. Although they are often committed to the notion of cultural structures, many culturally minded social theorists balk when the specter of "rules" is conjured. Even before the inception of cultural sociology, cultural anthropologist Victor Turner (1982, p. 80) was criticizing the notion that a cultural structure is simply a "combination of rules and vocabularies already laid down in the deep structures of mind and brain." And while Turner was

---

[3] Note that this is a reversal that carries with it a difference in how *semiotics* and *semantics* are being deployed: in Ricoeur's model, as already noted, the analytic level of the word corresponds to semiotics, while the level of the sentence corresponds to semantics.

[4] The notion of words and sentences are, of course, metaphorical. As the subsequent paragraph explains, the linguistic model is simply a helpful template for the new paradigm I put forward for the analysis of culture.

thinking more of mid-century structural anthropology, the same aversion can be seen in the context of its intellectual cousin that was born of the cognitive revolution. The idea of assorted rules carved deep inside the brain is not only part of structural anthropology, but also informs the cognitive science that developed during the mid-20th century. Cultural psychologist Jerome Bruner (1990, p. 4) argues that the concept of structured cognitive rules gives rise to the misguided metaphor of *computation*, where human cognition is more akin to "the *processing* of information" than to "the *construction* of meaning." And the problem with this (from Bruner's meaning-centered perspective) is that because information is independent of meaning, meaning is not "relevant to computation" (1990, p. 4). Based on this critique, Bruner goes on to assail the notion of syntax, as well:

> [In computation the] categories of possibility and the instances they comprise are processed according to the "syntax" of the system, its possible moves. Insofar as information in this dispensation can deal with meaning it is in the dictionary sense only: accessing stored lexical information according to a coded address. (1990, p. 5)

The trouble with this critique is that Bruner throws syntax out with the bathwater of cognitive science. His evident horror at the computational metaphor leads him to unnecessarily eschew the notion of rules—of syntax—entirely. In similar fashion, in order to sidestep this guilt by association, many cultural sociologists have been careful to temper their structuralist tendencies with notions of "dynamic" processes (Eyerman, 2008, p. 22; McCormick, 2012, p. 722), "spontaneity" (Wagner-Pacifici, 1986, p. 165), and "contingency" (Alexander, 2006, p. 29). However, in the present case all these caveats are really unnecessary. The syntactical rules I am describing as part of the new paradigm are not to be found in the physiology of the brain; they are just as socially constructed as meaning and cultural structures. Therefore, while not denying the importance of these scholars' considerations—and sharing Bruner's rejection of the computational metaphor—I will welcome the rigidity that cultural syntax implies. In the spirit of Kieran Healy's "Fuck Nuance" (2017), I will embrace the fullness of the concept.

## Semantics

If meaning and structure are the cherished children of cultural sociology, meaning is clearly the favorite. Isaac Reed (2009, p. 5) tells us that cultural sociology "is about meaning—specifically, the role of meaning in social life," while Jason Mast (2013, p. 9) explains that "At the core of cultural sociology is the insistence that social action is … meaningful." When reading the works of cultural sociologists, "meaning" is the clanging cowbell alerting us that culture is near. It sounds its familiar, tinny peal over every hill and dale throughout the corpus of this tradition. Lyn Spillman (2008, p. 1) explains that "Cultural sociology is about meaning-making. Cultural sociologists investigate how meaning-making happens, why meanings vary, how meanings influence human action, and the ways meaning-making is important in social cohesion, domination, and resistance." When Viviana Zelizer (1994, p. 213) wants to demonstrate that "cultural and social factors influence the uses and meaning of money," she shows how "monetary payments acquire powerful symbolic meanings" (1994, p. 211) through the "cultural transformation in children's value" (1994, p. 32); when Philip Smith (2008, p. 28) wants to develop "a truly cultural theory of punishment," he tells us that "punishment in its generalities and specificities cannot be understood without reference to public meaning" (2008, p. 1); when Frederick Wherry (2012, p. 134) wants to describe a "cultural sociology of markets," he deploys "a meaning-centered analysis" (2012, p. 134); when Iddo Tavory and Ann Swidler (2009, pp. 171–2) want to contribute "to the sociology of culture," they "examine the meanings of condom use" (2009, p. 172); and when Ronald Eyerman (2006, p. 20) outlines his program for a cultural sociology of the arts, he calls for "a return to meaning in the sociology of the arts."

The foregoing litany shines a light on the centrality of meaning to understanding the social world, and the insistence on this is one of the glories of cultural sociology. This unremitting focus on meaning derives in no small part from cultural sociology's genealogical roots in cultural anthropology, the field from which it draws much of its inspiration. The innovative thought of luminaries such as Mary Douglas, Victor Turner, Marshall Sahlins, and, most spectacularly, Clifford Geertz is the lifeblood pulsing through the veins of cultural sociology. Specifically, it was the cultural turn in anthropology that revivified the notion that the interpretation of meaning should be at the center of the social sciences.[5] Geertz (1973, p. 9) asserts that anthropological research is "an interpretive activity," that the analysis of culture is above all else "an interpretive [science] in search of meaning" (1973, p. 5), that the work of one who would analyze culture is "like that of a literary critic" (1973, p. 9), and therefore that cultural analysis "is like trying to read ... a manuscript" (1973, p. 10). This notion of culture as a text-in-need-of-interpretation has had far-reaching consequences for the social sciences broadly conceived, but

---

[5] "Revivified" because long before the cultural turn in anthropology, Max Weber (1978, p. 4) had asserted that "Sociology ... is a science concerning itself with the interpretive understanding of social action," and, furthermore, that "We shall speak of 'action' insofar as the acting individual attaches a subjective meaning to his behavior." Similarly, Wilhelm Dilthey claimed that "Understanding and interpretation is the method used throughout the human studies ... It contains all the truths of the human studies" (cited in Dilthey and Rickman, 1962, p. 116).

for the present purposes I will continue to focus on the repercussions across what would later emerge as the field of cultural sociology.

In Isaac Reed's (2011, pp. 89ff.) elucidation of a theory that gives interpretation its rightful place at the table of sociological explanation, he describes the concept of a specifically interpretive epistemic mode and lays this concept squarely at the feet of Geertz. This interpretivism is built on the idea that the social world can in some cogent sense be approached as a text and that the "problem for the social researcher is, then, to interpret [its] meaning" (Reed, 2011, p. 162). Of course, when Reed writes these words, he is building on what is already a powerful trope in cultural sociology, where the business of "hermeneutically reconstructing social texts" (Alexander and Smith, 2003a, p. 13) had been underway for some time. Richard Biernacki (2009, p. 120) makes the case with equal force: "textual and symbolic interpretation [is] the constitutive business of cultural sociology." Again, it is not the purpose of this chapter to deny the importance of this approach. Instead, the point I wish to make is that in the hands of cultural sociologists, the hammer of interpretation has had the habit of making all the aspects of culture look like nails of meaning.

In the midst of cultural sociologists' evident excitement about interpretation, it can be easy to forget that the social world is merely *like* a text (culture is not, in fact, a book). But one can skirt the simile by making the claim that culture *is in fact* a system of signs. And this is a move that had already been made even before the cultural turn in anthropology. When Geertz (1973, p. 5) claims that "The concept of culture I espouse ... is essentially a semiotic one," he is echoing a conceptual conceit that can be traced through Barthes, Lévi-Strauss, and all the way back to Saussure.[6] But Geertz is rather coy regarding this semiotic claim. While he is happy to wax eloquent about the interpretive nature of cultural analysis, the moment the implications of culture's semiotic qualities began to rear their heads, he demurs: "The besetting sin of interpretive approaches to anything—literature, dreams, symptoms, culture—is that they tend to resist, or to be permitted to resist, conceptual articulation" (Geertz, 1973, p. 24). Indeed, Geertz (1973, p. 30) warns that "Nothing will discredit a semiotic approach to culture more quickly than allowing it to drift into a combination of intuitionism and alchemy" ("alchemy" here being a euphemism for the more obscene expression, "theory"). And it would appear that while the semantic dimension of semiotics is for Geertz (1973, p. 30) sufficiently grounded in reality to escape his censure, the dimension of syntax—the rules governing the possibilities of meaning—smacks of "cabalism" and belonged to the province of the "dark sciences." Thankfully, cultural sociologists have

---

[6] I use the term *echo* advisedly, for while Geertz's theorizing of culture and meaning in "Thick Description" (1973) aligns closely with the tradition of Barthes, Lévi-Strauss, and Saussure, the genesis of his theorizing is to be found elsewhere (see Cossu, 2021).

largely ignored Geertz's imprecations against theorizing. Yet they have nevertheless mirrored his disregard for any sustained consideration of what could be thought of as cultural syntax. It is not the purpose of this chapter to determine why this is so, but it certainly makes one wonder if the present lacuna in theorizing on the rules governing meaning systems can, in part, be credited to its studied absence in the work of Geertz.

Despite the lack of explicit theorizing on cultural syntax, there is nevertheless a current running just below the surface of a good deal of cultural sociologists' work on the interpretation of social life, and this current suggests that there is something more than semantics afoot in the field, something sensed but not grasped. It is as though the concept of syntax rushes like an unseen subterranean river coursing just beneath one's feet. In his reflections on cultural sociologists' development of a Geertzean approach to their labor, Matthew Norton (2011a, p. 205) comments on the shared "theoretical insight that human interactions with the world are pervasively interpretive and that these interpretations can best be understood through the reconstruction of semiotic systems and the meanings that are generated within them." Yes, the cowbell of meaning is clanging here, but, more importantly, so is the idea of a "semiotic system." Since semiotic systems include more than just semantics, the fact that this concept has remained operative in the field means that there has always been the possibility that the rules governing the relationship between meanings could be taken up and theorized. Reed (2011, p. 161) has his ear to the same ground when he writes that "an essential aspect of social life as such is its dependence upon arrangements of meaning." And it is precisely the rules governing the "arrangements of meaning" that a cultural syntax seeks to explore. However, instead of identifying syntax as the source of this rumbling, Norton, Reed, and all the others veer back and head to familiar ground; they move from the individual meanings of signs and symbols to the higher, sentence-level analysis of structure.

## Structure

In their introduction to the *Oxford Handbook of Cultural Sociology*, Alexander et al (2012, p. 12) note that "While all cultural sociologists are committed to meaning-centered analysis, there are different levels of commitment to the idea that culture should be studied as if it is a language with a set of meaning structures." Despite the fact that some might not be as enthusiastic as others, cultural sociologists have nevertheless given ample consideration to the analytical level of structure. In their seminal article staking out the turf of cultural sociology, Alexander and Smith (2003a, p. 24) explain how their project seeks to understand culture "as a text that is underpinned by signs and symbols that are in patterned relationships to each other." This notion of patterned relationships between signs and symbols corresponds to Ricoeur's level of the sentence, what I have been referring to as the structural level of cultural analysis. And just as a certain combination of words will result in a declarative sentence, while another combination produces an imperative sentence, so one arrangement of meanings will constitute one cultural structure, while a different arrangement will result in another.

In the same way that the drive to interpret the meanings of social life didn't originate with cultural sociology, neither did the urge to discover the structures formed through the patterning of those meanings. And just as the immediate impetus to interpret social life came from the cultural turn in anthropology, so too did the urge to discover and describe cultural structures.[7] One example of this early anthropological exploration of structure can be found in the work of Mary Douglas and her illumination of the complex structures of *purity* and *pollution*. Douglas (1984 [1966], p. 156) writes compellingly of the human tendency to create symbolic structures based on these meanings: "Whatever we perceive is organized into patterns for which we, the perceivers, are largely responsible." She goes on to argue that the presence of these patterned structures in any given society creates the possibility that a member of that society might violate this symbolic structure, which can result in negative sanctions against the violator:

> Pollution powers ... inhere in the structure of ideas itself and punish a symbolic breaking of that which should be joined or joining that which should be separate. It follows from this that pollution is a type of danger which is not likely to occur except where lines of structure, cosmic or social, are clearly defined. (1984 [1966], pp. 158–9)

In a similar way, Victor Turner (1982, p. 75) identifies a meaning structure he calls *social drama*, a "process of converting particular values and ends, distributed over a range of actors, into a system (which is always temporary and provisional) of shared or consensual meaning." And these social dramas, as he asserts elsewhere, belong to "the dimension of 'structure'" (Turner, 1987 [1974], p. 33). Likewise, Marshall Sahlins (2005 [1976], p. 167), another representative of the cultural turn in anthropology, describes how an economy is a "symbolic system" based on structures built up of "the social meaning[s] of ... object[s]." He then elaborates on how this cultural structure is based on a specific pattern of meanings: "The goods stand as

---

[7] Of course, the cultural anthropologists weren't the first to emphasize the existence of structured meanings in the social world. In the late 19th and early 20th centuries, Wilhelm Dilthey (1979 [1910], pp. 170–2) was already theorizing about the "structure of experiences" and "systems of culture" that were built upon relationships between meanings.

an object code for the signification and valuation of persons and occasions, functions and situations. Operating on a specific logic of correspondence between material and social contrasts, production is thus the reproduction of the culture in a system of objects" (Sahlins, 2005 [1976], p. 176).

While not the raison d'être of cultural sociology in the way meaning has been, sussing out and describing cultural structures has been fruitful for those laboring in its orchards. Following the path cleared by the cultural turn in anthropology, cultural sociologists have blazed new trails. For example, when Akiko Hashimoto (2013, p. 30) elucidates the framework of the "fragmented meanings of the war [WWII]," she "shows how cultural trauma narratives may develop a splintered discursive structure"; when Ronald Jacobs (2008, pp. 273ff.) chronicles the crisis precipitated by the 1991 Rodney King beating by Los Angeles police officers (and the subsequent acquittal of those officers), he explains how the "same event can be narrated in a number of different ways" and how these structured plots influence people's evaluations of different communities; when Matthew Norton (2011b, p. 319) wants to illustrate the existence of "structures of meaning and the systematic interplay of different elements of these structures," he analyzes the "complex dynamics of meaning making" that structure a television news analysis program; when Bernhard Giesen (2004, p. 10) dilates on the particular trauma sometimes experienced by perpetrators, he considers the "symbolic structures" created by the plexus of meaningful stories, myths, rituals, and images (2004, p. 11); when Julia Sonnevend (2012, p. 228) theorizes what she calls the *image encounter*, she describes how the viewer of an image "constructs social and individual meanings," and depending on how those meanings are structured, the encounter might result in an *iconic ritual*; when Philip Smith (2005, p. 34) seeks to explain the reason why wars are waged, he sets out to "identify the basic structures of the genre war"; and when Jeffrey Alexander and Jason Mast (2011, p. 10) describe the felicity conditions for a social performance, they insist that we "must attend to the cultural structures," the "relations between signs in a cultural system that render a performative intelligible, meaningful, and capable of being interpreted as felicitous or infelicitous."

In each of these cases, "Symbols are the building blocks of cultural systems" (Kane, 2011, p. 12), and with these building blocks mighty edifices have been constructed. But even though these structures of meanings are complex and dynamic, none of their analyses really directly addresses the rules governing the combinations of their component parts. Their theoretical reconstructions *do* describe the various patterns of meanings and how the various signs and symbols are related to one another, but this is not the same thing as describing which patterns are permitted, and which are not, based on the symbolic logic of the particular cultural structure. Although all these theorists agree that meaning is organized in "representational structures consisting of symbolic codes, tropes, and narratives for constructing, interpreting, and maintaining 'reality'" (Kane, 2011, p. 15), none offers anything approaching a cultural syntax with which to explore the rules of what can and cannot be meant in a given context.

## Syntax

As I have been at pains to point out, there is a void in the analysis of culture that is in need of consideration. My argument is that when we take seriously the claim that culture is a system of signs (and therefore squarely within the purview of semiotics), we should also avail ourselves of the discipline's other relevant theoretical resources. The paradigm I am putting forward is a template comprising three levels of analysis—that of meanings ("words"), that of structures ("sentences"), and in between those two, that of the rules governing the ways in which such meanings can combine, and, indeed, the ways in which they cannot combine. This set of rules is, of course, the special province of syntax, a dimension of semiotics that is defined in various ways depending on one's theoretical commitments. For his part, Saussure (2009 [1996], p. 135), in the context of his semiology, uses "syntax" rather nonchalantly as "the theory of word sequences," hiding it under the umbrella of his more frequently invoked concept of "syntagmatic analysis," which he delineates as the examination of combinations of words arranged in a sequence (2009 [1996], p. 122). Similarly, although writing in the tradition of behaviorism, Charles Morris (1938, p. 13) conceives of "syntax" as "the study of the relations between certain combinations of signs within a language." Finally, Noam Chomsky (1965, p. 3), from the perspective of his theory of transformational grammar, describes "syntax" as comprising "the rules that specify the well-formed strings of minimal syntactically functioning units."

The point here is not to insist too rigidly on the exact definition of syntax, but rather to deploy the concept in the service of building a more robust paradigm that will in turn open up new vistas onto the social world. Using Ricoeur's hierarchical distinction between word and sentence (1976, p. 7), a simple series of examples from ordinary language should help make this model clear.

(a) *The book is bewildering.*

In the case of (a), we can see that in terms of semantics, there are four words whose meanings are easy to determine. At the structural level, the sentence is patterned such that it is declarative.[8]

---

[8] Obviously, punctuation plays a role at the sentence level of analysis, but in terms of the paradigm I am propounding by way of analogy, it has no independent part to play.

(b) *Is the book bewildering?*

In the case of (b), we can see that in terms of semantics, the same four words are used, and each has the same meaning as in (a). However, at the structural level, the sentence has been transformed into an interrogative by a rearranging of the words. Of course, there are a number of transformations we can make using just these four words. We can return them to their original order of (a), but still alter their structural level by rendering the sentence an exclamatory one, as in (c).

(c) *The book is bewildering!*

Furthermore, we can also return to the original structure of (a), a declarative sentence, but do so with an altered order of the same four words, as in (d).

(d) *Bewildering is the book.*

However, and this is the main point, the permutations are not limitless. While "Syntactic rules bear an arbitrary relationship to the functions they fulfill" (Bruner, 1990, p. 76), clearly, there are syntactic rules that not only enable the various permutations of (a), (b), (c), and (d), but also constrain and preclude others. To wit:

(e) *Book bewildering is the.*

Obviously, this is a pattern of words that is not permissible within the strictures of English syntax. Although (e) still comprises the four original words found in examples (a) through (d), and the individual meanings of those words are still recognizable, their disposition makes no sense. Taken as a whole, the arrangement has no recognizable structure, that is, it is not declarative, interrogative, exclamatory, or imperative, and therefore has no recognizable meaning at the structural level of the sentence.[9]

At this point, it is important to remember that what I am offering is a paradigm. It is a theoretical model whose purpose is not to perfectly describe the entirety

---

[9] There is another type of linguistic combination that could extend this series, one that Chomsky (1957) memorably exemplifies with the following declarative sentence: "Colorless green ideas sleep furiously." While semantically incoherent, the sentence is in fact syntactically sound, and it is interesting to contemplate an analogue for this case in the social world. Indeed, the notion of such an analogue is only conceivable with the theoretical model I am here elucidating, a model that fully integrates meaning, syntax, and structure.

of the social world, but rather to provide a heuristic that is generative of a new perspective on culture, one that can in turn provide useful and interesting insights. For example, the reduction of culture to Ricoeur's two hierarchical levels of word and sentence is an obvious simplification. We could easily complexify his model by noting that between the level of word and sentence—yet not reducible to either—is the level of *clauses*. Similarly, we could analyze words at the lower level of *morphology*, or reach above that of sentences by examining *paragraphs* or entire *texts*. And depending on one's interests, these additional layers of meaning might very well prove to be profitable avenues of exploration. In fact, a case can be made that cultural sociologists have long been busy analyzing culture at many of these different structural levels, determining how they coordinate and fit together to create larger structures of meaning.

My argument is that this conventional study of the coordination and patterning of meaningful units is akin to that of examining the patterns of words that constitute different kinds of sentences. Just as we saw above in our sample sentences, there are certain combinations of words that constitute declarative sentences, while others constitute interrogative sentences: "The book is bewildering," "Bewildering is the book," and "The book—it is bewildering" are all declarative sentences, while "Is the book bewildering?" "Is this the book that's bewildering?" and "Is that book bewildering?" are all interrogative. Specific patterns of words—and *only* specific patterns of words—yield specific types of sentences. When applying this analogy to the study of culture, it can yield important insights at the level of structural analysis, but this is not a matter of syntax. The well-established structural analysis of culture looks at the various patterns of meaning with an eye to how they coordinate within the constraints of a specific type of cultural structure (much in the same way that we can look at the specific patterns of words with an eye to a specific type of sentence).

So, for example, in the case of a social performance, codes, narratives, and events must coordinate and fit together in specific ways in order for the overarching drama to take place. If these component meanings do not fit together in the appropriate ways, we say things like *the performance was unsuccessful* (Alexander, 2006, p. 29). This would be the same as saying that "The ship is taking on water!" fails as an interrogative sentence.[10] However, from the perspective of syntax, the analysis is qualitatively different. "The ship is taking on water!" obeys the dictates of English syntax, even though the sentence might not fulfill its intended purpose as an interrogative (that is, to ask a question). But "Ship are taking on water the!" doesn't merely fail as an interrogative sentence; it isn't a sentence at all. This combination of words is not only an impermissible pattern within the context of a particular kind of sentence structure; it is a violation of

---

[10] Of course, with the right punctuation or vocal inflection, this arrangement of words might succeed as an interrogative sentence.

syntactical rules. And this is the distinction I want to make between what cultural sociologists have long been doing in terms of their analyses of cultural structures and what I am proposing they begin doing in terms of analyzing the rules of cultural syntax.

Although the concept of syntax has been largely ignored by even the most semiotically minded cultural sociologists,[11] this is not to say that syntax was completely unknown to the forebears of cultural sociology. Sahlins (2005 [1976], p. 176) looks to it explicitly. He argues that each area of social life—his empirical example is the American clothing system—forms "a complex scheme of cultural categories and the relations between them" and that this "scheme operates on a kind of general syntax: a set of rules for declining and combining classes of the clothing-form" (2005 [1976], p. 176). And writing before Sahlins, Roland Barthes (1990 [1967], p. 4) develops a semiological project wherein he describes the fashion photograph as belonging to a system of meaning with its own unique set of symbols and rules for patterning: "within photographic communication, [fashion photography] forms a specific language which no doubt has its own lexicon and syntax." However, despite these early suggestions, syntax never became a major concern for these or any of the other scholars working in the semiotic tradition of the human sciences; semantics and structure remain the focal points of their analysis.

Even within the reaches of cultural sociology we can point to some false starts in what looks prima facie like a move in the direction of cultural syntax. Eviatar Zerubavel (1998, p. 72) seemed on his way to introducing and building on the concept when he notes that if we wish to understand the semiotic nature of society, we "must first understand how [a particular symbol] is related to other symbols we use," and in our analyses of meaning we must always be mindful of the fact that "Semantics ... is inseparable from syntactics" (1998, p. 73). However, in spite of his reference to syntax, Zerubavel was traveling toward a destination very far away from the one I propose here. Or perhaps it is more correct to say that he was simply traveling back to the starting place: semantics. Instead of venturing toward an exploration of the unseen rules that govern the possibilities of meaning-making, Zerubavel explains that by "syntactics" he is simply referring to the idea that "The meaning of symbols generally derives not from their own inherent properties but from the way they are semiotically positioned ... vis-à-vis other symbols" (1999, p. 72; see also Zerubavel, 1987, for a similar claim). In the end, he is simply restating a version of Saussure's semiological dictum that "concepts are purely differential and defined not by their positive content but negatively by their relations with the other terms of the system. Their most precise characteristic is in being what the others are not" (Saussure, 2009 [1966], p. 117).

---

[11] This fact is odd, since in 1938 Charles Morris (1938, p. 13) claimed that syntactics "is the best developed of all the branches of semiotic."

Saussure's theory of "definition-by-opposition" is a mainstay for those studying the social world through a semiotic paradigm. It is reiterated by Ricoeur (1976, p. 5), when he asserts that "no entity belonging to the structure of the system has a meaning of its own; the meaning of a word, for example, results from its opposition to the other lexical units if the same system." And from there the idea was eagerly adopted by cultural sociologists. Bernhard Giesen (2012, p. 788) invokes it when he asserts that cultural structures are "generated by applying distinctions and classifications. Both sides of a distinction refer to contrasting or oppositional meanings that, by this opposition, constitute each other." Anne Kane (2011, p. 13) relies on it when she explains that "meaning is derived from symbols in relationship to one another. In other words, meaning is dependent on the internal structural arrangement of concepts in complex patterns of similarity, difference, and opposition." A productive use of this cultural semantics (that is, the theory of cultural meaning) can also be seen in Alexander and Smith's work (2003b, p. 123) on the binary structure of the discourse of American civil society. In this project, they first identify what they call "democratic and antidemocratic codes," then argue that these codes form lists of binary oppositions. On the democratic side are actors who are "active," "autonomous," "rational," "reasonable," "calm," "controlled," "realistic," and "sane"; and on the antidemocratic side are actors who are "passive," "dependent," "irrational," "hysterical," "excitable," "passionate," "unrealistic," and "mad." Taken as pairs of antonyms, these lists serve to give each other meaning: an actor who is rational is not irrational, and contrariwise, the actor who is irrational is not rational; similarly, the actor who is sane is not mad, and vice versa. This quality of mutual definition by opposition is explained by Alexander and Smith in the following way: "The formal logic of homology and opposition [is the means] through which meaning is created" (Alexander and Smith, 2003b, p. 124). Giesen (2012, p. 788) distills the semantic nature of this process when he notes simply that, "We do not know the meaning of a concept unless we can conceive of its opposite." Thus, while a cultural structure of oppositional relationships *could* be analyzed from the perspective of cultural syntax, the inclination of cultural sociologists has been to ignore these structures' ordering rules. Instead, as demonstrated above, these oppositional structures are seen solely through the lens of meaning, of semantics.

## The rules of meaning-making

Having described in abstract how a semiotic approach to the study of the social world might incorporate the concept of syntax into its foundational paradigm (alongside semantics and structure)—and how up until this point interpretive social science has yet to do so—I turn briefly to an empirical example to illustrate a cultural syntactic feature in more concrete terms. Specifically, the example will revolve around the dominant American narrative about the 9/11 terrorist attacks.

Narratives are cultural structures that can serve to *represent* the social world (Maines, 1993; Denzin, 2004), *explain* it (Polkinghorne, 1988; Hinchman and Hinchman, 2001; Danto, 2007), *transform* it (Bennett, 1978; Benford, 2002), and even in some strong sense *constitute* it (Sherwood, 1994; Somers, 1994; Kerby, 1997; Bruner, 2003; Straub, 2010). The subset of these narratives that claim to represent non-figuratively some aspect of social reality, so-called "social narratives" (cf. Steinmetz, 1992, p. 506; Somers, 1994, p. 606), spring from an effort to draw meaning from the would-be chaos of the social world and are therefore of particular interest to cultural sociologists and other social scientists working within the interpretive tradition. These social narratives constitute much of our journalism, histories, conversations, memories, orations, advertisements, and, while not coextensive with it, much of our art and literature, as well.

As cultural structures, every narrative (social or otherwise) has a plot, a particular arrangement of meaningful actions. And just as every sentence belongs to one of a small number of types (for example, declarative, interrogative, imperative, and exclamatory), so every plot belongs to one of a small number of types based on its *eudaemonic path*;[12] that is, every plot can be categorized according to the trajectory of its protagonist's complete movement between states of fortune (for example, a tragic plot structure traces the protagonist's fall from happiness to misery). Thus, if we are to analyze a social narrative through the semiotic paradigm I am proposing, we can view the narrative's constituent meaningful actions or episodes as the cultural *semantic elements* (that is, analogous to words), the narrative's plot type as the *cultural structure* (that is, analogous to a sentence), and the rules dictating how the narrative's meaningful actions or episodes can be combined as the *cultural syntax*.

With this paradigm at our disposal, we can begin by classifying the prevailing American narrative of 9/11 as comprising the plot type that has long been referred to as a *romance* (Frye, 2000 [1957]). In a romance, the protagonist begins in relative happiness, experiences a downward turn toward misery, and eventually reestablishes their state of happiness. And in some cases, this turn toward misery occurs suddenly in what Aristotle (1991) in his *Poetics* calls a *peripeteia*—a sudden reversal of fortune. Thus, if we take a

---

[12] Of course, just as sentences can be categorized in numerous ways (for example, according to their meter, their voice, their tense, and so on), classification according to eudaemonic path is merely one of many possible ways to categorize narratives. See my full elaboration of eudaemonic paths in "Farewell to Genre" (Madigan, forthcoming).

look at the established American social narrative of the 9/11 terrorist attacks, we can immediately recognize that it is emplotted as a romance that begins with a peripeteia: On an otherwise pleasant September morning in 2001, passenger jets smash into both World Trade Center towers and the Pentagon. These attacks "are popularly accepted as arriving 'out of the blue'" (Gibbs, 2014, p. 121) and send the American collectivity plummeting from happiness to misery. But this catastrophic moment of the planes' fiery impacts is, of course, only the initial episode of the narrative. Subsequent episodes include the collapse of the two towers later that morning, the ongoing search for survivors, the marshaling of American military forces, the ouster of the Taliban from Afghanistan, the disruption of al-Qaeda's worldwide terror network, and, ultimately, the killing of Osama bin Laden. The conclusion of the narrative positions the protagonist (the American people) as finally triumphant, and, indeed, having returned to a state of happiness.

Because America's shared narrative of 9/11 is emplotted as a romance that includes a significant peripeteia, any content prior to the peripeteia must be more or less consistent with America's collective wellbeing. If an episode that took place prior to the crashing of the planes is not coded this way—if the episode is understood to signify American misery—it will simply not be possible to include it in the narrative. In other words, *based on the rules of cultural syntax*, episodes that are inconsistent with American happiness are simply not permitted to precede the peripeteia. This is why even otherwise-relevant events are not included in the prevailing 9/11 narrative, events such as the 1993 bombing of the World Trade Center, Osama bin Laden's plot to assassinate President Clinton during the latter's visit to the Philippines in 1996, the al-Qaeda bombing of the US embassies in Kenya and Tanzania in 1998, as well as their bombing of the *USS Cole* in 2000. And this absence is significant, because these omissions from the narrative can lead to their omission from collective memory, which not only impacts how these events are represented in cultural productions, but also has consequential effects on the beliefs and actions of collectivities more broadly.

The value of the concept of cultural syntax in this case is that it provides a more persuasive alternative to ideological explanations. When analyzing the dominant American 9/11 narrative, the absence of al-Qaeda's other assaults on American interests immediately prior to the attack is puzzling. After all, these assaults are ideologically consistent with coding al-Qaeda as treacherous terrorists, so why would this clearly relevant material be selected for omission from the narrative? The answer is that in the context of this type of narrative structure, there is a syntactic rule that obviates the presence of these meaningful episodes. This syntactic rule is made even more evident when we look at alternative ways of relating these events.

As Hayden White (1990) explains, there are multiple methods for recording past events, including the non-narrative form of the chronicle;

that is, a record of past events that are related to one another but devoid of a recognizable beginning and conclusion. Thus, in the 9/11 museum that opened in 2011 on the site of the former World Trade Center in New York, visitors walk through a series of exhibits featuring text and artifacts that depict meaningful events that are purportedly relevant to the 9/11 attacks. But because these exhibits are not constructed as a narrative (they are, in fact, presented in the form of a chronicle), they are free to—*and do*—include the al-Qaeda assaults on American interests that preceded the 9/11 attacks, because, in the context of a chronicle, there is no cultural syntactic rule prohibiting their inclusion.

Similarly, when the 9/11 narrative is depicted as a tragedy, one in which the American collective falls from happiness to misery without returning to happiness as in the case of a romance, the depictions of these al-Qaeda assaults are syntactically permitted.[13] However, in this narrative form, the eventual victories and ultimate triumph are not permitted due to the cultural syntactical rules dictating the arrangement of meaningful episodes within the cultural form of a tragedy. And again, this explanation succeeds where an ideological one does not, for it is difficult to make a persuasive case that it is American material and ideological interests that consistently hew so closely to these omissions, differing as they do depending on the cultural structure through which the 9/11 story is being told.

## Conclusion

My central argument in this chapter is that semiotically inflected social sciences would be enhanced by including the concept of *cultural syntax* in their analyses. This is certainly not to suggest that every particular social analysis is incomplete without incorporating an investigation into the syntactical elements of their cases. Rather, it is to assert that the element of syntax should be made part of these social sciences' foundational paradigm alongside semantics and structure. Doing so means that when examining social life through an interpretive perspective, scholars would keep before them a modified version of Ricoeur's model of culture as a text: at the level of the word, there is semantic analysis; at the level of the sentence there is structural analysis; and between those levels is the examination of the syntactic rules for meaning-making.

Just as Saussure argues that a sign's signifier and signified are joined arbitrarily, so too do syntactic rules arbitrarily dictate the ways in which

---

[13] For example, some of these assaults are elaborated on in Hulu's 2018 US TV miniseries *The Looming Tower* (based on Lawrence Wright's 2007 book, *The Looming Tower: Al-Qaeda and the Road to 9/11*), which is emplotted as a tragedy.

meaningful phenomena may or may not be conjoined. The rules of cultural syntax thereby enable and constrain the cultural structures we experience every day throughout the social world. That is, these rules determine the limits of how we are able to combine signs and symbols within those cultural structures.[14] For this reason, having a theoretical model with the vision to identify these rules enriches the descriptive and explanatory powers of any semiotic approach to culture.

**References**

Alexander, J.C. (2003) *The Meanings of Social Life: A Cultural Sociology*, New York: Oxford University Press.

Alexander, J.C. (2006) "Cultural Pragmatics: Social Performance between Ritual and Strategy," in J.C. Alexander, B. Giesen and J. Mast (eds) *Social Performance: Symbolic Action, Cultural Pragmatics, and Ritual*, New York: Cambridge University Press, pp. 29–90.

Alexander, J.C. and Mast, J. (2011) "The Cultural Pragmatics of Symbolic Actions," in J.C. Alexander, *Performance and Power*, Malden, MA: Polity Press, pp. 7–23.

Alexander, J.C. and Smith, P. (2003a) "The Strong Program in Cultural Sociology," in J.C. Alexander, *The Meanings of Social Life: A Cultural Sociology*, New York: Oxford University Press, pp. 11–26.

Alexander, J.C. and Smith, P. (2003b) "The Discourse of American Civil Society," in J.C. Alexander, *The Meanings of Social Life: A Cultural Sociology*, New York: Oxford University Press, pp. 121–54.

Alexander, J.C., Jacobs R. and Smith, P. (2012) "Introduction: Cultural Sociology Today," in J.C. Alexander, R. Jacobs and P. Smith (eds) *The Oxford Handbook of Cultural Sociology*, New York: Oxford University Press, pp. 3–23.

Aristotle (1991) "Poetics," in J. Barnes (ed) *The Complete Works of Aristotle*, vol. 2, Princeton: Princeton University Press, pp. 2316–40.

Barthes, R. (1990 [1967]) *The Fashion System*, Los Angeles: University of California Press.

Benford, R. (2002) "Controlling Narratives and Narratives as Control within Social Movements," in J.E. Davis (ed) *Stories of Change: Narratives and Social Movements*, New York: State University of New York Press, pp. 53–78.

Bennett, W.L. (1978) "Storytelling in Criminal Trials: A Model of Social Judgment," *Quarterly Journal of Speech*, 64: 1–22.

---

14 However, just as in the case of a community of linguistically competent speakers, while syntactical violations are atypical, they are not necessarily completely absent. Undoubtedly, one could find exceptions, although these would, in all likelihood, be the sort that prove the rule.

Biernacki, R. (2009) "After Quantitative Sociology," in I. Reed and J.C. Alexander (eds) *Meaning and Method: The Cultural Approach to Sociology*, Boulder, CO: Paradigm, pp. 119–207.

Bruner, J. (1990) *Acts of Meaning*, Cambridge, MA: Harvard University Press.

Bruner, J. (2003) *Making Stories: Law, Literature, Life*, Cambridge, MA: Harvard University Press.

Chomsky, N. (1957) *Syntactic Structures*, The Hague/Paris: Mouton.

Chomsky, N. (1965) *Aspects of the Theory of Syntax*, Cambridge, MA: MIT Press.

Cossu, A. (2021) "Clifford Geertz, Intellectual Autonomy, and Interpretive Social Science," *American Journal of Cultural Sociology*, 9(3): 347–75.

Danto, A.C. (2007) *Narration and Knowledge*, New York: Columbia University Press.

Denzin, N.K. (2004) "Forward: Narrative's Moment," in M. Andrews, S.D. Sclater, C. Squire and A. Treacher (eds) *The Uses of Narrative: Explorations in Sociology, Psychology, and Cultural Studies*, New Brunswick, NJ: Transaction Publishers, pp. xi–xiii.

Dilthey, W. (1979 [1910]) "The Construction of the Historical World in the Human Studies," in W. Dilthey, *Selected Writings*, Cambridge: Cambridge University Press.

Dilthey, W. and Rickman, H.P. (1962). *Pattern and Meaning in History: Thoughts on History and Society*. New York: Harper.

Douglas, M. (1984 [1966]) *Purity and Danger: An Analysis of the Concepts of Pollution and Taboo*, New York: Routledge.

Eyerman, R. (2006) "Toward a Meaningful Sociology of the Arts," in R. Eyerman and L. McCormick (eds) *Myth, Meaning, and Performance: Toward a New Cultural Sociology of the Arts*, Boulder, CO: Paradigm, pp. 13–33.

Eyerman, R. (2008) *The Assassination of Theo Van Gogh: From Social Drama to Cultural Trauma*, Durham, NC: Duke University Press.

Fontdevila, J. (2010) "Indexes, Power, and Netdoms: A Multidimensional Model of Language in Social Action," *Poetics*, 38(6): 587–609.

Frye, N. (2000 [1957]) *Anatomy of Criticism*, Princeton: Princeton University Press.

Geertz, C. (1973) "Thick Description: Toward an Interpretive Theory of Culture," in C. Geertz, *The Interpretation of Cultures*, New York: Basic Books, pp. 3–30.

Gibbs, A. (2014) *Contemporary American Trauma Narratives*, Edinburgh: Edinburgh University Press.

Giesen, B. (2004) *Triumph and Trauma*, Boulder, CO: Paradigm.

Giesen, B. (2012) "Inbetweenness and Ambivalence," in J.C. Alexander, R. Jacobs and P. Smith (eds) *The Oxford Handbook of Cultural Sociology*, New York: Oxford University Press, pp. 788–803.

Hashimoto, A. (2013) "The Cultural Trauma of a Fallen Nation: Japan, 1945," in R. Eyerman, J.C. Alexander and E. Reese (eds) *Narrating Trauma: On the Impact of Collective Suffering*, Boulder, CO: Paradigm, pp. 27–51.

Healy, K. (2017) "Fuck Nuance," *Sociological Theory*, 35(2): 118–27.

Hinchman, L. and Hinchman, S. (2001) "Introduction: Toward a Definition of Narrative," in L. Hinchman and S. Hinchman (eds) *Memory, Identity, Community: The Idea of Narratives in the Human Sciences*, New York: SUNY Press, pp. xiii–xxxii.

Jacobs, R. (2008) "Civil Society and Crisis: Culture, Discourse, and the Rodney King Beating," in L. Spillman (ed) *Cultural Sociology*, Malden, MA: Blackwell, Ch. 25.

Kane, A. (2011) *Constructing Irish National Identity: Discourse and Ritual During the Land War, 1879–1882*, New York: Palgrave Macmillan.

Kerby, A.P. (1997) "The Language of the Self," in L. Hinchman and S. Hinchman (eds) *Memory, Identity, Community: The Idea of Narratives in the Human Sciences*, New York: SUNY Press, pp. 125–42.

Madigan, T. (forthcoming) "Farewell to Genre: Plot, Meaning, and Eudaemonic Paths in Social Narratives," *Current Sociology*.

Maines, D.R. (1993) "Narrative's Moment and Sociology's Phenomena: Toward a Narrative Sociology," *The Sociological Quarterly*, 34(1): 17–38.

Mast, Jason. (2013) *The Performative Presidency*. Cambridge: Cambridge University Press.

McCormick, L. (2012) "Music Sociology in a New Key," in J.C. Alexander, R. Jacobs and P. Smith (eds) *The Oxford Handbook of Cultural Sociology*, New York: Oxford University Press, pp. 722–42.

Morris, C. (1938) *Foundations of the Theory of Signs*, Chicago, IL: University of Chicago Press.

Norton, M. (2011a) "Afterword: The Geertz Effect," in J.C. Alexander, P. Smith and M. Norton (eds) *Interpreting Clifford Geertz: Cultural Investigations in the Social Sciences*, New York: Palgrave Macmillan, pp. 203–9.

Norton, M. (2011b) "A Structural Hermeneutics of The O'Reilly Factor," *Theory and Society*, 40(3): 315–46.

Pelc, J. (1982) "Semiotic and Nonsemiotic Concepts of Meaning," *American Journal of Semiotics*, 1(4): 1–19.

Polkinghorne, D. (1988) *Narrative Knowing and the Human Sciences*, New York: SUNY Press.

Reed, I. (2009) "Culture as Object and Approach in Sociology," in I. Reed and J.C. Alexander (eds) *Meaning and Method: The Cultural Approach to Sociology*, Boulder, CO: Paradigm, pp. 1–15.

Reed, I. (2011) *Interpretation and Social Knowledge: On the Use of Theory in the Human Sciences*, Chicago, IL: University of Chicago Press.

Ricoeur, P. (1976) *Interpretation Theory: Discourse and the Surplus of Meaning*, Fort Worth, TX: Texas Christian University Press.

Sahlins, M. (2005 [1976]) "La Pensée Bourgeoise: Western Society as Culture," in M. Sahlins, *Culture in Practice*, New York: Zone Books.

Saussure, F. de. (2009 [1966]) *Course in General Linguistics*, Chicago, IL: Open Court.

Sherwood, S.J. (1994) "Narrating the Social: Postmodernism and the Drama of Democracy," *Journal of Narrative and Life History*, 4(1/2): 69–88.

Smith, P. (2005) *Why War? The Cultural Logic of Iraq, the Gulf War, and Suez*, Chicago, IL: University of Chicago Press.

Smith, P. (2008) *Punishment and Culture*, Chicago, IL: University of Chicago Press.

Somers, M.R. (1994) "The Narrative Constitution of Identity: A Relational and Network Approach," *Theory and Society*, 23(5): 605–49.

Sonnevend, J. (2012) "Iconic Rituals: Toward a Local Theory of Encountering Images," in J.C. Alexander, D. Bartmanski and B. Giesen (eds) *Iconic Power: Materiality and Meaning in Social Life*, New York: Palgrave Macmillan, pp. 219–31.

Spillman, L. (2008) "Introduction: Culture and Cultural Sociology," in L. Spillman (ed) *Cultural Sociology*, Malden, MA: Blackwell, pp. 1–15.

Steinmetz, G. (1992) "Reflections on the Role of Social Narratives in Working-class Formation: Narrative Theory in the Social Sciences," *Social Science History*, 16(3): 489–516.

Straub, J. (2010) "Psychology, Narrative, and Cultural Memory: Past and Present," in A. Erll and A. Nunnig (eds) *A Companion to Cultural Memory Studies*, Berlin: Walter de Gruyter, pp. 215–28.

Tavory, I. and Swidler, A. (2009) "Condom Semiotics: Meaning and Condom Use in Rural Malawi," *American Sociological Review*, 74(2): 171–89.

Turner, V. (1982) *From Ritual to Theatre: The Human Seriousness of Play*, New York: PAJ Publications.

Turner, V. (1987 [1974]) *Dramas, Fields, and Metaphors: Symbolic Action in Human Society*, Ithaca, NY: Cornell University Press.

Wagner-Pacifici, R. (1986) *The Moro Morality Play: Terrorism as Social Drama*, Chicago, IL: University of Chicago Press.

Weber, M. (1978) *Economy and Society*, Oakland, CA: University of California Press.

Wherry, F.F. (2012) *The Culture of Markets*, Oxford: Polity Press.

White, H. (1990) *The Content of the Form: Narrative Discourse and Historical Representation*, Baltimore, MD: Johns Hopkins University Press.

Wright, L. (2007) *The Looming Tower: Al-Qaeda and the Road to 9/11*, New York: Vintage Books.

Zelizer, V.A. (1994) *Pricing the Priceless Child: The Changing Social Value of Children*, Princeton, NJ: Princeton University Press.

Zerubavel, E. (1987) "The Language of Time: Toward a Semiotics of Temporality," *The Sociological Quarterly*, 28(3): 343–56.

Zerubavel, E. (1998) *Social Mindscapes: An Invitation to Cognitive Sociology*, Cambridge, MA: Harvard University Press.

6

# Memory, Cultural Systems, and Anticipation

*Andrea Cossu*

The past, the present, and the future are different tonalities of temporality, which are best understood in a processual way. While memory studies have often approached the relation between the past and the present, the future still seems an uncharted territory, despite substantial contributions that investigate the issue of the "memory of the future" (Gutman et al, 2010). I connect the sociological reflection on memory and the past, the semiotic attention to semantic networks, and some recent literature on anticipation to argue that the future is a real territory for memory studies beyond the current state of the art. The direction the chapter proposes is that of a semiotic, cultural sociology. My analysis is grounded on a network-based formalization of the cultural system, and it attempts to depict an autonomous role of cultural encyclopedias and scripts (as a form of cultural memory) in the micro-level orientation to future action. This approach is useful to bring together—in the discussion of the interaction between memory and the future—the role of declarative and non-declarative culture (Lizardo, 2017), the nature of macro-micro mechanisms (Norton, 2014), and the process through which situations are made recognizable and orderly.

## Prologue (Springsteen and I)

Trento, February 2021. It is somehow soothing to look back at a simple walk around the streets of London, as Italy is locked down due to a COVID-19 pandemic outbreak. In some sense, that's what memories are for: to look back and select suitable parts of the past in order to use them as a measure of the normality or abnormality of the present, and also to make projects about the future ("and as soon as this is over, I *will* take a long walk in a crowded place").

Another long walk—London, September 2019, walking while rehearsing my talk for a conference—stopped in front of a movie theater, where I happily purchased a ticket to watch *Blinded by the Light*, a coming-of-age story of multicultural frictions and integrations, which is less notable for its originality in British cinema (*East is East*, *Bend It Like Beckham*) than it is for its focal point, its totemic reference, and its soundtrack: the myth and songs of Bruce Springsteen, at the time of his fast rush to global stardom in the 1980s.

I stopped walking in the streets, I entered the theater, took my seat, and started tracing comparisons with my own Springsteen-based coming-of-age story, which has involved all sorts of fandom and its accessories: live shows (peaking in the dream of a lifetime, seeing Springsteen in Jersey), endless exegesis, bootleg recordings, and failed attempts to secure tickets for his shows on Broadway. The usual stuff that dreams and para-social relations with celebrities are made of.

And yet, as I was watching and enjoying that pretty little movie, something grabbed my other self's, the sociologist's one, attention. It happened a little more than a third into the movie, when the instantly recognizable introductory notes to "Thunder Road" filled the room and left me with a grin. What more can you get out of a song about cars and girls (two of Springsteen's obsessions), beside memorable lines like "all the redemption I can offer, girl, is beneath this dirty hood"? If you have seen Springsteen live more than the customary couple of times (and I have), and have had an iPod full of bootlegs, you know that at some point *your* turn comes—your turn to sing, your turn to make a connection. Springsteen may sing the line "show a little faith, there's magic in the night, you ain't a beauty but, hey, you're alright" on the *Born to Run* album, but live and in concert, that is your duty. It is a tradition that was established some forty years ago, and requires a lot of performative memory and skill (knowledge of the scripts, knowledge of what to do, the readiness to be carried out by the audience in case you don't know it) to be accomplished seamlessly and perfectly.

However, this was a movie about Springsteen and a kid, and "Thunder Road" made its appearance in a collective scene—Bollywood meets *My Fair Lady* meets a multicultural *Bildungsroman*—where different characters sing different lines. So, the question was, who's going to sing the "show a little faith" line? Depending on who sang it, meanings could have been different, my projected meanings at least. And yet this hypothesizing revealed the complexity of my local knowledge about the song (the kind of web-based, rhizomatic knowledge that pragmatism and postmodernism usually thrive on), and how I was mobilizing it not only to live in the moment—to make sense of how "Thunder Road" made possible sense within the narrative of the movie—but also to create ideas about possible directions. Overinterpretation can be a daunting thing, but it built my connection to the narrative by focusing on the ways that narratives usually work: they lead you somewhere, somehow, but in order to get there, you need to provide to yourself multiple paths. As we were getting closer to the "show a little faith" line, I had multiple choices, and I also entertained multiple curiosities. In the end, I had my answer about who sang the line (at this point, no spoilers), while being true to my biography: I *hummed* the line like I often did in concert, and others in the audience did that. All was well. You cannot take the Bruce Springsteen fan out of the body and mind of a sociologist. There are priorities, and yes, the Boss often comes first.

## Introduction

When I watched *Blinded by the Light* for a second time, this time with a more focused sociological eye on it, I realized that the whole scene had taken place in the short time span of two minutes. These two minutes were filled by alternative hypotheses about a text, which were drawn in the range of possible interpretations, rejected or kept as the movie went on, and resulted in a continuous adjustment between the linearity of narrative and the progressively reduced ramifications that stemmed from my interpretive activity.

In this chapter, I will make a case in favor of taking these processes seriously, as they can contribute to a better understanding of the unstable interaction between memory, culture, and temporality. I will do that from within a perspective that, although indebted toward hermeneutics and literary theory in some parts, makes more sense as a way of practicing a *semiotic sociology* (Heiskala, 2021) that takes at the center of its preoccupations the questions about the formats of the cultural system, and its relations to social process.

In its intellectual development, the sociology of memory has entertained quite an uneasy relationship with these topics, whereas they should be at the center of our theorizing about the relationship between culture, agency, and the representation of the past. In its Halbwachsian and, most of all, Durkheimian lineage (Watts-Miller, 2001; Misztal, 2003; Cossu, 2010; Gensburger, 2016), sociological memory studies have focused on the semiotics of "collective memory" with an eye on social classifications and the externality of memory as a "social fact." Building upon these Durkheimian insights, the sociology of memory that fueled the memory boom of the 1980s and 1990s (for a review of that particular phase, see Olick and Robbins, 1998) has integrated the notion of memory as a social fact with an attention to its semiotic dimension (looking for a "specific semiotic" of the past and temporality: Eco, 1984; Zerubavel, 2003), and with an attention not only to the cultural structures of memory but also for their capacity to organize systems of meaning that organized, in a more or less integrated way, the set of representations about the past specific to a given system of action.

The relevance of these neostructural approaches to memory has been influential in uncovering the deeper organization of expressions to which discourses about the past could be anchored, but it has produced a conflation that equaled the mnemonic—or the commemorative—with the symbolic in terms of public, declarative culture (Lizardo, 2017), therefore erasing a crucial interface of how memory works, that is, the one between the individual and the collective (Olick, 1999; Erll, 2011).

A second, unfortunate consequence has consisted in the consolidation of a conceptual asymmetry between synchronic and processual understandings of memory (again, as a semiotic system of representation). Particularly in the first wave of the memory boom, scholars have benefited from a vision of memory as a system of signs held together by relations that contribute to its stability. However, with this stability also came a certain sense of reification of those relations (Fine and Beim, 2007), and a neglect for the micro-social (discursive, interactive, affective, and practical) dimension of how "memory" works. By claiming that memory is "produced through social interaction" (Fine and Beim, 2007, p. 2), collective memory is emphasized as a *process* rather than simply as a product, and yet many studies underplay the role of cultural structures as simultaneously the source and the outcome of memory work (see, for example, Van de Putte, 2022).

There is no easy way out of this conundrum, particularly if one aims to avoid the reduction of "memory" to exclusively individual processes or, on the contrary, to semiotic—and largely metaphorical—abstraction. The distinction has been clearly made by Jeffrey Olick (1999): according to individualistic principles, "memory" should be understood primarily as "collected" memory, defined as "the aggregated individual memories of members of a group" (Olick, 1999, p. 338). On the other hand, "collective" memory proper maintains that "certain patterns of sociation" are not "reducible to individual psychological processes," and certain extraindividual patterns, like group definitions, are independent of individual ones (Olick, 1999, p. 341). More crucially, other orientations to what collective memory is stress its relational and relatively independent features, particularly so if it is conceived as a system of relations between symbols as "long-term structures to what societies remember or commemorate that are stubbornly impervious to the efforts of individuals to escape them" (Olick, 1999, p. 342). Whether it is the *langue* as opposed to the *parole* in Saussurean terms, basic binary structures or "codes" (Alexander, 2003) or deep narratives that give shape to myths, traditions, or other forms of inscription of the past, these structures look, and sometimes are analytically constructed to look precisely this way, as reified or transcendent structures.

What I would like to offer in this chapter keeps a central focus on the semiotic character of memory and on its relevance to the functioning of cultural systems. Rather than describing memory as a "cultural system" (Schwartz, 1996) or as a "frame" (Irwin-Zarecka, 1994), I would like to address memory as a crucial *operation* of cultural systems, of how they organize themselves in a describable form (Esposito, 2001), and argue that this constitutes a preliminary step for a better appreciation of the organization of different varieties of temporality that organize different social times like the past, the present, and the future.

The latter, it seems, has been a missing social time in collective memory studies, although there is an abundance of literature on the normative role of remembering (a future-oriented, civic goal of social memory work), and one has to notice that an explicit or implicit attention to memory furnishes ideas both about nostalgia (Boym, 2001) and utopia. I am, however, interested in the future as the realization of other operations (and highly cultural ones) in which memory is involved; that is, operations that disentangle the complexity of our (human) capacity to orient ourselves (individually or as embedded in collectivities) to the future, and in which notoriously slippery processes of agency, imagination, heuristic projection, and anticipation take place. These processes are concerned with the future in a more mundane and ordinary way, and yet it is in its ordinary operations of communication and selection that memory plays its most powerful role, allowing humans to fulfill their role as pragmatic agents.

In order to describe what issues are fundamentally at stake in this vision of memory, I start from the widespread Weberian, Geertzean notion of culture as a "web of significance" (Geertz, 1973), which plays a role in many standard accounts of culture as a semiotic concept. I highlight that one of the problems inherent in this vision of culture is its reluctance to describe the format of culture, a task to which semiotics (and particularly those semiotic theories more interested in the operations of semantic networks) can come to the rescue. Yet, if we follow this line of argument, we need to consider not only the format of culture (culture at the analytic level: see Kane, 1991; Alexander, 2003), but also relations within semantic networks that can be understood both as states of the system and as the effect of sustained communication within the system. This brings temporality back in, as well as the future as a possible realization of these communications. In doing so, a semiotic sociological understanding of how culture works requires both an attention to operations of memory within the system, and to their capacity to handle possibilities as a contingent feature of any given cultural system. Therefore, a reflection on the link between memory and the anticipatory capacity of cultural systems is needed, and I try to inject it in my description of the interaction between memory, culture, and temporality. In the Conclusions, I will highlight possible interdisciplinary ways to advance the discussion on this crucial, and then sociologically neglected, aspect of memory work.

## "Memory" and the semiotic space

Approaches that insist on the networked character of both culture and memory are, simultaneously, problematic and fruitful, particularly if we connect them to a semiotic notion of culture. The seeds of the latter were successfully planted in the social sciences with the cultural turn and the rise of "interpretive social science" (Rabinow and Sullivan, 1979), which prompted an investigation of culture not as a set of internalized attitudes and ultimately values (Parsons and Shils, 1951), but as the background against which action is projected, an environment (Alexander, 1988) composed of signs, narratives, motives, and broad cosmologies that enable action and guarantee its mutual intelligibility.

Semiotics entered this picture by providing, if not a unified theory, at least the promise of achieving an understanding of these symbolic patterns with regards to their internal organization and their capacity of being mobilized for action. With the promise of semiotics as practiced within the boundaries of the cultural turn, however, came also a confusion that centered on the level at which semiotics had to be applied.

Semiotics entered the broad landscape of cultural sociology, and in many ways the then narrower sector of sociological collective memory studies, in the three main forms of applied, specific, and general semiotics (Eco, 1984). On the one hand, scholars applied semiotic concepts to practices and objects of commemoration understood as "texts" (broadly intended), the meaning of which had to be recovered through an analysis of the relations they entertained with other texts and with other systems organized semiotically— in the last instance, values. On the other, sociologists were more successful in building a "specific" semiotics of memory by adopting neostructural orientations of various kinds, which looked for deep grammatical relations of time and memory.

Both these orientations proved extremely successful in the affirmation of memory studies within sociological analysis, and contributed to the advancement of sociologists' understanding of collective memory and its role in the production of the temporal stability of cultural systems. At the same time, the explicit or implicit assumptions underlying the contribution of applied and specific semiotics seldom questioned the double character of cultural systems as working both as orientative and expressive systems of symbols (Schwartz, 1996), or as "models of" and "models for" (Geertz, 1966) social life and the apprehension of social reality.

Memory studies were not simply trapped in this dilemma (how to furnish a theory of the cultural system that is at the same time semiotically sound, and which accounts for the complexity of the cultural system): they actively contributed to its implementation thanks to its long lineage in the Halbwachs-Durkheim line (Olick, 1999), which made the analysis of memory almost naturally ready for an analysis of collective representations as foundational elements of cultural systems. Therefore, the fruitful encounter of memory, semiotics, and cultural sociology converged on a set of problems that represented the core set of assumptions of the sociological semiotics of memory: the Durkheimian focus on collective representations about the past; the autonomy of the cultural system; and the idea that both memory and culture are intimately structured through difference and opposition.

Many of these contributions, in some way or other, relied on the overarching notion of "code" as a fundamental component of cultural sociological analysis, moving away from a vision of culture that stressed its practical contingency while focusing on its formal stability. The notion of code was, indeed, successful in many ways, because it showed the promise of retrieving formal features of how memory and the past are socially constructed, while linking them to cognitive capabilities. The patterns of the past, as they are retrieved in a given group's representations about the past, are therefore not only ordered in symbols, narratives, discourses, and texts, but also the result of operations that connect individuals' activities (at the level of "collected" memories) and more group-level ones, by which what is remembered works simultaneously as an expression of cultural order and a prescription for social order. In another guise, therefore, what the sociological study of memory accomplished was a translation in symbolic terms of the sociological attention to a hierarchy of normative order, according to which symbolic expressions are related and/or connected to ultimate ends of action, like the societal values that are expressed by the selection of specific portions of the past, which in turn function as markers of identity and as desirable descriptions of a social "center" (Shils, 1975) of values and institutions. The common ground, on which both the sociological analysis of "collective memory" and the analysis of sociocultural order converged, was the idea that there is some solidarity within cultural systems, and that the latter can be analyzed in terms of their internal structure.

With the success of the notion of code, however, came also a set of assumptions that proved extremely problematic for a semiotic analysis of memory. As Risto Heiskala (2003, pp. 191–200) argued, neostructuralist thinking of the kind that momentarily triumphed within cultural sociology and the sociology of memory privileged cultural statics and cultural reductionism by advancing arguments that: structures are closed codes; structures consist only of associative relations; these associative relations have a paradigmatic form; the relations between elements are binary ones; structures are unconscious, and, therefore, universal. Saussure and Hjelmslev meet Durkheim, so to speak, with the latter providing a functional argument about social solidarity, and the former lending sociology the idea that the symbols that express and produce solidarity can be analyzed in terms of their relations and difference.

By relying on the "specificity" of a code of memory, sociology has embraced the structuralist assumption that syntax and semantics are at the center, while discarding, in theory if not in practice, an attention to the pragmatic dimension of the semiotics of memory. However, in the midst of a more general critique of code-based cultural sociology, scholars called for a more processual approach attentive to pragmatic factors and communications.

Jeffrey Olick (2007), for example, criticized the idea of the "unity" of memory, as well as the idea of its independence from other aspects of culture. For his part, Alon Confino (1997, p. 1391) stigmatized "studies of memory in symbolic isolation," detached from the historicity of time and of individuals as limits of memory work and cognition. These calls for a dialogic, process-centered approach have done much to problematize the idea that meaning is generated by deeper structures, which need to be uncovered in order to grasp the organization of memory in its formal terms. Semioticians like Mikhail Bakhtin (Olick, 1999, 2007), Yuri Lotman, or Umberto Eco (Desogus, 2012; Cossu, 2017; Salerno, 2021) have substituted, with a more hermeneutic focus, the Durkheimian sociology of culture and cognition, which was the broad theoretical perspective in which studies of memory as collective representation were originally carried out.

By pointing to the complexity of the semiosphere, of cultural memory as an encyclopedia, of the intimate connection between text and dialogue, these semiotic premises have also moved away from a consideration for the applied and specific semiotics in the direction of the contribution of general semiotics as a theory of symbolic system and, more crucially, as a theory of cultural organization. From this point of view, no mnemonic practice or object can be understood in isolation from other practices or objects and from culture as a whole, in which temporally antecedent discourses and texts influence how the text is received and produced in any given present. This activity, which links text to text(s) and texts with genres, generates pathways that can be understood (analytically) with a focus on the recursive operations (Esposito, 2008) that organize access to information, "engendering to this end an always new and always changing equilibrium of remembering and forgetting" (Esposito, 2008, p. 185), which is constrained both by the type of operations that a cultural system can allow and by the type of data that is generated (through communication and inference at the level of possibility and at the level of communication) by these operations.

In the next section, I argue that this assumption can be put to work effectively by mobilizing different semiotic assumptions about the format and the operations of culture. In particular, I focus on the strategic role that semiotic ontologies fulfill in warranting a pragmatic openness of cultural systems, and how this openness, which centers on the notion of scripting and implies consideration for the interface between semantics and pragmatics, is of absolute relevance for linking memory and the future.

## Semiotic ontologies, selectability, and the future

The transition from an analytic to the processual vision of memory described above endows the cultural system with a huge degree of dynamicity, not usually warranted by the reliance—implicit or explicit—of much cultural sociological theorizing on the normative dimension and its post-normative substitute, the idea of culture as a system of signs that has to be appreciated from a synchronic perspective. The former vision, which puts values at the center of a system of action by making them action's ultimate goals, offers a somewhat limited account of the orientation to the future. Action, so to speak, takes place in a condition in which values are both a requisite and a point of arrival. The future, while taken into account, is a realization or a confirmation of the past, with very little room for contingency. If we, on the other hand, consider a more semiotically oriented notion of culture as a sign structure or a system of symbols, a necessary condition for action is some sort of "memory" of symbols, and yet it must be noted that the realization of adequate symbolic behavior (utterances, performances) still relies on producing in the future symbols that are consistent with their past configuration and with their position within a cultural system.

Most crucially, however, this latter vision establishes a clear link between memory and culture, as explicit in the work of semioticians like Yuri Lotman (1990; see especially Tamm, 2015), for whom culture is essentially the "nonhereditary *memory* of a community" (Lotman and Uspenski, 1978, emphasis added), or Umberto Eco (2014), who sees the encyclopedia as a metaphor and a regulative idea to understand the semantics of culture, the networks that can be created in order to connect cultural units.

This form of memory is closer to the notion of the cultural system (Geertz, 1966, 1973) as a historically transmitted pattern. It is also, in the last instance, a holistic vision. Both Lotman's and Eco's approach to cultural memory, as a semiotic condition and as a necessary operation of any semiotic system, see—particularly in Eco's "maximal encyclopedia" and in Lotman's "semiosphere"—culture as everything that is thinkable (has been thought and preserved), and yet the maximal encyclopedia holds information that, in principle, burdens any given individual carrier. The idea is particularly developed in Lotman. First, he equates culture and memory, meaning that "from the viewpoint of semiotics, culture constitutes collective intellect and collective memory" thanks to the operations of a "supra-individual mechanism for the preservation and transmission of certain messages (texts) and the generation of new ones" (Lotman and Uspenski, 1978, p. 216). On the other hand, memory and culture walk hand in hand precisely because both are not primarily representations, but operations. Lotman writes: "Memory is not a storehouse of information, but a mechanism generating it" (Lotman 2000, cited in Tamm 2019).

This approach means a reversal of the relationship between memory and culture that usually gives form to memory studies. Culture is not a prerequisite for memory, like in the Durkheimian vision in which, if we follow some kind of culturalist orthodoxy, religious symbols as representations have a primacy over representations of the past. Memory is, on the contrary, an outcome of operations of remembering and forgetting, which constitute culture as a set of units that are dynamically assembled, connected, and disconnected. If we follow this line, however, more needs to be said about the ways the cultural units that constitute memory are assembled, and how temporality is involved in the assemblage of memory.

On this specific point, the focus on memory as a culture-generating mechanism ought to be complemented by a notion of how the internal relations of culture can be established. The concept of encyclopedia, Eco's contribution to a global theory of culture, is indeed what can contribute to the understanding of those mechanisms of operation that establish culture as a semiotic system of "relations between relations" (Kockelman, 2005, 2012). The concept, as it developed from Eco's (1976) first foray into the analysis of semantic memory (see, for Eco's direct antecedent, Quillian 1968), to the mature and final formulation of the distinction between a maximal and local or specialized encyclopedias (Eco, 2014), owes much to formal semantics but also to the general theory of semiosis first formulated by Charles Sanders Peirce. Both premises of Eco's work, semantic memory models and Peirce's theory of culture (Wiley, 1994), open the path for a consideration of the connection between cultural memory and the future (see next section).

In common with dynamic visions of semiotics, the cultural units that are inscribed in the general encyclopedia are linked together in complex chains that constitute at the same time the process and the product of semiotic activity. The semiotic space that results from these connections in turn constitutes an ontology, which is "the categorical organization of a portion of universe that may take the form of any kind of classificatory tree or semantic network" (Eco, 2014, p. 60). Thus, the encyclopedia, as a general format of knowledge, includes also those aspects (exemplified by the tree) that have achieved a higher degree of formalization or have reached the status of a code (such as language). In this sense, it includes both the elements and the rule for the transformation and the combination of its subsection. Yet, at the general level, what are these rules? Are they comparable to the ones that characterize formalized regions, or is a higher degree of contingency in place when it comes to the consideration of the links that are established between and across units?

The general process in place in the definition of the connections within any kind of encyclopedia is a *semiosic* one that involves association among different cultural units. Semiosis is, indeed, the core mechanism of culture, an idea that Eco (and other interpretivist semioticians and social scientists at large) derives from the philosophy of Peirce. In particular, it is the temporality of semiosis that can be mobilized in the construction of a cultural theory of memory that moves beyond commonsense visions of memory as storage, social scientific notions of memory as representation, and bring varieties of temporality back in.

Peirce's (1931–1958) notion of the interpretant, which is central in Peirce's account as well as in other, more contemporary, pragmatist attempts to build semiotic social science (Heiskala, 2003; Kockelman, 2005), offers an account of the basic process at work in the definition of the encyclopedia, as well as of its processual, action centered character:

> A sign or representamen, is something which stands to somebody for something in some respect or capacity. It addresses somebody, that is creates in the mind of that person an equivalent sign, or perhaps a more developed sign. That sign which it creates I call the interpretant of the first sign. The sign stands for something, its object. It stands for that object not in all respects, but in reference to some sort of idea, which I have sometimes called the ground of the representamen. (Peirce, 1931–1958, CP 2.228)

In the light of this process, which Peirce describes in this passage as filled with cognitive activity and working at the level of the *expressions* of signs (the representamen), a semiotic based on the concept of the encyclopedia displays peculiar features: "(a) it is structured according to *a network of interpretants*; (b) it is virtually *infinite* because it takes into account multiple interpretations realized by different cultures" (Eco, 1984, p. 83). An encyclopedic model is infinite, however, in two senses. At the systemic level, it contains all the possible paths that link interpretants (as well as the rules for the generation of those connections, sedimented in culture, which belong to the same encyclopedic level in which the artifacts or cultural units produced by the operations of those rules are generated); while at the processual level, and more importantly for a theory of the semiosic character of temporality, the unlimited semiosis suggested by Peirce and mobilized by Eco brings time back in as essential to the constitution of meaning as an interpretant (energetic, emotional, logical). In other words, semiosis, as a succession of associated interpretants, is not only past-oriented, with inferences drawn on the ground of an available body of knowledge, but also and always future-oriented, because any given sign in any given position of the network gives rise, through the process of interpretation, to selections within the system that are operative as interpretants (that is, they became themselves, in turn, the motor for further selection), and so on. Put another way, any selection that takes place in the present forces future selections, which are anticipated in the array of possible interpretations implied by the sign/interpretant.

This is an aspect of the general theory of culture as encyclopedia that has been often times overlooked, and yet it is the one that carries probably the most fertile sociological implications. One reason is that many semiotic approaches have moved at the level of an analytic description of culture, and have idealized both contexts and circumstances of social situations (as a consequence of their foundational interest for the *langue* as opposed to the *parole*). However, one can wonder to what extent the semiotic model can be brought into a more intimate bond with a theory of culture in action, which in turn brings into the picture the temporality of action and its pragmatic, future-oriented arrangement.

## The shapes of the future

If the encyclopedia is a network of interpretants, each inferred from others, then temporality is embedded in the ways it works concretely, and only a bird's-eye, frozen look can assume its synchronicity. It is more fruitful to engage it *as a network* by considering its character of a network as "flow," which implies considering culture as memory and as flow (Salerno, 2021). This notion is consistent with the ways semiotics has taken into account temporality as essential to the organization of meaning under different guises: narratives offer sequences of chained "events" that have causal power only insofar as they happen to be a selection among alternatives; semantic narrative programs (Greimas, 1966) are characterized by contingency; scripts (Tomkins, 1978) organize meaning as sequences of appropriate actions within the constraints of situations and circumstances provided by frames (Fillmore, 1976).

Thus, any relevant element of cultural memory, particularly as it is informed narratively and it is scripted, which entails temporally directed causality (Cossu, 2020), always contains the foreseeing of its intended and sometimes unintended consequences. When translated into the toolkit of the encyclopedia and its Peircean premises, this means that any interpretant, thanks to its position in a network, involves not only an organization of relations at the synchronic level, but also all the possible directions interpretation may take.

Here lies also, however, a fundamental distinction between the analytic level at which semiotic descriptions of the encyclopedia stand, and the uses one can make of them from the point of view of a theory of culture in action. An encyclopedic model of the semantic space has pragmatic implications, but it is not concerned with action per se—the way cultural units are selected in order to produce purportedly valid inferences about the state of the world. From the point of view of the organization of cultural memory, it is chiefly concerned with the encyclopedia as a hypothesis and a realm of possibility, independent of any pragmatic relation between an instigating object and a selecting subject (Kockelman, 2012). However, from the point of view of a contribution to the theory of action, instigation and selection are concrete social processes that simultaneously involve the mobilization of the past and the anticipation of the future in order to produce a sound and recognizable selection that can be accountable both for the ego and its alia in a social situation (Garfinkel, 1967; Scott and Lyman, 1968).

On the one hand, therefore, the encyclopedia offers a discussion of culture as memory that involves what in memory is dynamic and processual. On the other, the theory is not complemented by a general approach to action that can take into account the way the future is organized semiotically, beyond the activity of interpretation. It lacks reference, in other words, to a general framework for action that takes into account interpreting agents (not necessarily human), instigating artifacts (including, in some cases, humans), and the furnishing of situations in which interpretation occurs.

Sociology has always been vocal about the necessity to recognize action as process, but has done little until recently (with exceptions in the field of phenomenology: Geertz, 1976) to include a theory of future coordination within the general framework of action and culture. It has often relied on a deductive model, where action descends from adequate premises and in which each unit of action is, ideally, in accordance with the premises posed within the situations by actors (Goffman's analysis of face-to-face impression work, and Parsons's analysis of the double contingency of action being exemplar cases of this deductive origination from, respectively, the point of view of microsociology and macrosociology).

What elements of such a theory can be developed and framed in accordance with the ideas coming from a semiotic understanding of culture that stresses the centrality of semantic networks? And how can it be realized in such a way that it is consistent with sociological accounts of future coordination that take into consideration different aspects of action's extension to the future?

Tavory and Eliasoph (2013, see also Tavory 2018), for example, operate a distinction between "protensions" (moment by moment anticipation), trajectories, and broader plans and temporal landscapes, but their theoretical proposal is very much centered on actors-in-time at the expense of culture-in-time as a cultural system that is relatively independent of actors' realizations. Mandich (2020), in an extremely compelling article that builds on pragmatic sociology, evokes different regimes of the future, but subjects the anticipation of the future to assumptions that are, in the last instance, based on a tempered intentionalism. Suggestive and impressive as those theoretical advances are, they push, implicitly or explicitly, culture into an undesirable background where it works, sometimes seamlessly, sometimes less so, without being questioned.

On the contrary, a cultural sociology of the future should assign both logical predictability and practical contingency to culture in action, and the kind of cognitive semiotics that the notion of encyclopedic semantic models entail is useful as a way to link culture, cognition, and action in the planning and projecting of the future (Mische, 2009). There are three moves that can be taken so that culture, action, and future orientation can be brought together more harmoniously.

First, one should proceed with the recognition that cultural memory works in full force when it is creative and productive, rather than simply expressive (Joas 1996). Yet, if we take the alternative route and stress the productivity of memory, one should also recognize that this productivity is in some sense attributed to the cultural system as memory, as a network of interpretants that trace paths and allows for the production of new paths that link interpretants. Most work on anticipation is carried out within situations by knowing that some networks will be activated within a specific situation, and others can be activated when facing novelty.

Second, a theory of meaning should be formulated in accordance with the premises of memory as process and creativity. In this sense, theories that stress the associative character of meaning (a trait of semiotics since Saussure's mnemonic chains), and its contextual and historical character (Putnam, 1975) already contain important elements that can contribute to a dynamic theory of meaning and its mobilization, both when we consider declarative culture and non-declarative, embodied, and habitual forms of culture. The concept of encyclopedia, which is very liberal with regards to meaning and its pragmatic implications, seems almost ready-made for such an integration that can accommodate for the many levels at which meaning operates.

Third, a theory of memory that takes into consideration the future displays important pragmatic features that can integrate an attention to its formal features with one more directed at the situations in which meaning occurs and produces its consequences. The models that rely on the semantic encyclopedia already display a relevant degree of pragmatic openness at the analytic level (in terms of scripts and frames, or contextual and situational selections), and they successfully embed pragmatic implications in the semantics of cultural units. A step forward requires a cultural pragmatic (Alexander, 2004, Patterson, 2014) in which cultural units are reconnected with actors and situations.

These three fronts represent those on which a cultural theory of anticipation can prove most fruitful, not just and not really as a contribution to a theory of cultural memory, but also and more in general to a theory of action.

## Conclusions

I have argued that a semiotic sociology of memory should take temporality seriously, in order not only to reconcile synchrony and diachrony (or system and process), but also to bring to a theoretically fruitful and conceptually manageable synthesis the regimes of temporality at work in the traditional distinction between past, present, and future.

The main argument I have advanced is that memory studies have done little to extend the grasp of their implicit or explicit theories of temporality toward the theorizing of the relations between memory and the future. In part, this has happened as a consequence of their almost exclusive theorization of the future in normative terms, as a desired condition that bears the marks of how much "good memory" has worked. However, I have also identified a series of limitations—particularly as they are inscribed in the *sociology* of memory—that harm a comprehensive consideration of the potentially tight bond between "memory" and the future.

"Memory," in the broad sense I have used the concept here, is not limited to representation and it is certainly not limited to the past. By adopting the systemic and yet open-ended notion of memory I have explored in this chapter, the future can effectively be brought back in, as a selection among possible temporal landscapes and alternative courses that always has the possibility to become a "present" and "solidify" itself into a recognizable past that becomes a resource for further memory work. I argue that this dynamic is at the center of the interface between culture and action and, therefore, that a sociology of culture is, in many respects, always a sociology of memory.

The main characteristics of the approach I have outlined here, both as a tool for the critique of weaker approaches in memory studies and as a first step toward theory construction, highlight the centrality of a relational, processual, semiosic, and pragmatic notion of memory, which ends up working both as a *system* and as a *mechanism* for the harmonization of social time and the production of intertemporal stability.

A cultural sociology of memory—or, even better said, a cultural sociology *as* a sociology of memory—brings these systemic and mechanismal aspects to the fore as an integrated framework for linking actions and situations, narrative and practice, and the different social times that parse our experience. That memory is at the center of this complex configuration needs to be remembered, particularly in light of the broad and extensive concept of memory that I have outlined here, less concerned with the representation of the past than it is with the core operations of culture as a complex web of meanings.

Within this framework, the concept of memory enters not only as a reminder of the past but as an operation that connects the past with the present, and the planning and the consideration of the future. Indeed, the notion of cultural memory that I have adopted here, and its connection to a notion of semantic encyclopedia, helps in the configuration of typical paths to the future, and explores the latter as a set of possibilities that are inscribed into semiotic systems. At the analytic level of culture, memory is central for the construction of a less static and deterministic notion of culture, and brings at least the possibility of temporality in. At the level of the concreteness of culture, its inscription in actions and situations, memory serves as a crucial mechanism that reveals, simultaneously, the symbolic and pragmatic aspects of social life, and its general semioticity.

## References

Alexander, J.C. (1988) *Action and its Environments: Towards a New Synthesis*, New York: Columbia University Press.

Alexander, J.C. (2003) *The Meanings of Social Life: A Cultural Sociology*, Oxford: Oxford University Press.

Alexander, J.C. (2004) "Cultural Pragmatics: Social Performance between Ritual and Strategy," *Sociological Theory*, 22(4): 527–73.

Boym, S. (2001) *The Future of Nostalgia*, New York: Basic Books.

Confino, A. (1997) "Collective Memory and Cultural History: Problems of Method," *American Historical Review*, 102(5): 1386–403.

Cossu, A. (2010) "Durkheim's Argument on Ritual, Commemoration, and Aesthetic Life: A Classical Legacy for Contemporary Performance Theory?," *Journal of Classical Sociology*, 10(1): 33–49.

Cossu, A. (2017) "Signs, Webs, and Memories: Umberto Eco as a (Social) Theorist," *Thesis Eleven*, 140(1): 74–89.

Cossu, A. (2020) "From Lines to Networks: Calendars, Narrative, and Temporality," *Memory Studies*, 13(4): 502–18.

Desogus, P. (2012) "The Encyclopedia in Umberto Eco's Semiotics," *Semiotica*, 192(1/4): 501–21.

Eco, U. (1976) *A Theory of Semiotics*, Bloomington, IN: Indiana University Press.

Eco, U. (1984) *Semiotics and the Philosophy of Language*, Bloomington, IN: Indiana University Press.

Eco, U. (2014) *From the Tree to the Labyrinth: Historical Studies on the Sign and Interpretation*, Cambridge, MA: Harvard University Press.

Erll, A. (2011) *Memory in Culture*, Basingstoke: Palgrave Macmillan.

Esposito, E. (2001) *La memoria sociale. Mezzi per comunicare e modi per dimenticare*, Bari: Laterza.

Esposito, E. (2008) "Social Forgetting: A Systems Theory Approach," in A. Erll and A. Nunnig (eds) *Cultural Memory Studies: An International and Interdisciplinary Handbook*, Berlin: Walter de Gruyter, pp. 181–90.

Fillmore, C.J. (1976) "Frame Semantics and the Nature of Language," *Annals of the New York Academy of Language*, 280(1): 20–32.

Fine, G.A. and Beim, A. (2007) "Introduction: Interactionist Approaches to Collective Memory," *Symbolic Interaction*, 30(1): 1–6.

Garfinkel, H. (1967) *Studies in Ethnomethodology*, New York: Prentice-Hall.

Geertz, C. (1966) "Religion as a Cultural System," in M. Banton (ed) *Anthropological Approaches to the Study of Religion*, London: Tavistock: 1–46.

Geertz, C. (1973) *The Interpretation of Cultures*, New York: Basic Books.
Geertz, C. (1976) "Art as a Cultural System," *Modern Language Notes*, 91(6): 1473–99.
Gensburger, S. (2016) "Halbwachs' Studies in Collective Memory: A Founding Text for Contemporary 'Memory Studies'?," *Journal of Classical Sociology*, 16(4): 396–413.
Greimas, A.J. (1966) *Sèmantique Structurale*, Paris: Larousse.
Gutman, Y., Brown, A.D. and Sodaro, A. (eds) (2010) *Memory and the Future: Transnational Politics, Ethics and Society*, Basingstoke: Palgrave Macmillan.
Heiskala, R. (2003) *Society as Semiosis: Neostructuralist Theory of Culture and Society*, Frankfurt am Main: Peter Lang.
Heiskala, R. (2021) *Semiotic Sociology*, Basingstoke: Palgrave Macmillan.
Irwin-Zarecka, I. (1994) *Frames of Remembrance: The Dynamics of Collective Memory*, New Brunswick, NJ: Transaction.
Joas, H. (1996) *The Creativity of Action*, Chicago, IL: University of Chicago Press.
Kane, A. (1991) "Cultural Analysis in Historical Sociology: The Analytic and Concrete Forms of the Autonomy of Culture," *Sociological Theory*, 9(1): 53–69.
Kockelman, P. (2005) "The Semiotic Stance," *Semiotica*, 157(1/4): 233–304.
Kockelman, P. (2012) *Agent, Person, Subject, Self*, Oxford: Oxford University Press.
Lizardo, O. (2017) "Improving Cultural Analysis: Considering Personal Culture in its Declarative and Non-Declarative Modes," *American Sociological Review*, 82(1): 88–115.
Lotman, Y. (1990) *Universe of the Mind: A Semiotic Theory of Culture*, Bloomington, IN: Indiana University Press.
Lotman, Y. (2000) "Pamiat' Kul'turi," in Id. *Semiosfera*, Saint Petersburg: Iskusstvo-SSB.
Lotman, Y. and Uspenskii, B. (1978) "On the Semiotic Mechanism of Culture," *New Literary History*, 9(2): 211–32.
Mandich, G. (2020) "Modes of Engagement with the Future in Everyday Life," *Time and Society*, 29(3): 681–703.
Mische, A. (2009) "Projects and Possibilities: Researching Futures in Action," *Sociological Forum*, 24(3): 694–704.
Misztal, B. (2003) "Durkheim on Collective Memory," *Journal of Classical Sociology*, 3(2): 123–43.
Norton, M. (2014) "Mechanisms and Meaning Structures," *Sociological Theory*, 32(2): 162–87.
Olick, J. (1999) "Collective Memory: The Two Cultures," *Sociological Theory*, 17(3): 333–48.
Olick, J. (2007) *The Politics of Regret*, London: Routledge.

Olick, J. and Robbins, J. (1998) "Social Memory Studies: From Collective Memory to the Historical Sociology of Mnemonic Practices," *Annual Review of Sociology*, 24: 105–40.

Parsons, T. and Shils, E. (1951) "Values, Motives, and Systems of Action," in T. Parsons and E. Shils (eds) *Toward a General Theory of Action*, New York: Harper & Row, pp. 47– 278.

Patterson, O. (2014) "Making Sense of Culture," *Annual Review of Sociology*, 40(1): 1–30.

Peirce, C.S. (1931–1958) *Collected Papers of Charles Peirce*, 8 vols, Cambridge, MA: Harvard University Press.

Putnam, H. (1975) "The Meaning of Meaning," *Minnesota Studies in the Philosophy of Science*, 7: 131–93.

Quillian, R. (1968) "Semantic Networks," in M. Minsky (ed) *Semantic Information Processing*, Boston, MA: MIT Press.

Rabinow, P. and Sullivan, W. (eds) (1979) *Interpretive Social Science*, Berkeley, CA: University of California Press.

Salerno, D. (2021) "A Semiotic Theory of Memory: Between Movement and Form," *Semiotica*, 241: 87–119.

Schwartz, B. (1996) "Memory as a Cultural System: Abraham Lincoln in World War 2," *American Sociological Review*, 61(5): 908–27.

Scott, M. and Lyman, S. (1968) "Accounts," *American Sociological Review*, 33(1): 46–62.

Shils, E. (1975) *Center and Periphery: Essays in Macrosociology*, Chicago, IL: University of Chicago Press.

Tamm, M. (2015) "Semiotic Theory of Cultural Memory: In the Company of Yuri Lotman," in S. Kattago (ed) *The Ashgate Research Companion to Memory Studies*, Farnham: Ashgate, pp. 127–41.

Tamm, M. (2019) "Introduction: Juri Lotman's Semiotic Theory of History and Cultural Memory," in M. Tamm (ed) *Juri Lotman – Culture, Memory, and History. Essays in Cultural Semiotics*, Cham: Palgrave Macmillan, pp. 1–26.

Tavory, I. (2018) "Between Situations: Anticipation, Rhythm, and the Theory of Interaction," *Sociological Theory*, 36(2): 117–33.

Tavory, I. and Eliasoph, N. (2013) "Coordinating Futures: Toward a Theory of Anticipation," *American Journal of Sociology*, 118(4): 908–42.

Tomkins, S.S. (1978) "Script Theory: Differential Magnification of Affects," *Nebraska Symposium on Motivation*, 26: 201–36.

Van de Putte, T. (2022) "Collective Memory between Culture and Interaction," *Memory Studies*, 15(4): 751–66.

Watts-Miller, W. (2001) "Durkheimian Time," *Time & Society*, 9(1): 5–20.

Wiley, N. (1994) *The Semiotic Self*, Chicago, IL: University of Chicago Press.

Zerubavel, E. (2003) *Time Maps: Collective Memory and the Social Shape of the Past*, Chicago, IL: University of Chicago Press.

# 7

# Stigma-embedded Semiotics: Indexical Dilemmas of HIV across Local and Migrant Networks

*Jorge Fontdevila*

In his *Symposium*, Plato stages a dialogue between two male lovers—philosopher Socrates and military general Alcibiades—to reflect on tensions between a physical, baser love and a virtuous, nobler love. The latter is closer to a pure Form of Beauty. Throughout the *Symposium*, these two kinds of love are examined in a series of dialogues by banquet guests, who are distinguished men of Athenian society and many married to women:

> 'Socrates, are you asleep?' 'Not at all,' he said ... I said, 'you're the only lover I've ever had who's good enough for me, but you seem to be too shy to talk about it to me' ... And then he said ... 'My dear Alcibiades ... You must be seeing in me a beauty beyond comparison and one that's far superior to your own good looks. ... You're trying to get true beauty in return for its appearance, and so to make an exchange that is really 'gold for bronze'. ... 'When I heard this, I said ... 'It's now up to you to consider what you think is best for you and for me.' (Plato, 1999 [*c*. 385 BC], pp. 57–8)

For our purposes, what is remarkable about these dialogues is not so much their deep philosophical exploration of *Eros* but that such exploration is expressed in contexts of homoeroticism and the beauty of the male body. In fact, unlike most modern heterosexual men, these banquet men seem unconcerned about threats to their masculinity when publicly discussing same-sex desires or bisexual behaviors.

As other scholars have noted, one of the West's greatest ironies is that its first explicit philosophical reflection on love begins as a discussion of homoerotic love. In fact, in Archaic and Classical Greece male–female relations were rarely eroticized. The "romanticization" of male–female courtship develops later in Hellenistic and Roman times and flourishes in our Christian era with the troubadour literary phenomenon (Konstan, 1994). Eventually, in contrast to Ancient Greece where it could be signified as a virtue, in our modern West, male homoerotic desire became medically signified as a neurosis. To clarify, I am not claiming that homoerotic desires in Ancient Greece (typically intergenerational) and the modern West (typically among consenting adults) are of the same "kind." I am simply highlighting the semiotic fact that male homoeroticism can be valued or devalued in different social formations.

In this vein, Hacking (2002) argues that modern post-Victorian classifications of sexual orientation—heterosexual, homosexual—are not based on meaningful, long-established "causal histories" in the ontological sense and hence cannot be construed as biological "natural kinds." For one, such binary sexual classifications epistemologically "erase" bisexuality as a third, stable category in the modern world—unlike in Ancient Greece. Certainly, modern taxonomies are of the "interactive kind" in that they *loop back* on the people classified, transforming and partially constructing them in the process. As Hacking explains:

> Let a new way to classify human beings emerge, and let people become aware of how they are classified, then they will often behave differently … The truths about that category of people will change because the people have changed … that is, classifications interact with the classified. (Hacking, 2002, p. 104)

At any rate, the fact remains that same-sex and different-sex practices and desires have coexisted throughout history in complex degrees of institutional and semiotic signification—emerging from unique psychosocial etiologies across cultures (see Herdt, 1997, for ritualized same-sex practices in Melanesia).[1] With respect to the modern West, Butler (1990, p. 17) and

---

[1] The search for biological explanations (or "natural kinds") of homosexuality has a painful history in the West. The latest, most comprehensive iteration finds that all genetic effects account for about 25–32 percent of whether someone will have same-sex sex (Ganna et al, 2019). This makes it impossible to effectively predict whether a specific individual will engage in same-sex practices based on their genome alone. Moreover, in line with Hacking's (Foucauldian) argument, even if it was found that some individuals had predetermined sexual orientations, it would still be the case that "only at a certain [historical] time did the idea of the homosexual as a 'kind of person' come into being" or that at other times most men practiced culturally sanctioned bisexual behaviors (Hacking, 2002, p. 96).

others contend that "the [modern] heterosexualization of desire requires and institutes the production of discrete and asymmetrical oppositions between 'feminine' and 'masculine,' where these are understood as expressive attributes of 'male' and 'female'" (see Laqueur, 1990; Patil, 2018, for colonial racialized dimensions). Put another way, the institutionalization of "heterosexuality" and strict policing of its boundaries became an indispensable element of the modern asymmetrical production of gender ideologies. Whereas in antiquity women were often viewed as imperfect versions of men, modernity ushered in the construction of men and women as complementary albeit asymmetrical "opposites." Thus, unlike the semiosis of bisexual masculinity in Ancient Greece, heterosexuality itself in our era became the semiotic "index" par excellence to signal contexts of "true" masculinity and gender arrangements (Cameron and Kulick, 2003).[2]

## Stigma against gay and bisexual men

As indicated above, within modern orders of heteronormative classification, male homoerotic desire became devalued and semiotically marked as "indexing" a masculinity deficit. It is in these historical contexts of structural stigma and discrimination that we find that gay, bisexual, and other men who have sex with men (henceforth gay and bisexual men) remain the population most affected by HIV/AIDS in the US. Although constituting 2–10 percent of the population, in 2019 gay and bisexual men made up 69 percent of all new HIV diagnoses in the US (CDC, 2021a). Moreover, HIV disproportionately affects Latino and African-American gay and bisexual men—pointing to additional intersectional processes of racial/ethnic historical discrimination. Thus, in 2019 alone, Latino gay and bisexual men accounted for 32 percent of HIV new diagnosis compared to 25 percent for their white counterparts (CDC, 2021a, 2022). Such health disparities call for further research on the social and meaning-making mechanisms that produce excess burden of disease among Latino gay and bisexual men.

Epidemics do not exist in sociocultural vacuums. Sociocultural factors are often more instrumental to the disease burden of a population than the disease's causal pathogen. Ultimately, there is always a "need for a biosocial reconception of disease" to focus on the social determinants of health affecting a population (Singer and Clair, 2003, p. 434; Fontdevila, 2020,

---

[2] Within capitalist orders, the historical conditions that produce and enforce heteronormativity—and stigma against homoerotic desire—are complex but partly related to the differentiation of the family from its traditional productive role and its modern institutionalization as a separate nuclear unit of cathectic and emotional reproduction (D'Emilio, 1992, pp. 3–16; Katz, 2007).

on syndemics). Among social determinants, stigma and discrimination are considered fundamental causes of disease because they are linked to unequal prestige evaluations and access to resources that perpetuate health disparities (Link and Phelan, 1995; Hatzenbuehler et al, 2013; CDC, 2016). Homophobic stigma against sexual minorities significantly drives the HIV/AIDS epidemic by creating symbolic and material barriers to HIV disclosure, condom use, testing, access and adherence to treatment and care, as well as family rejections and job or housing denials. Sexual stigma is typically compounded with HIV-related stigma based on unfounded fears of contagion, illness, and death. Ultimately, stigma is part of the mechanisms of societal power and control that (re)produce the fault lines of sexual inequality and perpetuate health disparities (Link and Phelan, 2001; Parker and Aggleton, 2003; Teunis and Herdt, 2007).

To recap, in stigmatizing same-sex desire, modern heteronormative orders set the semiotic and institutional conditions that disproportionately affect the sexual health of sexual minority men, and this unfolds via complex pathways. In contexts of potential HIV transmission, I argue that these men are impacted by the interplay of three levels of social complexity—at the macro-level of sexual inequalities, at the epidemiological level of biosocial disease, and at the micro-level of sexual interaction (see Wiley, 1988, for emergent levels). Moreover, at the nexus of the interplay of these levels, I find powerful processes of semiotic mediation. Thus, to understand how stigma and discrimination against homoerotic desire (henceforth homoerotic stigma) operate via such processes of semiotic mediation requires deep interpretive knowledge of the lifeworlds of those populations affected by the epidemic. Precisely to this end, in this chapter I use ethnographic methods to explore the lifeworld of Latino gay and bisexual migrant men as they interact with local men in sexualized spaces. I have chosen this empirical case to illustrate the significance of semiotic tools to explain the creation of contextual meaning in social life, but also to examine the production of emergent contexts that can drive HIV.

First, I set the historical stage of the semiotics of condomless sex within the framework of HIV/AIDS as an epidemic of signification. Second, drawing on key analytical tools of Peircean semiotic mediation, I explain the constitutive role of indexical signs in the production of social context. Third, I apply these semiotic tools to a case of condomless sexual practices to show how indexical mechanisms produce risky contexts—"silence" of HIV disclosure indexing resistance to stigma. These contexts emerged at the turn of the 21st century, often producing risky polysemic (mis)interpretations across local and migrant networks. Finally, I conclude that HIV/AIDS is driven by processes that are essentially semiotic, and that higher level emergent properties—HIV disparities—result from multiple pathways of semiotic mediation embedded in structural stigma.

## Condomless sex semiotics

From the outset it became clear that HIV/AIDS is fundamentally an "epidemic of signification" immersed in signifiers of deviant sexualities and moral plague (Treichler, 1987; see Sontag, 2001, for AIDS and metaphor; Greteman, 2019). Moreover, over three decades of research show that framing condom use as a "simple choice between risky behavior and rational attempts to protect one's health ignores the complex semiotic space" that intimate partners navigate during sex (Tavory and Swidler, 2009, p. 171). I have argued elsewhere that selves during sex are often inconsistent and juggle multiple motivations—rooted in conflicting semiotic axes (Fontdevila, 2006, 2009). Despite strong intentions about HIV protection, individuals at key junctures feel more accountable to complex semiotic framings of their face-to-face sexual performances—such as metacommunicating masculinity or relationship trust by avoiding condom use—than their long-term health goals of preventing infection. Built-in performative pressures are typical of sexual encounters, underscoring the primacy of the interaction order over individual cognition (Goffman, 1983).

In this light, it is important to examine how a macro-level "epidemic of signification" such as HIV/AIDS built on widespread sexual phobias and inequalities becomes interactionally "realized" on the ground where the actual virus ultimately spreads via intimate exchange of bodily fluids. It is in these micro-interactional arenas "where semiotically charged objects and actions have powerful effects" upon behavior (Tavory and Swidler, 2009, p. 185). Research finds multiple pathways embedded in complex meaning systems by which HIV is transmitted. In the case of sexual interaction—where a physical barrier to sharing sexual fluids is crucial to prevent HIV—understanding the semiotics of condom signaling is paramount. Across different contexts, condom use or request is found to index a wide range of interpretations, from breaches of trust or love (Sobo, 1995; Fontdevila, 2009; Carrillo, 2017), threats to masculinity (Fontdevila, 2006), less commitment to provide modern consumption gifts (Mojola, 2014), to unhealthy postcolonial conspiracies (Tavory and Swidler, 2009), and exclusion from subcultural belonging (Dean, 2009), among others. These meaning systems are often polysemic and ambiguous—in some contexts anchored in conflicting semiotic axes but combined in synergistic ways in others.

Condom semiotics can be construed as proximal mechanisms of HIV transmission that mediate macro-structural drivers of HIV/AIDS, such as poverty, sexual stigma, gender or racial inequalities, and postcolonial relations. In these mediations, condoms create phenomenological contexts that often index sexual relationships of less intimate or lower status. In this light, the changes in the semiotics of condomless sex among gay and bisexual men in the US provide a relevant illustration of condom mediations on the ground. Throughout the 1980s, a deficient governmental response to the AIDS crisis largely fueled by societal homophobia provoked gay activism to "normalize" condom use as gay men's primary survival strategy. Sexual behavioral changes among gay men were such that by decade's end experts reported that "AIDS education and prevention campaigns have resulted in the most profound modifications of personal health-related behaviors ever recorded" (Stall et al, 1988, p. 878). Safe sex—consistent condom use for anal sex—became the "unmarked" and generalized semiotic practice in the gay community.³

By the early 2000s, however, it became clear that the full picture was more complicated and sexual behavioral change was not easily sustainable—long-term strategies of risk reduction rather than elimination appeared more feasible. Some gay men experienced "condom fatigue" and reverted to condomless behaviors. New generations of gay men who had not witnessed the epidemic's early devastation were not adopting safe sex. The steady resurgence of condomless sex was partly due to "treatment optimism" in the wake of new antiretroviral therapies (ART) that radically transformed AIDS from a deadly to a chronic and manageable disease.⁴ But other social forces were also at play. Among them, the ongoing sexual and disease stigma that many HIV-positive gay men experienced not just from society at large but from HIV-negative men's rejection as well. The unmarked practice of consistent condom use had, over time, become part of a complex semiotics of "homonormativity" and stigma against HIV-positive men.⁵ In response, some HIV-positive men and their sexual networks resisted rejection by

---

3   Markedness theory originates in the Prague linguistic circle and refers to the notion that oppositions within a linguistic or semiotic paradigm are typically hierarchical, in that some encoded signs are more general or specific than others; for example, "woman" is the patriarchal "marked" sign of a dual paradigmatic system in which "man" is signified as the generalized type of human, the "unmarked" type (see Steiner, 1982, for a review; Waugh, 1982). Here, I refer to "unmarked" condom practice to convey a semiotic practice that is perceived as the generalized and default form in most social contexts (for example, right-handedness, heterosexual marriage).

4   "Treatment optimism" in a post-ART era refers to decreased concerns about acquiring HIV by some gay men because AIDS is perceived as a manageable and chronic condition. Hence there is less commitment to safe sex.

5   Homonormativity is the idea that there is a "right way" of being gay in the gay community, including pressures to use condoms consistently. Perhaps a troubled moment in gay rights activism reflecting homonormative tensions was when Larry Kramer, a pioneer gay activist and writer, characterized "barebacking" (HIV-positive gay men having condomless sex) as a form of homicide (quoted in Dean, 2019, p. 277). As Katz (2020, p. xvi) has indicated, "AIDS gave new life to dying old canards long associated with queerness, such as the association of homosexuality with illness." It is worth noting that HIV stigma circulates not just in the larger society but in the gay community as well.

engaging in "marked" practices of "bareback sex," where condomless sex became a subcultural norm (Dean, 2009).

## Social context from indexicality and metacommunication

After setting the stage of the semiotics of condomless sex among gay and bisexual men in the US, I turn now to explaining the semiotic relevance of indexicality and metacommunication in the production of context in social life. These are the semiotic tools I apply below to show the production of HIV risky contexts at the intersection of local and migrant sexual networks.

*Indexicality*

Three broad perspectives explain semiosis or signification in social life. One perspective claims that signification occurs when signs "correspond" to their denotational objects (referential theory of meaning). From another perspective signification emerges when signs "relate" to each other via rules of contrasts in sign systems (structuralist or self-referential theory of meaning). Finally, a third perspective contends that signification occurs when signs "produce" interactional effects on sign users (pragmatic theory of meaning). Although all three signifying modes coexist in some combination, Silverstein (1976) claims that it is the pragmatic mode via indexical signs that anchors the other two—referential, self-referential—in meaningful contexts of everyday use, providing relevant cues and redundancies to interpret communicative messages in interaction.

A turning point in the pragmatic understanding of language's capacity to produce meaning in social context occurred when linguistic anthropologists—drawing mostly from Peirce (1931–1958) and Jakobson (1960)—foregrounded the indexical dimension of linguistic signs. For Peirce, semiotic mediation—contra Saussure's dyadic signifier/signified—is triadic in essence, including (1) a sign (representamen) that relates (2) an object (whatever the sign stands for, physical or mental object) to (3) an interpretant (cognitive effect or feeling created in a mind by the sign in its standing relationship to its object).[6] These three components typically enter an iterative dynamic, including the potential for unlimited semiosis, by which

---

[6] Additionally, Peirce claims that the sign stands for an object "not in all respects, but in reference to some sort of idea … called the ground of the representamen" (Peirce, 1931–1958, CP 2.228). This "ground" is an elementary preframing cognition, part of a universe of discourse, that selects "relevant attributes" of a "dynamic object" (that is, the object in itself) to constitute the perceived "immediate object," which then triggers the semiotic mediation via the sign to the interpretant (Eco, 1994, p. 28; Cossu, 2017).

interpretants become more elaborate signs of further triads (more on this later). Moreover, signs can relate to their objects by analogy or similarity (icon), arbitrary rule or convention (symbol), or spatiotemporal contiguity (index). This latter capacity—indexicality—constitutes the basis for the contextual function of language in sociocultural practice (Duranti, 2003; Mertz, 2007; Fontdevila, 2010).

Indexes, unlike symbols, are signs or sign elements that do not denote but point to the world to create or reproduce the contexts in which they are performed. They signify by virtue of their spatiotemporal contiguity to the contexts they stand for (for example, smoke signaling fire). In the case of the semiotic system of language, indexes are more or less grammaticalized elements that point to features of the physical or social world, and that speakers use reflexively to lay out the contextual parameters of their interactions. Thus, from deixis (for example, this, now), pronouns (for example, I, you), verb tenses to code-switching, registers, deference and status markers, prosodic tones, silences, and so on, indexes anchor the linguistic code in practical contexts of use. Austin's performatives carrying illocutionary force (for example, I promise you, I sentence you) are simply one example of indexical signs that so happen to be grammaticalized in most Indo-European languages (Silverstein, 1993). But other linguistic indexical strategies can also "constitute" or perform the contexts in which they are uttered. For instance, two people switching to first-name basis index (constitute) a new context of status proximity, co-workers switching from slang to formal register index the resumption of professional context, or male friends mocking effeminate mannerisms index their belonging to a heteronormative context.

Thus, indexes enable speakers to constitute and renegotiate their relative footings and social ties, rendering semiotic processes fully operational in communicative practice (Fontdevila and White, 2013).[7] Moreover, language is unique among semiotic systems because of its reflexive capacity. Silverstein (1976, 1993)—following Jakobson's (1960) insight on the ubiquitous metalingual function of language to speak about itself—claims that language's reflexivity is essentially metapragmatic. Most metalingual activities are not just about semantic understanding (glossing, translation) but fundamentally about indexing the (appropriate) pragmatic use of language in interaction. With

---

[7] Indexes are classified according to the degree in which their pragmatic use "presupposes" or "creates" the context that is being singled out (Silverstein, 1976). Many languages, like Javanese, include deference indexes that "create" status differences by stylistic and grammatical switches (Brown and Gilman, 1960, for tu/vous pronouns of address; Irvine, 1985). Others, like some Aboriginal languages, switch lexicon without changing referential content simply to index the presence within earshot of a mother-in-law or affine (Dixon, 1972).

variable awareness, we always use language metapragmatically—reflexively—to negotiate our social ties and relevant contexts (see Bauman and Briggs, 1990, for the "poetic" function also crucial for linguistic metapragmatics).

*Metacommunication*

Furthermore, communication is always metacommunication. For Bateson (1985 [1955], p. 188), "any message, which either explicitly or implicitly defines a frame, *ipso facto* gives the receiver instructions or aids in his attempt to understand the messages included within the frame." Thus, any message signals a framing context by providing indexical cues (context-markers) to actors to discern at what level of abstraction the interaction should be decoded to be understood. A basic example of metacommunicative messaging, typical among mammalian species, constitutive of context is indexing "this is play" by engaging in less intense physical contact than aggressive combat. Complex examples of metacommunication using language or paralanguage are changing the meaning of a remark into its ironic opposite by tone emphasis (index), or hyperbolic, indirect talk to index politeness and deferential context, such as "Could you pass the salt? That would be awesome!" Moreover, speakers use semantic content strategically to constitute context, as in "Did you bring condoms?" indexing nonmonogamy. In all cases, the meaning of the interaction—the type of metacontext among speakers—is signaled through contextualizing indexical devices.

The reflexive capacity to interpret metacommunicative indexes (for example, tone, silences, discourse markers, pronouns of address, register switches) is actually the capacity to understand the "meaning" of the interaction—the phenomenological question of relevance, "what is going on?" (Goffman, 1974, 1981; see Gumperz, 1982, for contextualization cues; Lucy, 1993). Meaning is accomplished via reflexive indexical switches of context-markers across metacommunicative levels. Any contextual interpretation that emerges from such indexical switches is inferred, albeit incompletely, via hard phenomenological work of abductive reasoning.[8] Moreover, such indexical signaling occurs in real time and so "the mechanisms by which relational information is signaled are inherently ambiguous, i.e., subject to

---

[8] Abductive reasoning refers to forms of cognitive inference by which deductive rules and formal principles become reflexively linked to local features of interactive settings that are known inductively from everyday life experience (Peirce, 1931–1958; Tavory and Timmermans, 2014). Thus, effective communication does not proceed just by following automatic rules of grammar but also by inductive knowledge of the practical meanings of a situation. In everyday life, these multiple contrasting levels of abstraction (deductive and inductive) become integrated and negotiated by abductive inference in the performance of speech.

multiple interpretations ... In conversation, such ambiguities are negotiated in the course of interaction" (Gumperz, 1982, p. 208).

In short, communication in social life is mostly about managing metacommunicative indexicalities, which typically entail great ambiguity and openness because they emerge in social networks and institutional practices that are anchored in different historical processes and times (Fontdevila and White, 2013). Meaning in social life is an interactional accomplishment that emerges reflexively between (ever-changing) grammar rules and speakers' phenomenological work at framing nested metalevels in speech situations (Garfinkel, 1967; Duranti, 2003; Mertz, 2007). Put differently, speakers do not passively decode ongoing utterances against a backdrop of culturally reified contexts but reflexively use their own verbal and nonverbal interactions as indexes to create such contexts (Duranti and Goodwin, 1992). Social context is never separate from talk. Social meaning is context-dependent but "speaking" itself via indexicalities is what creates the context that semiotically constitutes the nature of speakers' social ties.

## Silence indexing resistance to stigma[9]

After explaining the key analytical tools of contextual semiosis, I proceed now to apply them to an empirical case at the turn of the 21st century in order to illustrate indexical strategies of marked "bareback" practices of condomless sex. These strategies metacommunicate resistance to stigma but, as I show later, also produce HIV risky contexts. First, I examine the semiotic encoding of "silence" with regard to HIV disclosure as an index that signifies HIV-positive serosorting. In this context, serosorting means that two HIV-positive men decide to have sex without condoms because they assume or trust both are positive and not worried about infection (or reinfection). Then I show a pragmatics of serosorting dilemmas that migrant men may encounter in these risky contexts, and where polysemic (mis) interpretation of the semiosis of silence may produce a pathway to HIV transmission. Finally, I show a metapragmatic event where a US-born Latino man is aware of these subcultural norms and explains the semiotic code to a recent migrant man.

### *Code of silence*

Stigma and rejection against HIV-positive gay men have been pervasive throughout the HIV epidemic. In the following passage from the 2000s,

---

[9] Some excerpts and passages have been published elsewhere (Fontdevila, 2020). Published with the permission of Cambridge Scholars Publishing.

for example, Dustin, a 43-year-old white man, found it unusual that he was not rejected by an HIV-negative partner who requested condomless sex:[10]

> I said to him I'm HIV [positive] and I can't do that. He said he didn't care, and I said well I do. That was very unusual ... to me at least, because it's usually me who is getting rejected because of HIV, being positive. And now I'm having to reject somebody because they're negative.

Although many HIV-positive gay men, like Dustin, disclosed their status, some resisted stigma and rejection by adopting a discourse of "individual responsibility" that avoids disclosing HIV status. In many sexualized gay spaces (for example, bathhouses, sex parties, parks), the prevalent assumption has been that the moral responsibility of HIV protection and condom use does not fall on the HIV-positive partner but on anyone who freely enters the sexual encounter with the ultimate preference to remain uninfected (Bayer, 1996; Klitzman and Bayer, 2003; Wolitski and Bailey, 2005; Adam, 2006, 2016; Halperin, 2007; Offer et al, 2007).[11] To illustrate this semiotic code of individual responsibility, Austin, a 54-year-old white man, explicitly said that he did not want to infect anyone, but also clarified that:

> If someone's in the bathhouse, I usually don't tell them that I'm HIV. Okay. And my thinking—either correct or incorrect—is that, they're there and they're taking as much of a risk as I'm taking and they must

---

[10] The data I present here were collected as part of the larger ethnographic Trayectos Study, led by Dr. Héctor Carrillo, which explored contexts of HIV risk among gay and bisexual Mexican men who migrated to San Diego, California (Carrillo et al, 2008; Fontdevila, 2009; Carrillo, 2017). As ethnographer of the Trayectos team, I have selected for this analysis in-depth interview passages that illustrate relevant thematic findings, and translated them into English when necessary. Some excerpts and passages have been published elsewhere (Fontdevila, 2020, published with the permission of Cambridge Scholars Publishing). Participants were recruited between 2003 and 2005. To be eligible they were over 18, migrated or worked in the US within the past 10 years, and engaged in sex with men in the past 6 months. For comparison purposes, the larger study also included data collected from US-born Latino and non-Latino gay men who engaged in sex with Mexican-born men. All participants' names are pseudonyms. The content of this analysis is solely the responsibility of the author and does not necessarily represent the official views of the US National Institutes of Health.

[11] The concept of "discourse of individual responsibility" has been used in HIV prevention research to convey the contractual ethics of a sexual marketplace that is governed by the principle of "buyer beware" (see Race, 2001, for governmentality and HIV-positive men; Adam, 2006). The concept assigns responsibility to the individual who decides to have unprotected sex. It does not imply that HIV-negative men have a moral "responsibility" to avoid having sex with HIV-positive men.

be aware of this risk ... I think anybody who's very sexually active, if I meet you in a bathhouse you probably ... or if I were to meet you in the park, meet you where there's only the possibility of sex going on ... most likely you're probably HIV positive. That's my assumption.

Moreover, some HIV-positive gay men reflexively reclaimed such practices of HIV non-disclosure to metacommunicate "belonging" in a freer gay community unburdened by stigma and rejection. This practice of solidarity-building known as "barebacking" since the 1990s involves a deliberate decision—rather than an "accident" or "relapse"—by networks of some HIV-positive gay men to have condomless sex. It has been theorized as part of a subculture "to describe the distinctive styles and codes that make a practice intensely meaningful to those who undertake it" (Dean, 2019, p. 263, 2009; Carballo-Diéguez and Bauermeister, 2004).[12] Bareback practices resist stigma not only from homophobic orders but also from a homonormative gay community that all too often promoted condom use as an impossible "all or none" proposition (see note 5).

Peirce's triadic model of semiosis (signs, objects, interpretants) posits that interpretants become chains of signs to further interpretants. Applying this model, I contend that the indexical grammar of silencing HIV disclosure and condom request in sexualized spaces goes through at least two iterations of meaning-making. In its first iteration, silence[13] (indexical sign) about HIV disclosure indexes (points to) a marked and transgressive practice of condomless sex (immediate object) that greenlights permission effects (interpretant) in the minds of sex partners to engage in HIV-positive serosorting or individual responsibility.[14]

In its second iteration and typically in barebacking subcultures, such interpretant (that is, the meaningful permission effects to engage in serosorting) becomes a further sign (meta-index) that metacommunicates and constitutes a "morally safe" sexual context (meta-object) of ingroup

---

[12] The signifier "barebacking" is highly overdetermined in the literature, acquiring multiple meanings (Carballo-Diéguez et al, 2009; Dean, 2019, p. 258). It may refer, among others, to a subcultural movement, unprotected sex between HIV-positive partners who intentionally serosort to avoid infecting others, accidental unprotected sex with a partner of unknown status, or individuals who actively seek HIV infection (labeled "bug chasers," a phenomenon that prevention research considers to be rare). Here, I am using barebacking as a signifier of subcultural networks of gay men who intentionally practice condomless sex.

[13] For the general significance of "silence" in sexual scripting, see Cameron and Kulick, 2003, p. 131).

[14] Arguably, the "ground" that preselects as relevant such immediate object (condomless sex) is informed by its transgression vis-à-vis the universe of discourse of homonormativity, which presupposes rigid condom use as the only moral good (see note 6).

belonging and unrestrained sensualities triggering "feelings" of empowerment without judgement and rejection (meta-interpretant). These successive meaning-making iterations are constitutive of a pragmatics of resistance to HIV stigma that I argue becomes pleasure productive because of its "marked" transgression.

Given that every signifying triad produces an interpretant which then becomes the sign of another signifying triad and so on, semiosis could theoretically proceed ad infinitum according to Peirce (1931–1958). However, this infinite regress of unlimited semiosis is typically interrupted by the practical demands of everyday life, including cognitive limitations and intersubjective habits.[15] In the case of HIV-positive men, the second-order interpretant signifying "empowerment without judgement" is what I argue stabilizes this semiosis as a mutual and intersubjective interactional accomplishment of condomless sexual practices.

Needless to say, there may be third-order and further metalevel, more developed interpretants (pragmatic effects) of condomless sex for individual sexual partners, including freedom to express submissive or dominant innermost desires, intimate communicative needs, unconscious libidinal introjections, and so on.[16] At any rate, condomless sex is intersubjectively stabilized via a semiotic code that, although empowering to some, paradoxically may constitute a context of HIV transmission to others, as I show next.

*Pragmatics of serosorting dilemmas*

In contrast to the indexical grammar analyzed above, recent Latino gay and bisexual migrant men newly introduced to US sexualized spaces might have interpreted the "silence" of HIV as indexing sex with an HIV-negative or

---

[15] See Eco (1994, pp. 34–41) for the difference between Peirce's "unlimited semiosis" and Derrida's "deconstructive drift," where he claims that in Peircean semiotics there is "something" (in contrast to Derrida's "nothing") outside the text. In the Peircean view, semiosis is endlessly creative—interpretants are embedded in open-ended rhizomatic networks of multiple interpretations—but two extra-semiotic limiting cases anchor it to the world: indices (signs that acquire meaning by pointing to spatiotemporal objects of the world); and dynamic objects (the thing in itself, physical or mental, which provides resistances and affordances to the signifying action of perceiving the immediate object to be represented). Additionally, habits or dispositions to act on the world constitute another (upper) limiting case of semiosis. They act as an "absolute object" to a final interpretant provided by the intersubjective meanings of an external community, which always privileges some interpretations over others.

[16] See Halperin (2007) for gay subjectivity and deeper meanings that can motivate some gay men to engage in risky sex, including edgework sublimity, identification with HIV-positive men, ambivalence about survival, and rejection of a normalized life.

unknown status partner.[17] If they migrated from towns or rural areas with limited information about HIV, their premigration interpretations may frame partners who do not disclose HIV during sex as not knowingly seropositive. "Silence" for some migrant men may metacommunicate a tolerable level of assumed HIV-negative serosorting. In this case, this means that two HIV-negative or unknown status men decide to have sex without condoms because they assume both are likely negative and cannot get infected.

To illustrate these sexual pragmatics of HIV serosorting dilemmas that migrant men may encounter, Heriberto, a 21-year-old man from Durango, Mexico, who met his sex partner at a porn theatre, explains:

> We undressed and I realized the guy had a nice body … I didn't have condoms handy … I was hesitant whether to penetrate him or not … And so I said to myself, 'what shall I do?'… Then we started with oral sex first, oral sex with caresses and everything … I positioned myself and began teasing him with my penis [as if penetrating] … waiting for his response. He didn't say anything … that is, he didn't say, 'put on a condom' or anything. And I was so horny that I recall that I simply put some lube on me and him, and I penetrated him without a condom.

In this passage, Heriberto—who in the interview assumed he was HIV negative—is hesitant about penetrating his sex partner without a condom. At some performative juncture, he attempts to reduce HIV uncertainty by teasing his partner with his erect penis. In other words, he metacommunicates permission to engage in anal sex without condoms expecting consent. He is concerned about the risks involved but since his partner "didn't say anything," he proceeds to penetrate. Note that in asking "what shall I do?" he is posing the phenomenological question of "relevance" to himself, including seeking indexes to metacommunicatively frame whether or not the context is risky.

In its first iteration of meaning-making, silence (indexical sign) regarding condom request or HIV disclosure (in response to penis teasing) is the index pointing to a practice of condomless sex (immediate object), which has the pragmatic effect (interpretant) in Heriberto's mind of assuming both consent and HIV-negative or unknown serosorting. Then, in its immediate second-order iteration, such consensual interpretant becomes the further sign (meta-index) that signifies a tolerable level of HIV-safe condomless

---

[17] It is important to recognize that Latino gay and bisexual men do not constitute a monolithic group. Carrillo and Fontdevila (2014) challenge the reification of Latino same-sex categories—activo/pasivo, gay, homosocial—found in the literature, and show various contexts where individuals adapt to various interpretations, blendings, or move between categories. These flexibilities are captured by the concept of sexual hybridity (Carrillo, 2017).

context (meta-object) producing feelings of trust and unconstrained pleasure (meta-interpretant). Although in this passage he is not explicit about his assumptions, Heriberto expressed great concern about HIV after risky encounters, and it is likely he trusted this partner would have disclosed had he "knowingly" been HIV positive. In fact, trusting assumptions circulated widely among migrant men unfamiliar with sexualized spaces or engaging in new sexual relationships in the US (Fontdevila, 2009).

*Metapragmatic awareness*

As I have analyzed elsewhere, Heriberto's passage illustrates a semiotic grammar where "silence" is the indexical sign that contextually switches "condom protective" frames to "trusting" frames in sexual encounters (Fontdevila, 2009). These HIV dilemmas redirect actors' phenomenological attention from the pragmatics of desire to the metapragmatics of health-related assumptions. The epidemiological challenge here is that two "polysemic" interpretations on the indexical meaning of "silence" can bypass each other during sexual exchanges between local and migrant networks. Thus, meta-(mis)communication on the indexical meaning of "silence" in such sexualized spaces has HIV implications, given that ultimately condom protection is not used.

Metapragmatics is the reflexive knowledge, more or less explicit, of the pragmatic rules that guide a semiotic paradigm or code in context. To illustrate metapragmatic awareness of the semiotic code of silence that may be misinterpreted in cross-cultural encounters, Lance, a 35-year-old US-born Latino man from northern California, describes an incident at a sex party:

> When I went to one of those [sex] parties, this older man had … some Latino boy … barely speaks English, he's from Mexico. All of a sudden, he lets this [man] fuck him and he's not wearing a condom. And this guy is young … I'm like, what the … And I, and he had taken G [recreational drug] and he was really dizzy … I took him outside to the balcony and said, "*¿qué estás haciendo?*" [what are you doing?] … I'm telling him in Spanish … why are you having unprotected sex? you cannot have unprotected sex with these guys … they could have HIV, do you know what that means? … you could die … you cannot be coming to these [parties] … if you're going to be doing drugs, you cannot be having unprotected sex. I don't think he realizes the consequences of what could happen.

In this metapragmatic exhortation, Lance explicitly lays out the rules of the game (see Jacquemet, 1996, for metapragmatic awareness). In a few words, he instructs the young man, a recent Mexican immigrant, to avoid sex and drugs in sexualized spaces unless he "code-switches" to the "unmarked" practice of condom protection generalized to all sexual contexts.[18] Lance is metapragmatically telling the young man that he is being oblivious of the contextualization cues (Gumperz, 1982) that index this event as "marked," including the key contextual marker—silence of HIV disclosure—that metacommunicates (and constitutes) this sexual context as a risky "barebacking" event. I have indicated elsewhere that at least half of the Mexican gay and bisexual migrant men who were of HIV-negative or unknown status participated in US sexual networks and spaces where semiotic codes of HIV silence circulated unabated (Fontdevila, 2009). In adjusting to US gay life, some migrant men followed their own trust assumptions in contexts where barebacking subcultures were dominant.

## Conclusion

In this chapter I have reflected on rich ethnographic data to examine indexical grammars of sexual interaction that produce semiotic contexts where HIV can be transmitted through polysemic (mis)interpretation. In these contexts, silencing HIV disclosure can constitute a semiotic mechanism of transmission embedded in stigma against HIV-positive gay men who resist rejection. For local sexual networks, silence indexes condomless "bareback" subcultures of belonging or simply the individual responsibilities of a contractual sexual arena regarding self-protection. For recent migrant men, silence during sex may index differently—that sex partners consent and can be trusted to disclose if HIV positive. Paradoxically, it is the empowering and agential semiotic response to sexual and disease stigma by some HIV-positive gay men in sexualized spaces that creates the contexts of HIV transmission that migrant men then encounter.

Sawyer (2005), following Fodor's theories of emergence, distinguishes between "tokens" and "types" to argue that when a higher level emergent type (in this analysis, structural stigma or HIV disparities) can be realized by multiple "wildly disjunctive" tokens—different instantiations or mechanisms—then the higher level type can be theorized in effect as carrying causal powers. Undoubtedly, in any one instance the higher level

---

[18] Code-switching (for example, diglossia, multilingualism) functions as an indexical metapragmatic device used by speakers to create context, identity affiliation, and illocutionary force (Bailey, 2000; Fontdevila and White, 2013). For instance, by switching from low to high-status language varieties, a speaker can create a new context of authority. Here, I apply code-switching to condomless semiotics to convey that in "switching" practices—for instance, from condomless sex (marked) to condom protected sex (unmarked)—actors metacommunicate the interactional creation of their sexual context types, whether about being HIV stigma-free or HIV safe.

type is realized by a particular "supervenient" token base, which acts as its specific interactional and productive mechanism (for example, polysemic misinterpretation of indexing silence examined here as just one mechanism among many that drive HIV disparities). But the higher level emergent type has been so ubiquitously "institutionalized" throughout the social formation that it is irreducible to one single mechanism. Multiple different interactional mechanisms or token instantiations may realize its emergence. In turn, the higher level type can exert a sort of "downward causation" in shaping new supervenient bases of lower level token units (for example, persistent HIV disparities among groups further create the conditions for new meaning-making mechanisms of HIV transmission).

In light of this model of social emergence, I argue that two higher level property types—homoerotic stigma and HIV disparities—emerging from complex systems of sexual inequalities and biosocial epidemic, respectively, become historically coupled and realized via multiple interactional pathways of semiotic mediation. In this chapter, I have analyzed one semiotic mechanism (that is, one supervenient base) that takes place at the nexus of local and migrant sexual networks. Elsewhere, I examine other meaning-making semiotic mechanisms that produce risky sexual contexts driving HIV, including "liminal spaces" among non-gay identified Latino bisexual men, and "double-edged" semiotic tensions surrounding new biomedical interventions among young Latino gay men (Fontdevila, 2020).

With respect to recent biomedical technologies that prevent HIV, including pre-exposure prophylaxis (PrEP),[19] space limits prevent me from offering detailed accounts but I find in my recent qualitative research that these innovations are shifting the semiotic space of risk among gay men (see Lotman, 2000, for semiotic spaces; Fontdevila, 2020). Condomless practices are becoming increasingly generalized and unmarked, and HIV-positive men are experiencing less stigma by HIV-negative men who use PrEP. Moreover, geolocation sexual networking mobile applications have revolutionized the way gay men meet for sex (Race, 2015). Yet my qualitative data show new internalized stigma signifiers emerging via complex semioticizing mechanisms—for instance, among young Latino gay men in southern California, using and disclosing PrEP to sex partners or friends may index perceptions of promiscuous or unfaithful sexualities with detrimental effects for consistent pill adherence and access.

In the final analysis, many of the meaning-making mechanisms of HIV transmission among gay and bisexual men point to deeply institutionalized

---

[19] PrEP involves HIV-negative individuals taking one pill made of an antiretroviral combination to (in this case) prevent HIV infection. Studies show that when taken daily, it reduces the risk of getting HIV by 99 percent (CDC, 2021b).

processes of sexual inequalities and oppression. At the outset, I explained that in modern heteronormative orders, post-Victorian classifications—heterosexual, homosexual—devalued and medicalized homoerotic sexualities as diseased and signifying a masculinity deficit, as part of nonreproductive, disorderly sexualities. In consequence, sexual and disease stigma became compounded as fundamental cause affecting the health of modern gay and bisexual men. When HIV/AIDS hit this oppressed population in the late 20th century, ongoing compounded stigma frameworks became (re)enacted via multiple mechanisms of semiotic mediation. In turn, emerging disparities of HIV resulting partly from the workings of such semiotic mechanisms exerted relentless "downward causation" effects feeding back into the system by deepening health inequalities and the marginalization of sexual minorities.

It is important, however, to emphasize that although the synergistic association between sexual inequalities and HIV disparities proves hard to sever, it is crucial to explore the specific semiotic pathways that transmit HIV on the ground.[20] In the spirit of a pragmatist approach to social mechanisms—epistemologically between the radical contingency of interactionism and the reproductive habitus of practice theory—the question whether semiotic mediation is about social change or reproduction is ultimately a multilayered empirical question (Gross, 2009). A question that needs to consider the meso- and micro-level problem-solving challenges that actors confront in everyday life, along with the formal and substantive forces that work behind their backs. Ultimately, it is only through our deep understanding of contextual mechanisms of HIV transmission that the specific prevention and care needs of a vulnerable population in a particular time and place can be addressed.

In this connection, Peircean triadic mediation with its analytical tools of indexicality and metacommunication is key to capture how contexts of risk are interactionally constituted. I have examined processes by which a potential unlimited semiosis of interpretants about condomless sex becomes stabilized as a practical accomplishment of intersubjective stigma resistance—in Peirce's parlance, a habit or disposition to act upon the world. These condomless sex contexts can, on the one hand, become immediate objects of indexical signifiers of empowerment and agency to some sexual actors, but

---

[20] As Link and Phelan (1995, p. 87) indicate, the reason why the association between fundamental causes of disease and health outcomes are hard to break is because "resources like knowledge, money, power, prestige, and social connectedness are transportable from one situation to another, and as health-related situations change, those who command the most resources are best able to avoid risks, diseases, and the consequences of disease." In contrast, those who command the least resources, material or symbolic, are unable to avoid risky pathways leading to disease. Even if a pathway is intervened, often others appear—for instance, with respect to the links between poverty and chronic disease, if one pathway is intervened (such as taxing tobacco), others persist (such as unaffordable healthy foods).

on the other, be semiotically misinterpreted by new sexual actors—migrant men. Contexts that in the process unintentionally reproduce emergent HIV disparities. A duality of agency and reproduction at the nexus of polysemic (mis)interpretation.

My goal has been to show how emergent properties—structural stigma, HIV disparities—of interacting complex systems are realized through semiotic mechanisms at the meso- and micro-level of social interaction. Ethnographic and qualitative methods are in this respect indispensable as a first point of entry to begin unpacking such semiotic complexity. Moreover, these methods are ideally suited to deliver deep insights on interpretive mechanisms that can then be used to model larger scale epidemiological processes (Patton, 1999; UNAIDS, 2010; Auerbach et al, 2011). It is ultimately through data triangulation at multiple levels—biomedical, interactional, semiotic, structural—that we can tackle HIV/AIDS epidemic complexity and design efficient combination prevention strategies tailored to specific vulnerable populations.

## References

Adam, B.D. (2006) "Infectious Behaviour: Imputing Subjectivity to HIV Transmission," *Social Theory & Health*, 4(2): 168–79.

Adam, B.D. (2016) "Neoliberalism, Masculinity, and HIV Risk," *Sexuality Research and Social Policy*, 13(4): 321–9.

Auerbach, J.D., Parkhurst, J.O. and Cáceres, C.F. (2011) "Addressing Social Drivers of HIV/AIDS for the Long-term Response: Conceptual and Methodological Considerations," *Global Public Health*, 6(Sup3): 1–17.

Bailey, B. (2000) "Switching," *Journal of Linguistic Anthropology*, 9(1/2): 241–3.

Bateson, G. (1985 [1955]) "A Theory of Play and Fantasy," in R. Ignis (ed) *Semiotics: An Introductory Anthology*, Bloomington, IN: Indiana University Press, pp. 129–44.

Bauman, R. and Briggs, C.L. (1990) "Poetics and Performance as Critical Perspectives on Language and Social Life," *Annual Review of Anthropology*, 19: 59–88.

Bayer, R. (1996) "AIDS Prevention: Sexual Ethics and Responsibility," *The New England Journal of Medicine*, 334(23): 1540–2.

Brown, R. and Gilman, A. (1960) "The Pronouns of Power and Solidarity," *American Anthropologist*, 4(6): 24–9.

Butler, J. (1990) *Gender Trouble: Feminism and the Subversion of Identity*, New York: Routledge.

Cameron, D. and Kulick, D. (2003) *Language and Sexuality*, Cambridge: Cambridge University Press.

Carballo-Diéguez, A. and Bauermeister, J. (2004) "'Barebacking': Intentional Condomless Anal Sex in HIV-Risk Contexts," *Journal of Homosexuality*, 47(1): 1–16.

Carballo-Diéguez, A., Ventuneac, A., Bauermeister, J., Dowsett, G., Dolezal, C. et al. (2009) "Is 'Bareback' a Useful Construct in Primary HIV-prevention? Definitions, Identity and Research," *Culture, Health & Sexuality*, 11(1): 51– 65.

Carrillo, H. (2017) *Pathways of Desire: The Sexual Migration of Mexican Gay Men*, Chicago, IL: University of Chicago Press.

Carrillo, H. and Fontdevila, J. (2014) "Border Crossings and Shifting Sexualities among Mexican Gay Immigrant Men: Beyond Monolithic Conceptions," *Sexualities*, 17(8): 919–38.

Carrillo, H., Fontdevila, J., Brown, J. and Gómez, W. (2008) *Risk across Borders: Sexual Contexts and HIV Prevention Challenges among Mexican Gay and Bisexual Immigrant Men. Findings and Recommendations from the Trayectos Study*, San Francisco, CA: UCSF Center for AIDS Prevention Studies.

CDC (Centers for Disease Control and Prevention) (2016) "Stigma and Discrimination." Available from www.cdc.gov/msmhealth/stigma-and-discrimination.htm.

CDC (2021a) "HIV and Gay and Bisexual Men." Available from www.cdc.gov/hiv/group/msm/index.html.

CDC (2021b) "Pre-Exposure Prophylaxis (PrEP)." Available from: www.cdc.gov/hiv/risk/prep/index.html.

CDC (2022) "HIV and Hispanic/Latino Gay and Bisexual Men." Available from www.cdc.gov/hiv/group/gay-bisexual-men/hispanic-latino/index.html.

Cossu, A. (2017) "Signs, Webs, and Memories: Umberto Eco as a (Social) Theorist," *Thesis Eleven*, 140(1): 74–89.

Dean, T. (2009) *Unlimited Intimacy: Reflections on the Subculture of Barebacking*, Chicago, IL: University of Chicago Press.

Dean, T. (2019) "The Raw and the Fucked," in R. Varghese (ed) *Raw: PrEP, Pedagogy, and the Politics of Barebacking*, Regina: University of Regina Press, pp. 257–81.

D'Emilio, J. (1992) *Making Trouble: Essays on Gay History, Politics, and the University*, New York: Routledge.

Dixon, R.M.W. (1972) *The Dyirbal Language of North Queensland*, Cambridge: Cambridge University Press.

Duranti, A. (2003) "Language as Culture in U.S. Anthropology: Three Paradigms," *Current Anthropology*, 44(3): 323–47.

Duranti, A. and Goodwin, C. (1992) *Rethinking Context: Language as an Interactive Phenomenon*, Cambridge: Cambridge University Press.

Eco, U. (1994) *The Limits of Interpretation*, Bloomington, IN: Indiana University Press.

Fontdevila, J. (2006) "Phenomenologies of the Akratic Self: Masculinity, Regrets, and HIV among Men on Methadone," *Journal of Urban Health*, 83(4): 586–601.

Fontdevila, J. (2009) "Framing Dilemmas during Sex: A Micro-sociological Approach to HIV Risk," *Social Theory & Health*, 7(3): 241–63.

Fontdevila, J. (2010) "Indexes, Power, and Netdoms: A Multidimensional Model of Language in Social Action," *Poetics*, 38(6): 587–609.

Fontdevila, J. (2020) "Epidemics as Complex Systems: Sexual Meanings and HIV among Latino Gay and Bisexual Men," in A. Patterson and I. Read (eds) *The SHAPES of Epidemics and Global Disease*, Newcastle: Cambridge Scholars Publishing, pp. 132–67.

Fontdevila, J. and White, H.C. (2013) "Relational Power from Switching across Netdoms through Reflexive and Indexical Language," in F. Dépelteau and C. Powell (eds) *Applying Relational Sociology: Relations, Networks, & Society*, New York: Palgrave Macmillan, pp. 155–79.

Ganna, A., Verweij, K., Nivard, M., Maier, R., Wedow, R. et al. (2019) "Large-scale GWAS Reveals Insights into the Genetic Architecture of Same-sex Sexual Behavior," *Science*, 365(6456): eaat7693, doi: 10.1126/science.aat7693.

Garfinkel, H. (1967) *Studies in Ethnomethodology*, Cambridge, MA: Polity Press.

Goffman, E. (1974) *Frame Analysis: An Essay on the Organization of Experience*, New York: Harper & Row.

Goffman, E. (1981) *Forms of Talk*, Philadelphia, PA: University of Pennsylvania Press.

Goffman, E. (1983) "The Interaction Order," *American Sociological Review*, 48(1): 1–17.

Greteman, A.J. (2019) "Raw Education: PrEP and the Ethics of Updating Sexual Education," in R. Varghese (ed) *Raw: PrEP, Pedagogy, and the Politics of Barebacking*, Regina: University of Regina Press, pp. 211–33.

Gross, N. (2009) "A Pragmatist Theory of Social Mechanisms," *American Sociological Review*, 74(3): 358–79.

Gumperz, J.J. (1982) *Discourse Strategies*, New York: Cambridge University Press.

Hacking, I. (2002) "How 'Natural' are 'Kinds' of Sexual Orientation?," *Law and Philosophy*, 21(1): 95–107.

Halperin, D.M. (2007) *What Do Gay Men Want?: An Essay on Sex, Risk, and Subjectivity*, Ann Arbor, MI: University of Michigan Press.

Hatzenbuehler, M.L., Phelan, J.C. and Link, B.G. (2013) "Stigma as a Fundamental Cause of Population Health Inequalities," *American Journal of Public Health*, 103(5): 813–21.

Herdt, G.H. (1997) *Same Sex, Different Cultures: Exploring Gay and Lesbian Lives*, Boulder, CO: Westview Press.

Irvine, J.T. (1985) "Status and Style in Language," *Annual Review of Anthropology*, 14(1): 557–81.

Jacquemet, M. (1996) *Credibility in Court: Communicative Practices in the Camorra Trials*, Cambridge: Cambridge University Press.

Jakobson, R. (1960) "Closing Statement: Linguistic and Poetics," in T.A. Sebeok (ed) *Style in Language*, Cambridge, MA: MIT Press, pp. 350–77.

Katz, J.D. (2007) *The Invention of Heterosexuality*, Chicago, IL: University of Chicago Press.

Katz, J.D. (2020) "Foreword," in A. Patterson and I. Read (eds) *The SHAPES of Epidemics and Global Disease*, Newcastle: Cambridge Scholars Publishing, pp. xv–xvii.

Klitzman, R. and Bayer, R. (2003) *Mortal Secrets: Truth and Lies in the Age of AIDS*, Baltimore, MD: Johns Hopkins University Press.

Konstan, D. (1994) *Sexual Symmetry: Love in the Ancient Novel and Related Genres*, Princeton, NJ: Princeton University Press.

Laqueur, T. (1990) *Making Sex: Body and Gender from the Greeks to Freud*, Cambridge, MA: Harvard University Press.

Link, B.G. and Phelan, J.C. (1995) "Social Conditions as Fundamental Causes of Disease," *Journal of Health and Social Behavior*, 35: 80–94.

Link, B.G. and Phelan, J.C. (2001) "Conceptualizing Stigma," *Annual Review of Sociology*, 27(1): 363–85.

Lotman, Y.M. (2000) *Universe of the Mind: A Semiotic Theory of Culture*, Bloomington, IN: Indiana University Press.

Lucy, J.A. (1993) *Reflexive Language: Reported Speech and Metapragmatics*, Cambridge: Cambridge University Press.

Mertz, E. (2007) "Semiotic Anthropology," *Annual Review of Anthropology*, 36(1): 337–57.

Mojola, S.A. (2014) *Love, Money, and HIV: Becoming a Modern African Woman in the Age of AIDS*, Oakland, CA: University of California Press.

Offer, C., Grinstead, O., Golstein, E., Mamary, E., Alvarado, N. et al. (2007) "Responsibility for HIV Prevention: Patterns of Attribution among HIV-seropositive Gay and Bisexual Men," *AIDS Education and Prevention*, 19(1): 24–35.

Parker, R. and Aggleton, P. (2003) "HIV and AIDS-related Stigma and Discrimination: A Conceptual Framework and Implications for Action," *Social Science and Medicine*, 57(1): 13–24.

Patil, V. (2018) "The Heterosexual Matrix as Imperial Effect," *Sociological Theory*, 36(1): 1–26.

Patton, M.Q. (1999) "Enhancing the Quality and Credibility of Qualitative Analysis," *Health Services Research*, 34(5 Part II): 1189–208.

Peirce, C.S. (1931–1958) *Collected Papers of Charles Peirce*, 8 vols, Cambridge, MA: Harvard University Press.

Plato (1999 [c. 385 BC]) *The Symposium*, trans. C. Gill, London: Penguin Books.

Race, K. (2001) "The Undetectable Crisis: Changing Technologies of Risk," *Sexualities*, 4(2): 167–89.

Race, K. (2015) "'Party and Play': Online Hook-up Devices and the Emergence of PNP Practices among Gay Men," *Sexualities*, 18(3): 253–75.

Sawyer, R.K. (2005) *Social Emergence: Societies as Complex Systems*, New York: Cambridge University Press.

Silverstein, M. (1976) "Shifters, Linguistic Categories and Cultural Description," in K. Basso and H. Selby (eds) *Meaning in Anthropology*, Albuquerque, NM: University of New Mexico Press, pp. 11–55.

Silverstein, M. (1993) "Metapragmatic Discourse and Metapragmatic Function," in J.A. Lucy (ed) *Reflexive Language: Reported Speech and Metapragmatics*, Cambridge, MA: Cambridge University Press, pp. 33–58.

Singer, M. and Clair, S. (2003) "Syndemics and Public Health: Reconceptualizing Disease in Bio-social Context," *Medical Anthropology Quarterly*, 17(4): 423–41.

Sobo, E.J. (1995) *Choosing Unsafe Sex: AIDS-risk Denial among Disadvantaged Women*, Philadelphia, PA: University of Pennsylvania Press.

Sontag, S. (2001) *Illness as Metaphor and AIDS and Its Metaphors*, New York: Picador.

Stall, R.D., Coates, T.J. and Hoff, C. (1988) "Behavioral Risk Reduction for HIV Infection among Gay and Bisexual Men," *American Psychologist*, 43(1): 878–85.

Steiner, P. (ed) (1982) *The Prague School: Selected Writings 1929–1946*, Austin, TX: University of Texas Press.

Tavory, I. and Swidler, A. (2009) "Condom Semiotics: Meaning and Condom Use in Rural Malawi," *American Sociological Review*, 74(2): 171–89.

Tavory, I. and Timmermans, S. (2014) *Abductive Analysis: Theorizing Qualitative Research*, Chicago, IL: University of Chicago Press.

Teunis, N. and Herdt, G. (eds) (2007) *Sexual Inequalities and Social Justice*, Berkeley, CA: University of California Press.

Treichler, P. (1987) "AIDS, Homophobia, and Biomedical Discourse: An Epidemic of Signification," *Cultural Studies*, 1(3): 263–305.

UNAIDS (2010) *Combination HIV Prevention: Tailoring and Coordinating Biomedical, Behavioural and Structural Strategies to Reduce New HIV Infections*. Available from www.unaids.org/en/resources/documents/2010/20101006_JC2007_Combination_Prevention_paper.

Waugh, L. (1982) "Marked and Unmarked: A Choice between Unequals in Semiotic Structure," *Semiotica*, 38(3/4): 299–318.

Wiley, N. (1988) "The Micro-Macro Problem in Social Theory," *Sociological Theory*, 6(2): 254–61.

Wolitski, R.J. and Bailey, C.J. (2005) "It Takes Two to Tango: HIV-positive Gay and Bisexual Men's Beliefs about their Responsibility to Protect Others from HIV Infection," in P. Halkitis, C. Gómez and R. Wolitski (eds) *HIV+ Sex: The Psychological and Interpersonal Dynamics of HIV Seropositive Gay and Bisexual Men's Relationships*, Washington, DC: American Psychological Association, pp. 147–62.

8

# Supremacy or Symbiosis? The Effect of Gendered Ideologies of the Transhuman versus Posthuman on Wearable Technology and Biodesign

*Elizabeth Wissinger*

In March 2021, Dolce and Gabbana (D&G) showed its women's fall/winter 21 collection in a windowless, audienceless, mirrored fantasia of flashing lights glancing off reflective surfaces. The video showed models sweeping down the runway in shiny metallic garb, glossy white robots rolling along beside them. One "MC" robot seemed to be running the show, strobing lights, and pulsing the music with dramatic sweeps of its humanoid hands. The COVID-19 pandemic may have nixed the customary live show, but not the futuristic exuberance of the presentation. Ostensibly informed by "robotics research and Artificial Intelligence," D&G's Instagram (@dolcegabbana, 3/1/21) claimed that this collection was "an attempt to reveal how technology and craftsmanship, two apparently different worlds" can come together. By eliding the notion that technology *is* craftsmanship, the post invokes a rift in signification that has far-reaching consequences.

The idea that high fashion and high tech are mutually exclusive has a long history. Fashion, traditionally associated with the feminine, is a luxury world of silk, fur, and leather. The "hand" of a fabric, its feel to the touch, is just as important as how it drapes or looks on the body. The notion of "handmade" is also highly valued, evoking images of patient seamstresses painstakingly beading a one-of-a-kind creation. As the organizers of the 2016 Manus x Machina show at the Metropolitan Museum of Art aptly pointed out, the "oppositional relationship" of the "hand/machine dichotomy" (Bolton and

Cope, 2016, p. 9) has governed the culture of fashion since the birth of haute couture in the mid-19th century.

While the curators of the Machina show ultimately asserted that this dichotomy is false, its semiotic power remains. The apparently "different worlds" of machine technology versus human-centered craft is deeply felt in the culture of fashion, profoundly shaping its practices. The symbolic resonance of this dichotomy runs deep, in part because it dovetails so seamlessly with broader divides cleaving the culture at large—the traditional oppositions of soft and hard sciences; nature and culture; emotion and reason; female and male. This chapter explores how these symbolic divides also resonate through the utopian dreams of the transhuman, and the pragmatics of the posthuman, reasoning frameworks that animate design practice in the fields of wearable technology—for example, computational devices worn on the body—and biodesign, the field of design that employs living organisms or biologically grown outputs in its designs' functioning. In the situated practices of wearable tech and biodesign, the symbolic resonance of each field has inflected how, and which, materials and objects to-be-worn are designed.

Drawing on interviews and participant observation of designers of embodied technology, my analysis employs "design sociology" to explore how different constellations of associations inflect the "discursive and material practices which professional designers enact" (Lupton, 2018, pp. 1–2). Design sociology examines practitioner culture, to analyze and critique the social and technical contexts of designs before they are produced and reach consumers. The interrogation seeks to head off problematic practices before they are embedded in products and deployed in consumer settings. It is cognizant of the science and technology studies' claim that "there is a social component in all knowledge" (Bloor, 1976, p. 82) and the human–computer interaction tenet that "there are social dimensions to every physical context and social conditions for every physical aspect, particularly when considering design and technology" (Rousi and Alanen, 2021, p. 53).

Design sociology is also deeply informed by feminist materialism, and its feminist practice of developing

> an approach where we recognize the natural and cultural worlds, science and society and politics as being inextricably interconnected—co-constituted and co-produced. We want to develop a feminist practice that does not approach matter through the binaries of natures and cultures, but also proceeds with a recognition of the 'uneven epistemological weight' of certain ways of knowing. (Roy and Subramaniam, 2016, p. 38)

This "uneven epistemological weight" accorded different ways of knowing is particularly important—my respondents described not only gender divides in personnel, but also gendered symbolic dichotomies governing technology design practice.

Exploring the underlying symbolic ramifications of design practice in the wearable tech and biodesign fields revealed how gendered meanings played across people and practices, shaping design trajectories and real-world outcomes that reflect not only technological and material constraints on possibilities and design, but also what sociologists and communication scholars Peter Nagy and Gina Neff (2015) have referred to as the 'imagined affordances' of those designs. "At stake here are the very lenses we use to see ourselves and others" (Neff and Nafus, 2016, p. 9). As such, the design culture my respondents described suggested how gender inflects "expectations for technology that are not fully realized in conscious, rational knowledge but are nonetheless concretized or materialized in socio-technical systems" (Nagy and Neff, 2015, p. 1) in a manner that led to diverging design outcomes.

While the symbolic impact of gender differences on design culture and practice may seem to delineate the intuitively obvious, what matters here is the way my respondents used this symbolic gendered dichotomy to explain their own doing—of design, of their sense of the body they design for, and the goal of their making. These inflections shaped practitioner notions of what a body is and is good for, producing quite different outcomes. The lens employed by practitioners to see the human body is key to understanding the symbolic differences that govern much of design practice and outcomes. Seeking to enmesh the body with data-gathering technology, merging the body with technology ostensibly to perfect it, can nonetheless give rise to outward-turning data broadcasting that lays the groundwork for damaging data exploitation, for instance. Alternatively, exploring cooperative designs that create symbiosis between wearer and environment, while still providing self-knowledge by means of haptic feedback that is not necessarily wired or interfaced with the broader datasphere or providing comfort and knowledge that the material being worn has not created harm in its production, results in gadgets and garments that interface with the body in ways that are arguably less exploitative of human tendencies and natural resources. My respondents may not have employed these terms, yet the gendered inflections of their practice can be traced to paradigmatic concerns within conceptualizations of the transhuman and posthuman. On one hand, transhuman practices idealize merging technology with the body. On the other, posthuman practices imbricate humans with their environments to minimize harm to humans and nonhumans alike.

Technology design is supposedly as neutral as technology itself. Yet these findings indicate that the gender of both the practitioner and the practice affected outcomes in a manner that belies this notion. My analysis builds on ongoing findings in critical race and technology studies, which pinpoint how seemingly neutral design nonetheless comes with "socially embedded assumptions about race, gender, and sexuality that become encoded and perpetuated into hardware and software" (Schwartz and Neff, 2019, p. 2407). The transfer of embedded assumptions stems in part from the lack of diversity in science and design settings, which can lead to biased or discriminatory design outputs from these sectors (Nakamura, 2014; Levy, 2015; Lupton, 2015; Marwick, 2015; Neff and Nafus, 2016; Massanari, 2017; Sanders, 2017; Wissinger, 2016, 2017; Broussard, 2018; Noble, 2018; Rosner, 2018; Benjamin, 2019; McIlwain, 2019).

The analysis calls on the idea of "gendered affordances," that is, "social affordances that enable different users to take different actions based on the gendered social and cultural repertoires available to users and technology designers" (Schwartz and Neff, 2019, p. 2407), to sketch out how the practitioners I've studied draw on not only gendered social and cultural repertoires within their design environments, but also gendered technological practices, such as coding versus knitting, data broadcasting versus data privacy, and visual versus haptic, whose dichotomous associations and semiotic resonances inform how they are adopted, for whom, and why. Thus, in wearable tech and biodesign, not only the gender of the practitioner, but also the gender of the practice matters when seeking outcomes that value either transhuman or posthuman ends. A sociosemiotic lens allows us to see how gender maps onto the values we associate with various materials and practices of technology as it intersects with bodies, along with the objectives of certain actors in these fields.

## Wearable tech and biodesign

Both fashionable wearable tech and biodesign are "human-centered design." This concept has various permutations (Retail Info Systems, 2017). Here, it denotes gadgets and garments to be worn on the body.

From smart fibers and tattoos, biosensing devices and implants, networked jewelry, or an LED-encrusted dress, wearable technology generally denotes e-textiles and garments, connected biosensing devices, and wearable computers. Functions range from eminently practical, like tracking heart rate or counting steps, to utterly fantastical, when, for instance, a dress responds to biometric indicators of interest or attraction by gradually becoming more transparent (Wipprecht, 2011). Experimental sweat analyzing biofueled clothing and devices may eventually wield the power of microbiology to augment health, seek wellness, and promote a better environment. Generally, wearable technology design values perfecting the body, making its functions transparent and manageable, while maximizing it for optimum performance (Wissinger, 2017).

Rather than total control and domination over the body, the value of thinking about and cooperating with organisms, humans or otherwise, is central to many biodesign practitioners' design ethos. While its exact definition and concrete parameters are the subject of some debate, the term "biodesign" commonly refers to the practice of design with living organisms. As biodesign pioneer and curator Will Myers (2018, p. 8) has explained: "Biodesign harnesses biological processes for use in design … [it] refers specifically to the incorporation of living organisms or ecosystems as essential components … of function of the finished work." The term is a source of some contention, partly because it gets easily mired in debates about genetically modified organisms (GMOs) and the idea that we should not try to play god. Consequently, Orkan Telhan, well-known proponent of biodesign, interdisciplinary artist, designer, and researcher, argued, in his opening remarks for a recent design sprint, for the term "biological design:"

> It's about understanding the logic, the logos … so we understand the needs of other species to grow them for design. This is a design practice aimed not only at the needs of humans to exploit [organisms] but to find new ways to work with them. For a fashion designer, [biological design asks] how can you change your materiality and all of the amazing things that are available in nature? How can you think *with* them?

Biodesign in fashion ranges from one-off speculative designs created in the lab, to commercially produced, splashy, high-end collaborations. Living organisms have been incorporated into an MIT prototyped workout shirt in which microbes responded to the wearer's sweat by changing shape, thereby opening up cooling vents along the shirt's back (Chu, 2017). Designer Natsai Audrey Chieza is using a wild strain of soil-dwelling organism's naturally secreted pigment for dyeing textiles such as silk (Feldman, 2019; Faber Futures, 2021).

Early biodesign pioneer Suzanne Lee grew a bomber jacket from green tea and microbes to showcase materials for growing with biological methods (Lee, 2011; Levitt, 2011). Others have experimented with spider silk, combining growing compounds with spider DNA by means of synthetic biology, to create fully biodegradable, durable fabrics grown from sugar, yeast, and water (Paton, 2020; Bolt Threads, https://boltthreads.com). Mycelium, a mushroom-derived, weblike component that can be tanned into a leather-like material, has inspired several startups, with names like Mylo, Mycoworks, and other references to their source material (Paton, 2020; Hahn, 2021a, 2021b; Modern Meadow, www.modernmeadow.com; MycoWorks, www.mycoworks.com). While wearable technology is common, biodesign's commercial viability has yet to be proven.

I analyze the gendered affordances of these fields of design by drawing on theoretical conceptions that parse out the symbolic and material ramifications of embodied technologies, to examine how "humans are inextricably intertwined in the physical as well as the symbolic contexts in which they live" (Lupton, 2020, p. 51). Technological embodiment describes the way bodies are sensed, perceived, and lived through communication devices, clothing, biometric gadgets, distributed networks, interfaces, and biological interdependencies.

To explore technological embodiment, I take a feminist materialist stance, shaped by theoretical legacies from Spinoza, Deleuze and Guattari, Latour, and Merleau-Ponty. Of particular interest is the feminist materialist conceit that, as sociologist Deborah Lupton (2020, p. 51) iterates, the "post-structuralist emphasis on language, discourse, and symbolic representation is enhanced by a turn toward the material: human embodied practices and interactions with objects, space, and place." From this angle, the body must always be taken in context, as a "material semiotic node," which technofeminist Donna Haraway (1990, p. 200) famously theorized as a cyborg emanating from a confluence of human, nonhuman, and symbolic factors. Working with my respondents' chosen symbolic classification of their actions, my analysis maps out how masculine-identified practices tended toward individualistic, atomic, instrumental/rational, transhumanist ends; while feminine-associated practices aligned more with cooperative, inclusive, emotional/haptic, posthuman-oriented goals.

This chapter explores the wide-ranging consequences of meaning systems within two cultures of design. The first section will sketch out in broad terms the dichotomies governing how each type of design practice is perceived. The binaries laid out in this section emanate from a sense of the field developed over several years of work observing the wearable technology and biodesign communities. These dynamic oppositions sketch the terrain of meaning within which goals of action, and the value accorded to them, are shaped. The second section traces the masculine versus the feminine in respondents' descriptions of their own enterprise, which fall roughly along the lines of transhuman versus posthuman conceptions of the body. These conceptions shape how practitioners envision their design goals, and evidence ideologies informing what gets produced in these domains and for whom. The third section explores how gendered aspects of different significations play out in real terms with respect to design practices, practitioners, for example who is considered an expert, and how assumptions about gender influence choices of design method. These divides are not neatly aligned, however. Respondents arguably push back against what semiotician Ferdinand de Saussure (1986 [1916], p . 13) has called the "social crystallization" of the "necessary conventions" from which meaning is derived in "collectivity," which can sometimes be a messy process.

This creative misreading of Saussure's sense of the system's coherence can elucidate the social crystallization of meaning in action, as these practitioners negotiate the boundaries of the dynamic interchange between humans and embodied technologies in their design communities. Highlighting assumptions about what a body is and what it is good for draws out the causal factors of the data exploitation tendencies in many wearable tech designs, as opposed to the cooperative interdependencies centering much feminist wearable technology and biodesign practice.

## Methods and messy taxonomies

As sociologist Jorge Fontdevila (2020, p. 661) has argued, lived taxonomies refract established binaries and complicate them. He noted that the "dangers of closed classificatory systems" solidify identities in limiting ways. He explored how his respondents negotiated the complexity of sexual desire within rigid heteronormative binaries. Similarly, my respondents negotiate the complexity of material limitations and design exigencies within the rigid binaries of the masculine and feminine, from which emanate oppositions governing their design practices. These oppositions were gleaned from interviews, fieldnotes, participant observation, and analysis of the presentation of each realm in media treatments, ranging from Kickstarter pages and product websites, to established industry publications.

Ethnographic evidence regarding wearable technology was drawn from attendance at fashion tech summits, tech conferences, trade shows, and meet-ups. The 24 interview respondents included fashion and tech designers, intellectual property/patent attorneys working in the field of biotech, synthetic biologists, biodesigners, biofabricators, and wearables designers who engage with biological materials.

Semiotic scholar Valentin Volosinov (1973, p. 98) once observed that "the laws of language generation are 'sociological' laws." The sociological aspects of the language I identify here emerged from a "sense of the field" developed over several years of observation and thematic analysis of interviews. When respondents invoked binaries to explain their design practice, they frequently began with the broad category of *masculine* and *feminine*. They used this opposition to describe everything from their own gender to the connotations of scientific approaches they chose in their work.

Even when players in the field delineated the goals and outcomes of design in their practice in technical terms, notable symbolic oppositions emerged from this gendered divide. Symbolic oppositions describing concrete scientific and design practices revealed how gendered worldviews and everyday practices inflected technological practice. Within the broad categorization of feminine and masculine, respondents relied on specific subcategories to delineate their practice. The reader might be familiar with the semiotic connotations of female and male, such as nature/culture; private/public; low tech/high tech. The terms did not map perfectly, but patterns emerged along thematic lines. Roughly associating the biological with femininity and the digital with masculinity led to telling observations of selves and practices that differentiated design goals. Taking feminine first, and masculine second, the oppositions found in the field, and in interviews, lined up with biological/digital; analog/binary; unknowable/transparent; and energy harnessing versus consuming; the posthuman versus the transhuman. Some respondents were particularly interested in helping me understand the difference in approach to design that these meanings pulled forth. Their evocation of gender difference fed directly into practices such as working *with* materials as opposed to working *on* them; conceiving the body as organic versus the body as machine; while juicy or gross processes contrasted with dry and clean technologies. Put differently, these symbolic oppositions nonetheless shaped the concrete scientific practices and design outcomes for the designers I encountered.

Positing these taxonomies helped my respondents explain the lived meanings associated with design and innovation practices. Mapping the organizing principles of masculine and feminine onto complex categories of seemingly neutral action revealed how technological design is inflected by social concerns.

## I'm not in marketing! Gendered assumptions of expertise

At professional gatherings, hanging out at summits and conferences, and in interviews, respondents eagerly spoke of the clear gender disparities between hard and soft sciences, engineering and biology, experienced in their working lives. Perceived gender, for instance, governed who was considered an "expert" in professional settings. Several respondents reported using clothing and language to "signal" their status as engineers in meetings and professional gatherings, to be taken seriously and not dismissed as an irrelevant rep from marketing. They described the paucity of women engineers and the ignorance of women's perspectives in these design spaces. They experienced sexist assumptions about who they were, and found these assumptions embedded in the areas of design they encountered.

My respondents evinced the male association with engineering clearly and frequently. A wearable technology instructor and designer described how she and her female colleagues combatted the assumptions that they were "in marketing," detailing the steps they took to be recognized as a fellow engineer:

> All of my female engineering colleagues had these strategies so that when we went to a meeting with people we didn't know, how do you immediately inform people that you are not in marketing and that you are an engineer? What signals do you have to send? … sometimes

it's the way you dress, and it sometimes is the way you talk. When it happens over and over and over again, it gets quite old really fast. Fashion and all these outward signals become important when you're a female engineer.

Another explained that she and her fellow engineers were not "girly," but did alter their speaking patterns in order to "be taken seriously:"

> None of us would call ourselves girly but we all have to try to adopt the way men talk about work and behave in meetings in order to be taken seriously as engineers or to be seen as an engineer at all. If people don't know you, they always assume you're in marketing.

Another female-identified engineer and designer did not mince words when describing the problem: "In development spaces, we still have a lack of balance in gender. They're predominately male engineers and they're not necessarily thinking about women's issues or from a woman's perspective." A male respondent from a wearable tech design hardware company echoed this concern. He explained that many design companies use their existing cadre of engineers to create the product, and then call on focus groups to vet it after the fact. He felt strongly that addressing gendered design issues called for more inclusiveness, integrating women "into the design process" at the outset, not "just some women sitting in a room, not just paying for some research," but rather: "If they are designing for women, then you might want to have them involved and get their feedback. You need women on the team; not just one but several. Sometimes they see things differently."

Whether or not the women at the table can "see things differently" simply by nature of their gender socialization, the idea that there is a female perspective that can shape the design process is key.

## The visual and the haptic

Gender composition in these fields is documented and consonant with what my respondents perceived (Cech et al, 2011; Trafton, 2014; Bonham and Stefan, 2017; Cheryan et al, 2017). In addition to gender imbalance, perceptions of gendered practice also came into play. Digging deeper into how they imagined their "doings" when creating and innovating revealed how gendered meanings filtered my respondents' approach to materials, their function, and, ultimately, which problems they sought to solve with their designs. The difference between the visual and the haptic figured prominently in these discussions.

In popular understandings, men are supposedly more visual than women. Psychological explanations derived from Sigmund Freud (1955) and Simone de Beauvoir (2011) track this visuality to male rationality, insofar as their sexual identification is concretely defined by the body parts they can see. Groups of thinkers who can loosely be termed "postmodernists" have had a field day with the notion that the visual/rational dominated much of Western discourse (Jay, 1993). Similarly, "scopophilia," the love and elevation of vision to privilege it over other senses, was seen as a direct outcome of reifying rationality and the power of logical thinking. The primacy of the visual in achieving objectivity was blamed for much masculine scientific myopia when it came to grasping the complex nature of the world, and the tendency to essentialize in ways that were exclusionary (Harding, 1986; Hilary, 1986).

Donna Haraway (1988, p. 581) and other technoscientific feminists have critiqued this stance as falsely godlike, the "god trick" position giving the illusion of complete dominance and control. In real terms, many digital technologies incorporating screens arguably privilege sight, with its inherent separation between perceiver and perceived. The haptic, the tactile, nonverbal, bodily senses have been less valued in digital wearable technology design. The design dominance of the screen, and externalizing data for display, can arguably track onto this realm's masculinist and transhuman associations. Many of my female-identified respondents, however, looked beyond this need for screen technology, with its controllable inputs that effect visual outputs, while broadcasting data to be gathered and parsed. They were more interested in design coded feminine, the inward, the private, the sensed, rather than seen, ideas associated with the posthuman.

This difference in focus stemmed in part from the marginalized femme-identified status of the designers with whom I spoke. Arguably, this feminine association led these designers to rely on a different paradigm from the ideas generally governing wearable technology, and which are still in flux in the field of biodesign.

## A bizarre assault ... it's really sick, especially when we're talking about body data

My respondents' openness to feminine associations led them to design choices resonating with an ethos of cooperation, co-creation, and interdependence. These choices steered outcomes away from bodily optimization and exploitation toward more haptic, comfort-oriented, and humble goals. Significantly, the common, arguably masculinist-oriented digitization technologies that optimize for human perfection were not the prevalent model for the feminist wearable tech designers and biodesigners I interviewed. Technology should be designed to engage with the human body's interiority. This theme emerged across the responses gathered from feminist designers in the field of wearable technology and biodesign. They were at pains to contrast these "feminine" design practices with masculinist applications aimed at mastery and control.

At stake here are wearables aimed at "conspicuous wellness" (Neff and Nafus, 2016, p. 127), designed for mastery of human foibles by means of technology, aligning them with the masculinist side of the dichotomies my respondents invoked. The popular Oura Ring, for instance, clearly aims for bodily mastery and empowerment. The company website claims: "The new Oura Ring monitors your heart rate around the clock, giving you the insights you need to make the most out of your days and nights. Oura never forgets to check in on your body to confirm and optimize your predictions." The website (https://ouraring.com) promises that wearers tracking their sleep, activity, and stress levels will "realize" their "potential." In seeking to be fully optimized, users end up being fully datafied.

The privacy of data, and the body's role in data gathering, were key to the feminist wearable tech designers' conceptions, prioritizing ostensibly feminine, haptic, and inward-looking goals. Regarding data exploitation in wearable tech design, for instance, a speculative wearables designer observed:

> so much of the business models are based on selling data. You can get free this and free that or we can lower the price on the hardware because we're going to be making money on the data. I mean, it's really sick, especially when we're talking about body data.

Several of my respondents critiqued the exploitative nature of designs for gathering bodily data. Another wearable tech user experience designer described these practices as invasive, an "assault" on the body:

> Technology has this habit of taking us away from … There's this very bizarre thing that's going on with wearable technology and the way we're integrating with the body where technology is both invading our space and invading our bodies. I use this word "invading" because I think it is a little bit of an assault if you look at the spectrum of where we've been in humanity and how much we've allowed to influence the body in these ways on a consistent, regular basis … I just think that in the form of data, it has this way of still not creating a type of intimacy that I think is one with the body, when we're really connecting to our body. We are datafying everything and then it becomes this externalized mental thinking process as opposed to a real connection itself.

The assault of datafication resonates with transhuman ideals. Examining the values underlying practice helps uncover the Volosinovian "ideological threads" woven through design discourse. Transhumanism, in general terms, values the optimizable body, viewing the body as a machine that can be tweaked to achieve perfection. An anthropocentric technocentric human enhancement ideology, transhumanism is a continuation of Western European enlightenment ideals, which privilege rationality and suggest that science and technology can innovate around physical limits and social inequities. It reifies hierarchies and binaries of human/nonhuman, man/woman, while adopting a managerial stance in relation to subaltern bodies, regions, environmental resources. It uses "posthuman" to describe the end stage of transhumanism, an ultimate fusion of humanity and technology (Miller and Wissinger, 2018). Transhumanism's endgame is to achieve a "post" human state, a perfect union between body and machine in a techno-utopian conglomeration where machines overcome the weakness of the flesh.

My respondents claimed they push back against these transhuman tendencies using feminine associated practices. To design away from data externalization, for instance, a speculative designer prototyped a wearable—the "Embodisuit"—a coat that gathered data and sent it inward, rather than "harvesting" it to broadcast to corporations:

> The thing that was really driving me is it seems like almost all wearables are harvesting data from the body and sending them to corporations. This project for me was a direct critique on that and a reversal of that dynamic. Instead of your information being harvested and sent to another place for them to analyze and make recommendations to you and send you notifications, this is a wearable that was designed to take data from elsewhere and then send it to your body. Instead of data going out, data's coming in. So that you are really the one who's more … You're increasing your own awareness and become … It's about empowering yourself.

Reversing the dynamic of harvesting bodily data to be sent out empowered the wearer through increased awareness of their surroundings, of pollution exposure, or being tracked. This design focused on the feminine, toward inwardness, intimacy, and privacy, to oppose the masculinist transhuman goals of resourcing the body as so much data to be parsed and sold for corporate profit.

The masculinist, scopophilic, visually oriented side of tech design employs atomistic, context-ignoring ideas, which ignore long-term effects on the environment. A feminist biodesigner bemoaned how these technologies get a lot of press, yet a "sexy image of a glowing tree" ignores questions of "what it means to design living matter," saying:

> [You need to] … make projects that actually critique and challenge the status quo, without just getting swept along. So, for me, glowing trees are a real problem because they're often described saying "Oh,

this will be really sustainable, we won't need streetlights." And … both sides do it, ignoring all the other questions around that, and you just get a sexy image of a glowing tree, kinda Avatar style … why is it sustainable and is it possible? That's all ignored. And it doesn't really get to the bottom of questioning what it means to design living matter and should we be designing and releasing it on a large scale.

They described how "sexy" or "blinky" designs often won the lion's share of funding, claiming that money has been thrown at the ostensibly masculinist inflected show-and-tell goals of wearable tech, that focus on displays, lighting up, and putting screens on the body, which dominate the press. But what about how a wearable feels, one speculative designer asked:

It should be … about how something feels. It's very difficult to communicate that through a video, and [tech publications] *Wired* and *Gizmodo* and *Fast Company*, they're all … They want to write a nice article with a great video that captures people's attention. But a video is not the best way to talk about what it feels like to *wear* this wearable … we're seeing more wearables that have this, "I'm going to tell everybody what I'm feeling on a display." I see that project all the time. … A lot of interactions that are possible with a wearable don't communicate well over video, so you don't read about them.

This designer's work prioritized the haptic and tactile, the sense of touch in a body. The ostensibly non-rational feminine side of the symbolic binaries within which my respondents designed was an experiential, rather than rational/logical parsing of biometrics for data analysis. In contrast to the transhuman, masculinist associations of design in most wearable technology, the study's feminist wearable technology designers and biodesigners hewed to a posthuman design ethos.

## The posthuman

The posthuman interprets the human body as post-anthropocentric, via a critical philosophy that acknowledges the multiplicity of human selfhood, intermingled with data technologies (Braidotti, 2013). It incorporates critiques from postcolonial, feminist, critical race, and science and technology studies. It rejects humanist perspectives in favor of "the recognition of non-human dignity" to reach a "larger interconnected picture, which does not stand on human supremacy" (Ferrando, 2020, p. 3). Rejecting the goal of human mastery in favor of interdependence and cooperation, it seeks to level hierarchies and decenter the human; making room for the nonhuman in its analysis as well as accounting for power in the differential production of bodies. Drawing from non-essentialist theories of the cyborg, hybridity, and relationality (Haraway, 1990; Barad, 2007), it informs a design ethos valuing the haptic, openness to the unplanned, accidents, and cooperation. These values were cited by the feminist wearable tech designers and biodesigners I interviewed.

Eschewing designs that were not necessarily "sexy," visual, or easy to photograph resonated with my respondents' ability to embrace practices that were neither high tech, nor exciting. They were open to ideas for on-body technologies employing feminine-associated practices such as knitting and weaving. A femme-identified wearable tech designer I spoke to observed: "Knitting is really, really technical but has not been taken seriously. But it is real engineering."

One does not have to be female to think in this way, but rather adopt a perspective disassociating design practices from the strong signification systems from which they are normally emerge. One experimental wearable tech designer worked with knitting and weaving to circumnavigate the expense and production problems of wearable's dependence on thin layers of silicon embedded with "circuitry, sensors and microprocessors, stacked like a layer cake" (Kelley, 2021). Leaving aside traditional associations organizing fabrication techniques into technical and not technical, this researcher found feminine-associated knitting and weaving could solve bedeviling design problems of discomfort and bulky energy sources. Leveling hierarchies privileging one design practice as more "scientific" than another allowed a solution to longstanding problems to appear. Eschewing gendered perceptions of engineering silicon chips versus humble practices of knitting or weaving shaped design decisions toward these posthuman ends.

## Cogs, machines, and circuits versus bodies, guts, and insides

To distance themselves from transhumanist technologies that render the body a dataset to be manipulated or controlled, the biodesigners would sometimes invoke the bogey of the "gadget." For one synthetic biologist, the gadget was a strong signifier, which distanced her work from the digital. As she explained: "it's funny because I don't work on wearables at all ... I'm not really into gadgets. [In our work] we're kind of trying to say like well, maybe the intersection between the body and technology is different than electronics and the body and that kind of gadget."

She also called on the male/female binary quite blatantly, to explain which areas of her field are "coded female:"

> Daisy and I would be on panels together sometimes, and we were like the floofy ones who are gonna talk about art and society. And then

… the guys there … would be on the panel with us to explain what synthetic biology is, like, the technical stuff … It is certainly … coded female, that, like, there are the hard sciences that are, like, oh, I have the data and the facts. And I can engineer whatever I want. And then there's the women who worry about how it looks and how it affects our society.

Similar to testimony from wearable tech designers, biodesign's gender composition as a field surfaced frequently in interviews with biodesigners. The biodesigners, however, eagerly emphasize the female-friendly nature of the biodesign community:

The fact that the leading people in this space are female, I think is really important to note. … I think biology is, I don't have any evidence of this, but biology is notably more female and there is lots written about that, I think. And there is a greater … far more women doing biology than other sciences.

They contrasted this female friendliness with attitudes colloquially known "tech bro," which they encountered in engineering and traditional synthetic biology settings.

The "tech bro" stance was keenly evident in the experience of this biodesigner, who related that "the engineering side … is a bit, a very male dominated space." To elaborate, she cited the mindset that sees the body as a mere vehicle for scientific innovation, a "portal" as she put it. She told a story of how she felt like a "flesh donor" during an "extreme" conversation at a conference in her field. While he did not use the term, this scientist arguably worked from a transhumanist mindset, in which the body can be fully engineered and controlled. The bodies in question were cows' bodies; the topic was ideas for artificial insemination. She told the story of how the mostly male audience didn't blink, however, when faced with a "surprising" and "extreme" depiction of how the body can be manipulated for scientific ends:

I've encountered some extraordinary things over time, as always … At a conference where a male scientist was talking about encapsulating bull sperm to inseminate cows more efficiently … this particular scientist said, "Well, you know," something along these lines … "the vagina is not a one-way street. You can put things in and take them out—technically, the uterus is outside the body" … I sat there, and I looked around … and I counted less than 10 women, it was probably 10% women or less, in the room. And I was left feeling, like, whoa I didn't know I was just a flesh donor … It just was such an extraordinary …

> he was talking about cows, he wasn't talking about women … It just … it was so casual. He was so distanced as a scientist, in thinking about the body in that way, that it was just a portal. It was really, really, really, surprising. But there was this moment where … no one objected or, no one … there was no, sort of, gasp. It was just me going, huh, and one other … and the other women in the room and one guy I know who is gay who also noticed it and was not a scientist. So, there's moments like that.

Thinking about the body as a portal is an identifiably transhumanist point of view. No one objected to or remarked on what he was saying due to the dearth of women in the room; but also these statements evidenced a cultural mindset in which a scientist can refer to the vagina as "a street," and the comment goes unremarked. My respondents often sought to contrast their practice against this type of masculinist mindset. Arguably, the perceived female dominance of the biodesign field, coupled with the desire to reject the "tech bro" approach, helped them embrace ideas that tended toward the posthuman, the uncontrolled, private, and cognizant of interdependence between humans and nonhumans.

A well-known female biodesigner, for instance, famously made the rounds of the synthetic biology conference circuit with a steel case full of multicolored poo. The idea was that health problems could be detected by introducing biologically engineered components producing detectably different fecal hues. The project was named, tongue firmly in cheek, E. chromi (Pavlus, 2011). Speaking to me via Skype from her sunny London kitchen, she told me the idea was sensational because,

> we … you know, it wasn't a common way to talk about what synthetic biology could do. No one was talking about poo in the microbiome in that way. You're talking about cogs and machines and circuits, and we're talking about shit and our bodies and our guts and, inside us. And private spaces and private acts.

This statement richly invokes the dynamic oppositions I found in the field. The powerful contrast between the clean and controlled cog or circuit, with the messy, smelly, colored poo clearly delineated very different values. The fact that the poo was "engineered" by the somewhat unpredictable behavior of bacteria and used intimate bodily waste to gain health knowledge associated with the domestic, private, and personal clearly indicated that this researcher operated from a different mindset than the one that produces circuits, cogs, and gadgets.

For biodesigners, seeing differently was a favorite mantra. For them, biodesign can change the world because biodesigners have a profoundly different vision of it. Practical and material limitations do play a role in how biodesigners imagine their goals, but biodesign culture exhibits a marked openness to the unplanned, accidental, and cooperative. Feminist wearable technology designers and biodesigners often cited these values. One researcher I met at a Community Bio Summit at MIT, for instance, explained that she found the source for her biogrown fabrics "in the garbage" at her lab in Buenos Aires. Her professed goal was to "design differently," and she passionately described this practice at her poster session:

> It's a mindset, a paradigm shift in which the designer can no longer dictate from the top down. There has to be room for the organism to respond and do what it is going to do. Sometimes it doesn't grow. You can't make it just do what you want it to do, but that is the process of designing, you design with it. We are used to being in control but in this process, you have to give that up. They are living organisms that have their own process.

The highly esteemed value in the biodesign community is cooperation with organisms, giving up control rather than top-down design. This shift toward profound humility has not been a common ethos in masculinist-leaning transhumanist designs. As one panelist at a 2018 Biofabricate gathering explained, "when we look at microbes, we don't tend to think of them as partners for creativity." Another biodesigner proclaimed from the stage of an event celebrating biodesign at the New York City Kickstarter headquarters: "We are collaborating with the organisms. We are not telling them what to do. We have to work with them and respond to what they bring to the process."

A similar message from the stage of the Biodesign Challenge was clear: "Cells are NOT machines. DNA is NOT a programming language. Cells are analog and imperfect self-replicators. We are decades away from engineering bacteria the way the analogy would have us think—Forget control! We have been extremely successful with cooperation!" As they would have it, biodesign must reject the top-down model if it is to have a meaningful effect on embodied technologies moving forward.

As these practitioners were at pains to point out, one must work with the cells, not on them, a mantra I heard at many biodesign gatherings and summits. In practice, on-body biodesign technology frequently involves genetic manipulation, tweaking of cells to grow in ways the designer wants. This synthetic biology is at the heart of the pigment producing algae employed by Natalie Chieza's Faber Futures to dye silk, or the fermented fibers grown into spider silk-like cellulose, called Microsilk, produced by Bolt Threads (https://boltthreads.com), which Stella McCartney has woven into high-profile athletic garments (Paton, 2020).

There are key differences in the structure of the field of practice, however, when biology is involved. The perceived gender composition of the field, coupled with the mindset and design stance adopted by practitioners regardless of their gender identity, could lead to different outcomes. The problems with wearable technology are fairly well established, but biodesign may circumnavigate these. My respondents' community values and adoption of a posthumanist stance allows more consideration of the context-specific and long-term effects of their designs. As a female speculative wearable technology designer observed:

> Even if I'm not actually working with microbes I'm thinking about privacy, who's in power, who's vulnerable, what is the interaction design that … What is the interaction that we should be aiming for? You could prototype that in various ways. You don't have to be the person to invent the thing that goes into production. But you do have to think about how do you communicate the concerns early, and how do you communicate the alternatives early—while there's still time to influence the trajectory.

Is there time to influence the trajectory? Biodesigners' values of collaboration, cooperation, and letting go have not dampened corporate and scientific enthusiasm for developing it for profit. Limiting cultural attitudes baked into accepted design mindsets and practices threaten biodesign culture with long-term, unanticipated, detrimental outcomes on the field's potential.

A head of innovation at a synthetic design incubator explained that biodesign's language of empowerment and decentralization could mask far more mercenary goals:

> Then there's a community—certainly in biology; that's what I know best—of people who are wanting to do science in non-institutional spaces … I have some problems with a lot of the rhetoric though, because it can be like garage biotech but with like a Silicon Valley theme to it. Like, oh, we'll start the next big thing out of our labs. And so, in that case, it feels less like we're actually empowering people. They're using this language about empowerment and democratization, but what they really want is to be the next Steve Jobs.

Can a difference in vision produce the results biodesigners promise? A recent study of the viability of biodesign for fashion found that biotech and synthetic biology-derived textiles threaten to produce new forms of biowaste, and threaten the livelihoods of workers engaged in traditional textile production (Fibershed and ETC Group, 2018).

Critical and engaged study of the cultures of design from which biodesigned embodied technologies are emerging can elucidate the "imagined affordances" of the technology (Nagy and Neff, 2015) that facilitate more equitable and earth-friendly designs. As communication scholars Bucher and Helmond (2018, p. 6) have aptly observed, it is technology designers "who have the power to enable and constrain certain action possibilities through their design choices." My respondents were keenly aware of this world shaping power; expressing hope that their practice may lead the way to a more sustainable future.

## Conclusion: Why semiotics?

As Valentin Volosinov (1973, p. 19) reminded us, "Countless ideological threads running through all areas of social intercourse register effect in the world." These threads inform perceptions of the human body's inter-imbrication with technology, and shape what technology should be developed. Semiotic analysis highlights metaphors for technological embodiment, which affects what gets made, for whom, and why. This chapter examined designers' ideas to highlight semiotic connotations' impact on practical outcomes. Clearly, symbolic resonances shape the modes of technological embodiment for which my respondents design. A semiotic analysis bridges the gaps between sociological, media/communication, feminist, and fashion studies analyses to show how signifying factors deeply affect designers' imaginations of constraints and functionalities, with outcomes as much a product of signification systems as they are of science.

Analysis of these fields' gendered affordances called on the idea that "humans are inextricably intertwined in the physical as well as the symbolic contexts in which they live" (Lupton, 2020, p. 51). I relied on the feminist materialist conceit that, as Deborah Lupton (2020, p. 51) iterates, the "post-structuralist emphasis on language, discourse, and symbolic representation is enhanced by a turn toward the material: human embodied practices and interactions with objects, space, and place." The body must always be taken in context, as a "material semiotic node," which Donna Haraway (1990, p. 200) famously theorized as a cyborg emanating from a confluence of human, nonhuman, and symbolic factors.

This book's central argument, that the "discipline of sociology … needs to engage with semiosis mediation rigorously" addresses sociologists' notable hesitation to employ semiotic methods in sociological inquiry. The discipline-defining promise of empiricism's untrammeled access to reality partly explains this hesitation. The exigencies of symbolic analysis may also be to blame. How can one conduct analysis of fast-moving social complexities when some demand an exhaustive interrogation of the terms of analysis before one can even begin? When semiotician Algirdas Greimas (1990, p. 41) suggested that to study the semiotics of social scientific practice, one must first analyze the foundations of scientific discourse all the way down to the very "paper upon which ideas are formulated," it is little surprise that some sociologists threw up their hands and abandoned the enterprise.

Yet, to face embodied technology's ontological puzzles head on, sociologists must adopt the inherent uncertainty of semiotics' theoretical complexity. Embodied technology blends humans and data, extends human sensory and physical capabilities, and highlights our tenuous understandings of what constitutes a digitized "self" on the one hand, while engaging the nonhuman/human interdependencies and volatilities of biologically designed materials on the other. Perhaps this uncertainty explains why sociologists, traditionally, have not been interested in wearable tech in general, and fashionable wearable tech in particular; and the sociology of biodesign, like the technology it examines, is virtually nonexistent.

Tackling issues inherent to these domains demands complicating sociological assumptions about human beings as a subject of study. By "fetishizing the values of methodological rigour," geographer Nigel Thrift (2007, p. 18) has argued, sociologists miss the point of social science, to "hear the world and to make sure that it can speak back." This kind of active listening expands sociologists' methodological reach to grasp theoretical tools that elucidate human subjects within the symbolic systems shaping their existence. Only a semiotic analysis can elicit the bodily metaphors that practitioners use in conceiving their designs. Pinpointing these metaphors can help critique and reshape design practice for the better, or head off problematic and damaging design outcomes before they are realized.

The D&G show glamorized notions of AI and computing that capture the cultural imagination. Digitization has promised that we can conquer nature, overcome our biology, and leave our bodies and this ailing earth behind. In contrast to this transhuman paradigm, biodesign's posthuman values may offer a different path. Mapping and interrogating semiotic dichotomies shaping design practice invokes key sociological questions, which move the needle toward social justice. Asking who is in power and who is vulnerable orients researchers and designers toward seeking out and creating forms of just and equitable technological embodiment, which reject supremacy in favor of a more symbiotic future.

**References**

Barad, K. (2007) *Meeting the Universe Halfway: Quantum Physics and the Entanglement of Matter and Meaning*, 2nd edn, Durham, NC: Duke University Press Books.

Benjamin, R. (2019) *Race after Technology: Abolitionist Tools for the New Jim Code*, Medford, MA: Polity Press.

Bloor, D. (1976) *Knowledge and Social Imagery*, 2nd edn, Chicago, IL: University of Chicago Press.

Bolton, A. and Cope, N.A. (2016) *Manus X Machina: Fashion in an Age of Technology*, New York: Metropolitan Museum of Art.

Bonham, K.S. and Stefan, M.I. (2017) "Women are Underrepresented in Computational Biology: An Analysis of the Scholarly Literature in Biology, Computer Science and Computational Biology," *PLOS Computational Biology*, 13(10): e1005134, doi: 10.1371/journal.pcbi.1005134.

Braidotti, R. (2013) *The Posthuman*, Cambridge: Polity Press.

Broussard, M. (2018) *Artificial Unintelligence: How Computers Misunderstand the World*, Cambridge, MA: MIT Press.

Bucher, T. and Helmond, A. (2018) "The Affordances of Social Media Platforms," in J. Burgess, T. Poell, and A. Marwick (eds) *The SAGE Handbook of Social Media*, New York: Sage Publications, pp. 233–53.

Cech, E., Rubineau, B., Silbey, S. and Seron, C. (2011) "Professional Role Confidence and Gendered Persistence in Engineering," *American Sociological Review*, 76(5): 641–66.

Cheryan, S., Ziegler, S.A., Montoya, A.K. and Jiang, L. (2017) "Why Are Some STEM Fields More Gender Balanced Than Others?," *Psychological Bulletin*, 143(1): 1–35.

Chu, J. (2017) "Researchers Design Moisture-responsive Workout Suit," *MIT News*, May 19. Available from https://news.mit.edu/2017/moisture-responsive-workout-suit-0519

de Beauvoir, S. (2011) *The Second Sex*, New York: Vintage.

Faber Futures (2021) "Scale, Void, Assemblage 001," Faber Futures. Available from https://faberfutures.com/projects/project-coelicolor/scale-void-print/

Feldman, A. (2019) "Synthetic Biology Company Ginkgo Bioworks Tops $4 Billion Valuation, Pushing Its Ph.D. Founders' Stakes To Some $250 Million Each," Forbes, September 19. Available from www.forbes.com/sites/amyfeldman/2019/09/19/synthetic-biology-company-ginkgo-bioworks-tops-4-billion-valuation-with-t-rowe-investment-pushing-its-phd-founders-stakes-to-some-250-million-each/

Ferrando, F. (2020) "Leveling the Posthuman Playing Field," *Theology and Science*, 18(1): 1–6.

Fibershed and ETC Group (2018) "Genetically-Engineered Clothes: Synthetic Biology's New Spin on Fast Fashion," ETC Group, September 17. Available from www.etcgroup.org/content/genetically-engineered-clothes

Fontdevila, J. (2020) "Productive Pleasures across Binary Regimes: Phenomenologies of Bisexual Desires among Latino Men," *Sexualities*, 23(4): 645–65.

Freud, S. (1955) *The Interpretation of Dreams: The Complete and Definitive Text*, Philadelphia, PA: Basic Books.

Greimas, A.J. (1990) *The Social Sciences: A Semiotic View*, Minneapolis, MN: University of Minnesota Press.

Hahn, J. (2021a) "Hermès Creates Mycelium Version of its Classic Leather Victoria Bag," Dezeen. Available from www.dezeen.com/2021/03/18/hermes-mycelium-leather-victoria-bag-mycoworks/

Hahn, J. (2021b) "Adidas Unveils Stan Smith Mylo Trainers Made from Mycelium Leather," Dezeen. Available from www.dezeen.com/2021/04/19/stan-smith-mylo-trainers-adidas-mycelium-leather/

Haraway, D. (1988) "Situated Knowledges: The Science Question in Feminism and the Privilege of Partial Perspective," *Feminist Studies*, 14(3): 575–99.

Haraway, D. (1990) *Simians, Cyborgs, and Women: The Reinvention of Nature*, New York: Routledge.

Harding, S.G. (1986) *The Science Question in Feminism*, Ithaca, NY: Cornell University Press.

Hilary, R. (1986) "Beyond Masculinist Realities: A Feminist Epistemology for the Science," in R. Bleier (ed) *Feminist Approaches to Science*, Oxford: Pergamon Press, pp. 57–76.

Jay, M. (1993) *Downcast Eyes: The Denigration of Vision in Twentieth-century French Thought*, Berkeley, CA: University of California Press.

Kelley, S. (2021) "Weaving Inclusivity, Style into Wearable Tech," *Cornell Chronicle*, September 9. Available from https://news.cornell.edu/stories/2021/09/weaving-inclusivity-style-wearable-tech

Lee, S. (2011) "Grow Your Own Clothes," TED. Available from www.ted.com/talks/suzanne_lee_grow_your_own_clothes?language=en

Levitt, K. (2011) "Suzanne Lee Grows Her Own BioCouture Bomber Jackets," Vice, November 17. Available from www.vice.com/en/article/xyvjpa/suzanne-lee-grows-her-own-biocouture-bomber-jackets

Levy, K.E.C. (2015) "Intimate Surveillance," *Idaho Law Review*, 51: 679–93.

Lupton, D. (2015) "The Cultural Specificity of Digital Health Technologies," *This Sociological Life*, January 25. Available from https://simplysociology.wordpress.com/2015/01/

Lupton, D. (2018) "Towards Design Sociology," *Sociology Compass*, 12(1): 1–11.

Lupton, D. (2020) "Wearable Devices: Sociotechnical Imaginaries and Agental Capacities," in I. Pedersen and A. Iliadis (eds) (2020) *Embodied Computing: Wearables, Implantables, Embeddables, Ingestibles*, Cambridge, MA: MIT Press, Ch 3.

Marwick, A.E. (2015) *Status Update: Celebrity, Publicity, and Branding in the Social Media Age*, New Haven, CT: Yale University Press.

Massanari, A. (2017) "#Gamergate and The Fappening: How Reddit's Algorithm, Governance, and Culture Support Toxic Technocultures," *New Media & Society*, 19(3): 329–46.

McIlwain, C.D. (2019) *Black Software: The Internet and Racial Justice, from the AfroNet to Black Lives Matter*, New York: Oxford University Press.

Miller, K. and Wissinger, E. (2018) "Possible Futures of Embodied Biotech," paper presented at the Theorizing the Web conference, New York City.

Myers, W. (2018) *Bio Design: Nature, Science, Creativity*, New York: Museum of Modern Art.

Nagy, P. and Neff, G. (2015) "Imagined Affordance: Reconstructing a Keyword for Communication Theory," *Social Media + Society*, 1(2): 1–9.

Nakamura, L. (2014) "Gender and Race Online," in M. Graham and W.H. Dutton (eds) *Society and the Internet: How Networks of Information and Communication Are Changing Our Lives*, Oxford: Oxford University Press, pp. 81–96.

Neff, G. and Nafus, D. (2016) *Self-Tracking*, Cambridge, MA: MIT Press.

Noble, S.U. (2018) *Algorithms of Oppression: How Search Engines Reinforce Racism*, New York: New York University Press.

Paton, E. (2020) "Fungus May Be Fall's Hottest Fashion Trend," *The New York Times*, October 5. Available from www.nytimes.com/2020/10/02/fashion/mylo-mushroom-leather-adidas-stella-mccartney.html

Pavlus, J. (2011) "What If You Could Gauge Your Health With Color-Coded Poo?" Fast Company. Available from www.fastcompany.com

Pedersen, I. and Iliadis, A. (eds) (2020) *Embodied Computing: Wearables, Implantables, Embeddables, Ingestibles*, Cambridge, MA: MIT Press.

Retail Info Systems (2017) "Why the Future's Fashion Supply Chains Need a Human-Centric Model," Retail Info Systems, October 23. Available from https://risnews.com/why-futures-fashion-supply-chains-need-human-centric-model

Rosner, D. (2018) *Critical Fabulations*, Cambridge, MA: MIT Press.

Rousi, R. and Alanen, H.K. (2021) "Socio-emotional Experience in Human Technology Interaction Design: A Fashion Framework Proposal," in M. Rauterberg (ed) *Culture and Computing: Design Thinking and Cultural Computing, Lecture Notes in Computer Science*, Cham: Springer, pp. 131–50.

Roy, D. and Subramaniam, B. (2016) "Matter in the Shadows: Feminist New Materialism and the Practices of Colonialism," in V. Pitts-Taylor (ed) *Mattering: Feminism, Science, and Materialism*, New York: New York University Press.

Sanders, R. (2017) "Self-tracking in the Digital Era: Biopower, Patriarchy, and the New Biometric Body Projects," *Body & Society*, 23(1): 36–63.

Saussure, F. de (1986 [1916]) *Course in General Linguistics*, ed C. Bally and A. Sechehaye, with A. Riedlinger, LaSalle, IL: Open Court.

Schwartz, B. and Neff, G. (2019) "The Gendered Affordances of Craigslist 'New-in-town Girls Wanted' Ads," *New Media & Society*, 21(11/12): 2404–21.

Thrift, N. (2007) *Non-Representational Theory: Space, Politics, Affect*, New York: Routledge.

Trafton, A. (2014) "Research Reveals a Gender Gap in the Nation's Biology Labs," MIT News. Available from https://news.mit.edu/2014/research-reveals-gender-gap-nations-biology-labs-0630

Volosinov, V.N. (1973) *Marxism and the Philosophy of Language*, vol. 1, New York: Seminar Press.

Wipprecht, A. (2011) "Anouk Wipprecht on Intimacy 2.0," V2_Institute for the Unstable Media. Available from http://v2.nl/lab/blog/anouk-wipprecht-on-intimacy

Wissinger, E. (2016) "From 'Geek' to 'Chic': Wearable Technology and the Woman Question," in J. Daniels, K. Gregory and T.M. Cottom (eds) *Digital Sociologies*, Bristol: Policy Press, pp. 369–86.

Wissinger, E. (2017) "Wearable Tech, Bodies, and Gender," *Sociology Compass*, 11(11): 1–14.

# Index

References to footnotes show both the page number and the note number (166n8).

**A**

abductive reasoning 9, 14–16, 166, 166n8
addressivity 13
agency 19, 22, 74–5, 100–1, 142, 144, 175–6
 group 74
 individual/collective 80–1, 83–4
 personal 83
aggressive behavior 101
Alexander, Jeffrey 18, 120, 126, 131
ambage 107, *see also* communication ambiguity/ambage
anthropology 2, 4, 5, 7, 35, 118, 121–3, 126
 linguistic anthropology 4
anticipation 140, 144, 152–3
antiretroviral therapies 16, *see also* pre–exposure prophylaxis
application conditions 77, 79
Archer, Margaret 19, 83–4, 92
Aristotle 132
Ashimoto, Akiko 126
assimilation
 strategic 43
associative relations 8–9, 19, 146, 153 *see also* signification Saussurean tradition and mnemonic chains 153
Ásta (Sveinsdottir) 76, 78–80
audience 22–3, 87, 96, 97, 99, 101–4, 110, 113, 141–2, 195
avatars, disciplinary 3–4

**B**

Bakhtin, Mikhail 13–14, 13n4, 147
Bakhtin school 13–14, 15n5
Bakker, J.I. (Hans) 22, 52, 55, 61–2, 61n7, 68–9
barebacking practices 164, 167, 169, 169n12, 173
Barthes, Roland 3, 7–8, 123, 130
Bateson, Gregory 14, 166
Bauman, Richard 14n5, 111, 166
Beauvoir, Simone de 189–90

Bellah, Robert 53
Berger, Peter 16
Biernacki, Richard 123
big tent, *see* metaparadigmatic synthesis
bin Laden, Osama 133
binary classifications 4, 159, 187, 194, *see also* heteronormativity
biodesign 182, 184–7, 195–9, 200, *see also* posthumanism
biological systems 5
Bloor, David 182
Blumer, Herbert 52–4, 56–7, 62–4, 66–7
Boas, Franz 7
Boasian school 7
body 24, 75, 90, 182–4, 186–8, 191–7, 199
boundary
 social group 105, 109
 work 43
Bourdieu, Pierre 17, 36, 65
Brekhus, Wayne 21, 31–8, 40–2, 44–7
Briggs, Charles 14n5, 111, 166
Bruner, Jerome 121
Burt, Ronald 109
Butler, Judith 17, 159–160

**C**

Callejas, Laura 101
Carrillo, Héctor 162, 168n10, 171n17
category 32, 33, 35–7, 75, 77n, 79, 129, 189
 social categories 75
Chan, Tak 65
Charmaz, Kathy 58, 67
Chase, Ivan 109
Chicago school 63–4
chimpanzee politics 98–9, *see also* de Waal, Frans
Chomsky, Noam 127, 128n9
Clarke, Lee 45
classroom dynamics 99–101, *see also* McFarland, Daniel

205

code 4, 14–5, 17, 19, 44, 126, 129, 131, 143, 146, 149, 168–70, 173
  binary 8, 19, 146
  crude notions 6, 8
  linguistic 6, 11
  nonverbal 44
  self-referential 6–9, *see also* signification Saussurean tradition
  of silence 167–70, 169n13
code-switching 11, 44, 106, 111, 165, 173, 173n18
Collins, Randal 59, 59n6
cognition 10n1, 11, 18, 20–1, 31, 33, 35–6, 121, 147, 153, 162, 164
  deliberative 36
cognitive science 121
communication
  and ambiguity/ambage 107, 107n17, *see also* White, Harrison
  and complexity 12, 106
  digital 102–3
  and emergence 5–6
  and heteroglossia 13
  possibility of 1
  and predication 9
  and side-directed behavior 98, 100, *see also* side-directed behavior
  and social relationships 9, 12, 15
communicative practice 12, 165
comparative historical sociology 18, 54, 61–3
complexity levels 5, 61, 161, *see also* emergence
computation 121, 182
computational text analysis 113–4
condom semiotics 122, 162
  and masculinity 162
  and postcolonial relations 162
  and trust 162
condomless semiotics 162–4
conferralism 78–9
Confino, Alon 147
conflationism 19
consciousness 7, 13, 17, 60, 74, 82–3, 85
  collective consciousness 7, *see also* langue/parole
context-making function 11–15, *see also* indexicality
context-markers 166
contextual parameters 165
contextualization cues 14, 166, 173
contingency 22, 121, 146, 148–9, 152, 175
  double 152
cosmopolitanism 42
Cossu, Andrea 10, 23–4, 53, 55, 118n1, 123n6, 151, 164n6
courtroom dynamics 108, 112
Crenshaw, Kimberlé 40–1
critical race studies 183, 193
critical realism 22, 68

cultural autonomy 118
cultural sociology 23, 118–26, 130, 140, 145–7, 152, 154
  of arts 122
  of the future 152
  of markets 122
cultural structure 120–1, 124–6, 130–2, 135, 142–3
cultural syntax 119–120, 123, 126–7, 130, 132–5
  and rules of meaning-making 120, 132–4
cultural system 19, 23–5, 142, 144–8, 152–3
  and social system 18, 53
cultural trauma 126
cultural turn 2, 19, 118, 125, 145
culture 62, 68
  autonomy of 18–20, 25, 119, 144, 146, 151
  of attention 44
  and cognition 18–21
  declarative/nondeclarative 36, 140, 143, 153
  as encyclopedia 20, *see also* encyclopedia
  and indexicality 15
  and language 12
  metaphors of 18
  and networks 98
  as nonhereditary memory 148
  and practice 5
  and social structure 4, 18–19
  and structuralism 7–8, 19, 129
  as succession of interpretants 20, *see also* interpretant
  as system of signs 123, 127, 148–9
  as text 122, 124

**D**

Darwin, Charles 64
data exploitation 182
Dean, Tim 162, 164, 169, 169n12
deixis 11, 111, 165
D'Emilio, John 160n2
Derrida, Jacques 15n6, 16n8, 17, 170n15
design
  design culture 182–3, 186
  design sociology 182
  gender affordances 184–5, 199
  gender differences/inflections 183, 188–9
  gendered technological practices 183–4, 188
de Waal, Frans 97, 98–9
diachronic linguistics 8, *see also* signification Saussurean tradition
dialogicality 13, 87, 89
disclosure, theory of 76
discourse 6, 10n1, 17–18, 19, 86, 105, 107, 113, 146
discourse markers 11
discursive consolidation 75, 86–9
  degrees of 89

Dilthey, Wilhelm 62, 64, 122n5, 125n7
Douglas, Mary 122, 125
doxa 17–18
DuBois, W.E.B. 39
Duranti, Alessandro 5, 7, 107
Durkheim, Emile
  influences 2, 142, 145, 146, 147, 149
dyadic ties
  action 99, 103
  behavioral gesture 96
  as reductionist 107
  relationship 101
dynamic object, *see* sign object

**E**

Eco, Umberto 5, 8–10, 14–15, 20, 16n8, 148–9, 170n15
EGP class scheme 59, 63, 65
Ehrlich, Susan 112
Elias, Norbert 110n21
eliminativism 80–1
emergence 4–5, 75, 85
  causal powers 173
  complex systems 12, 18, 174, 176
  downward causation 174, 175
  higher level properties 161, 174, 176
  productive mechanism 173, 175
  of social ties 106
  of the subject 90
  supervenient base 173
Emirbayer, Mustafa 104
encyclopedia 8, 15n1, 20, 23, 140, 147–54
  *see also* associative relations
  maximal 148
  as a network 150–1, 153
entextualization 111
epistemes 17
Erikson, Emily 103–4, 104n14
ethnographic methods 18, 161, 168n10, 173, 176, 182, 187
ethnopoetics 14n5, 166, *see also* Bakhtin school

**F**

fashion
  culture of 181–2
  hand/machine dichotomy 181–2
  oppositional relationships 181–2
feminist materialism 182–3, 186
feminist studies 193
Fine, Gary 57, 59, 67, 99n8
Ferrando, Francesca 193
Fodor, Jerry 173
Fontaine, William 39
Fontdevila, Jorge 10, 12, 14, 17, 24, 85, 103n13, 106–7, 107n17, 119n2, 162, 165, 167, 171n17, 172, 174, 187
footings 12, 165
forgetting 147, 149

Foucault, Michel 17
frames 18, 23, 144, 151, 153
  condom protective 172
  metacommunicative 14, 166, *see also* Bateson, Gregory
  of interaction 106, *see also* Goffman, Erving
  trusting 172
Freud, Sigmund 189
Fuhse, Jan 103n12, 113
Fujimoto, Kayo 101
functionalism 2, 18–19, 53, 67
fundamental causes of disease 161, 175n20

**G**

gay activism 163
gay and bisexual men
  stigma against 160–1
  and HIV/AIDS 160
Geertz, Clifford 18, 19, 53, 55, 61–2, 61n7, 122–3
gender ideologies 17, 160, 183–4, 186–8
gender imbalances 189
gendered assumptions
  professional settings 188–9, 195
  sexist assumptions 188–9
gendered perceptions
  male rationality 190
  scopophilia 190
  visual versus haptic 189–90, 193
Gibson, David 102, 102n11
Giesen, Bernhard 126, 131
Go, Julian 38–9
Goffman, Erving 14, 100, 104, 111–2, 112n23, 162, 166
Goldthorpe, John 65
Gorski, Philip 68
grammar 6, 8, 13, 17, *see also* signification
  Saussurean tradition
grammaticalization 11, 13, 17, *see also* Bakhtin school
Greimas, Algirdas 151, 199
Gross, Neil 175
grounded theory 15, 55, 58, 67
Gumperz, John 14, 15, 105, 107, 111, 166–7, 173

**H**

Habermas, Jurgen 67
habit 10–1, 16–18, 16n8, 35
habituation 4, 7, 16–18, 17n10, 35
Hacking, Ian 159
Hanks, William 111
haptic 183–4, 189–90, 193
Haraway, Donna 76, 186, 190, 194, 199
Hawthorne, Nathaniel 33
health disparities 160–1, 174
Healy, Kieran 121
Heath, Melanie 38
Hegel, Georg 60, 64, 67

Heise, David 67–8
Heiskala, Risto 3, 6, 8, 17, 17n10, 142, 146
heteroglossia 13–14, 17
heteronormativity
　binary classifications 160, 165, 175, 187, 194
　historical conditions 17, 160n2
heterosexuality 18, 42, 160
homoeroticism 158–9
homonormativity 163, 163n5
homophobia 163
Herdt, Gilbert 159
HIV disparities 161, 174–5
HIV epidemic
　biosocial reconception 160, 174
　modeling of 176
　of signification 162
　social determinants of health 160–1
　syndemics 160
HIV-positive gay men
　discourse of individual responsibility 168, 168n11
　rejection 167–8
　stigma resistance 167–9, 174
HIV prevention needs 175
HIV serosorting
　dilemmas 170–2
　HIV-negative serosorting 171
　HIV-positive serosorting 167
Hjelmslev, Louis 79, 146

**I**

iconicity 11, *see also* sign icon
ideal type models 54, 61–3
identity 43–4, 47
　commuting 44
　and control 17, 106, *see also* White, Harrison
　gay 32–3, 160–1
　integrating 44
　sexual 31
　and uncertainty, *see also* White, Harrison
imagined community 87n8
immediate object, *see* sign object
"I-mode" 83–4, 91
indexes, *see* indexicality, *also* sign
indexical shifters 12n3
indexicality 6, 9–15, 17, 24, 107–8, 164–6, 165n7, 175
inequality
　racial 37, 47
　social 31, 36, 39, 41, 47
　sexual 161–2, 174–5
informal organization 99
information
　and bodily data 192
　and collective subjects 91
　and complex systems 5
　and linguistic communication 15, 85, 166

　and memory 147–8
　processing of 121
in-group membership 101
insider joke 100, *see also* classroom dynamics
instrumental targeting 101
intentionalism 152
intentionality 85, 111
interaction order 37, 162
interpretant 9–10, 10n1, 16–18, 16n8, 20, 150–1, 153, 164–5, 164n6, 169–72, 170n15, 175, *see also* sign
interpretation 4, 11, 15, 22, 68, 119, 122–4, 150–2, 167, 170n2, 172, *see also* abductive reasoning
interpretive sociology 15, 47–8, 61, 123, 131, 145
intersectionality 40–2, 44, 47–8, 53

**J**

Jacobs, Ron 126
Jakobson, Roman 2, 12, 14n1, 21, 31, 164–5
James, William 2, 64

**K**

Kane, Anne 19, 131
Kant, Immanuel 64, 67
keying exchanges 100, *see also* indexicality
kinds 77–9, 159
　natural/social distinction 77
　natural versus interactive kinds 159
Kockelman, Paul 5
Koshul, Basit 67

**L**

Lacan, Jacques 7
Lacy, Karyn 43
Lamont, Michele 15
language 4–7, 9–17, 34, 37–8, 40, 44, 66, 75–7, 79–80, 82, 84–5, 107, 111–3, 124, 127, 130, 149, 164–7, 173, 186–8, 199
　metalingual function of language 12, 165
langue/parole 7, 15, 143, 151, *see also* signification Saussurean tradition
Latino gay and bisexual men 160, 171n17, 174
Leap, Braiden 42
Lee, Suzanne 185
Lemert, Charles 4, 18
Levi–Strauss, Claude 2, 7–8, 19, 123
linguistic relativism 7, *also see* Sapir–Whorf hypothesis
linguistic self-awareness 82–5, 87, 92–3
Link, Bruce 161, 175n20
Lizardo, Omar 3, 20, 36, 140, 143
Lotman, Yuri 147–8, 174
Luckmann, Thomas 16–7, 64
Lupton, Deborah 183, 186, 199

**M**

Mackinnon, Neil 68
macrosociology 152

macro-structural drivers 162
Madigan, Todd 23, 132n12
marked/unmarked 17–8, 21, 32–46, 163, 169–70
  attention 32
  epistemic structure 38–9, 47
  marked condom practices 164
  markedness semiotic theory 16, 16n9, 163, 163n3
  and race 36–9
  semiotic asymmetry of 34, 38, 40
  sociology of 33, 35
Marx, Karl 13, 59, 61–5
  philosophy of praxis 13
  superstructure 62–3, 65
Martin, John L. 4, 20, 97n6, 113
masculinity deficit 160, 175
Mast, Jason 20, 121, 126
McFarland, Daniel 99–101
McLean, Paul 22–3, 98, 107n18, 109
McVeigh, Timothy 37
Mead, George H. 52, 61–2, 64, 66–7, 104
meaning 4–20, 22–3, 31, 34, 52, 57, 61, 74, 76, 79–83, 92, 96, 104, 106–7, 109–13, 117–32, 142, 145, 147–8, 150–4, 161–2, 164, 166–7
  constitution of 77
  innovative 80
  of money 122
  Peircean 10, *see also* interpretant
  Saussurean 6, *see also* signifier/signified
  and semiotization 34
meaning–making processes 4, 11, 122, 160, 169–70, 171–2, 174
memory 24, 53, 82, 85, 90, 92, 142–7, 152–3
  collected 143, 146
  collective 133, 143, 145, 148
  cultural 154
  as encyclopedia 147
  frames of 144
  as mechanism 148–9, 154
  operations of 144
  performative 141
  as process 143, 152
  and remembering 144, 147, 149
  semantic 149
  semiotics of 143, 146–7
  as a social fact 142
  sociology of 142, 154
  as storage 91, 149
  structural approaches 143, 145
memory studies 140, 144–5, 148, 154
mental states 74
Mertz, Elizabeth 4
metacommunication 14, 166–7, 175
metaparadigmatic synthesis 52–6, 66–9
metaphor 6, 11, 79, 121, 148, 162, 199, 200

metapragmatic awareness 12, 171–3
metapragmatics 5, 12–14, 17, 110, 165–6, 172
methodological individualism 80–1
methodological pluralism 15, 18
microsociology 152
migrant sexual networks 173–4
mind 10, 13, 17n10, 74–6, 82, 140, 171
  independence 78–9
  theories of the extended 75, 81, 91–2
Mische, Ann 104
morphology 129
Morris, Charles 23, 39, 64, 127, 130
Mullaney, Jamie 44
multiple semiotic pathways 162, 174–5
myth 6, 126, 141, 143

N

narrative 2, 4, 6, 9, 18, 22, 42, 46, 52, 76, 77, 80, 85, 90, 120, 126, 129, 132–4, 142–3, 145–6, 151, 154
  programs 151
  selfhood 90n11
  social 132–3
  versus chronicle 133–4
Nash, Jennifer 41
neo-Blumerian synthesis 58–60, 66
neo-Marxian political economy 58, 60
neo-Weberian sociology 54, 61–3
neoclassical economics 52
network analysis 112–4, *see also* social networks
network domains 106, *see also* White, Harrison
network theory 97
  formalism 103–4
  relationalism 103–4
network tools, *see also* social networks
  brokerage 108–9
  dominance 108–9
  negative ties 109–10
  temporality 110–11, 151
nomenclaturism 6
Norton, Matthew 20, 124, 126, 140
nostalgia 42, 144

O

Olick, Jeffrey 18, 20, 142, 143, 145, 147
online communication, *see* communication digital
ontology 75–7, 149
  object-centered 74
  process 92
  semiotic 147

P

Padgett, John 109
parole, *see* sign langue/parole
Parsons, Talcott 18, 53

participant observation, *see* ethnographic methods
participation shifts 102
Patil, Vrushali 18, 160
Peirce, Charles 2, 6, 9–10, 12, 14–15, 16, 20, 55, 63–6, 164, 169–70
Pelc, Jerzy 120
performance 14
  and competence 4, 8
  gender 17
  identity 44
  performance-based studies 14n5, *see also* ethnopoetics
  social 87, 89, 120, 126, 129, 148
  of speech 14, 166n8
  sexual 162
  and wearable technology design 184
Petrilli, Susan 61n7
Phelan, Jo 161, 175n20
phenomenological sociology 16
phenomenology 60, 97, 162, 166–7, 169, 171–2
Plato
  *Symposium* 158
plot 126, 132–4
politeness/deference markers 7, 11–12, 12n2, 110, 111, 165–6, 165n7
pollution 125, *see also* Douglas, Mary
polysemic interpretations 172–3, 175–6
possibilistic thinking 45
postcolonial studies 162, 193
posthuman design ethos 193–4, *see also* posthumanism
posthumanism
  body as organic 188
  design coded feminine 190
  feminine–associated practices 186, 190, 192, 194
  feminine oppositions 188, 192–3
  frameworks 182, 194–99
poststructuralism 2, 25, 199
power 16–18, 63, 65
pragmatic sociology 52–3, 55
pragmatics 4, 15, 147, 167, 170–2
  cultural 153
pragmatism 52, 54, 64, 104, 175
pre–exposure prophylaxis 174, 174n19
pretension 152
probabilistic thinking 45
properties
  communal 78
  emergence of 80, 161, 174, 176, *see also* emergence
  institutional 78
proximal mechanisms 162
Putnam, Hilary 20, 64, 153

**Q**

qualifiers
  linguistic 34

qualitative methodologies 15, *see also* ethnographic methods
queer expressions 8, *see also* associative relations

**R**

racism 37
Rainwater, Lee 36
Raud, Rein 22, 76, 80
Reed, Isaac 122–4
reflexivity 9–10, 12–14, *see also* indexicalities
remembering 149
rhizome 9, 16, 141, 170n15 *see also* encyclopedia, associative relations
Ricoeur, Paul 4, 119, 125, 127, 134
risk 21, 31, 44–8, 161–7
risk reduction 163
ritual 2, 6–7, 18, 75, 126, 159, *see also* signification Saussurean tradition
  iconicity of 126
Rouse, Joseph 76

**S**

Sabetta, Lorenzo 47
safe sex 163
Sahlins, Marshall 122, 125–6, 130
Sapir, Edward 7
Sapir-Whorf hypothesis 7, *also see* linguistic relativism
Saussure, Ferdinand de 6–11, 13, 19, 123, 127, 130–1, 134, 143, 146, 153, 164, 186
Sawyer, Keith 5, 12, 18, 173
Schutz, Alfred 64
science and technology studies 182–3, 193
Scott, Monster Kody 37
scripts 82, 100, 106, 140–1, 147, 151, 153, 169n13
Searle, John 74, 76, 85
secondness 12n3
secrecy 105–6, *see also* Simmel, Georg
selfhood 81, 82, 85, 90, 92, 193
self-referentiality 6–9, *see also* signification Saussurean tradition
semantics 6, 12, 15, 23, 123, 130, 132, 147
  cultural 120
semantic field 79
semantic network 140, 144, 152
semantic system 79
semiology 6–7, 127
semiosis 5, 9, 11, 20, 149–50
semiosphere 147–8
semiotic analysis 199–200
semiotic imagination 33, 48, 61
semiotic mediation
  Peircean triadic 9–11, 16, 52, 55, 164, 169, 175
  processes 4, 8, 161, 175
semiotic power 47
semiotic process 82
semiotic self 60

# INDEX

semiotic sociology 3, 20, 21, 52–4, 54n2, 55, 66–7, 140, 142, 153
semiotic, structuralist 4, 6, 8, 81, 147
semiotic system 124
semiotic traditions, *see* signification
semiotic weight 41, 43–4, 48
semiotics 1–21, 31, 53–5, 61, 63–6, 68, 111–2, 127, 146
  applied 145
  cognitive 153
  general 145
  specific 145
sentence 125, 129
sexual orientation 159
Shepherd, Hana 101
side-directed behavior
  definition 97, 98, 112
  empirical examples 98–103, 108–11
  and interpretation 113
  as social form 103, 105, 105n16, 114
  and semiotic gestures 104, 112–4
  and situations 108
  and social networks 108–12
  theoretical framework 103–8
sign 6–20, 34, 52, 57, 60, 119–20, 123, 124–7, 143, 145, 148, 150, 164–5, 164n6, 169–70, 171–2
  historical contexts 63–4, 68
  ground 10n1, 150, 164n6
  icon 10, 60, 165
  index 5–6, 10–11, 60, 107–8, 165, 165n7, *see also* indexicality
  interpretant, *see* interpretant
  linguistic 5–9, 11, 164
  object of 9–10, 10n1, 164, 164n6
  paralinguistic 11
  representamen 9–10, 150, 164
  signifier/signified 4, 6–9, 24–5, 134, 162, 164, 169, 174–5, 194
  symbol 10–11, 54–5, 57, 60, 61n7, 63, 65–6, 68, 126, 145–6, 165
  vehicle of meaning 4, 11, 120, 126
signification
  constitutive nature of 5
  Peircean tradition 6, 9–10, 16
  Saussurean tradition 6–9, 130
signifier *see* sign
signified *see* sign
Silverstein, Michael 12, 15, 164–5, 165n7
Simko, Christina 18, 20
Simmel, Georg 104–6, 105n16
Singer, Merrill 160
situated knowledge 76
skill 35, 141
Small, Mario 97n6
small group dynamics 101
Smith, Dorothy 58
Smith, Philip 120, 122, 126, 131
social class 63, 65

social context 9, 11–15, 164–7
social contract, theory of 85
social drama 125
social entity 80
social interaction 57, 60, 143
social mechanisms 140, 175
social networks 98, 108–14, *see also* side–directed behavior
social status 62–3, 65, 101–2, 165n7
social topology 106
sociality 3, 9, 11, 15
sociocultural systems 5, *see also* emergence
sociolinguistics 106
socio-logic 3
sociology
  as concept-driven 21, 35–6
  cultural, *see* cultural sociology
  relational 75, 97, 103–4, *see also* network theory relationalism
  and semiotics 1–6, 11–21
Song, Eunkyung 22–3, 98, 108, 108n19, 111n22
Sonnevend, Julia 126
Spillman, Lyn 4, 122
status markers 11, 12n2
stigma 24, 41, 43
  homophobic 160–61, 174
  sexual 161, 175
  against HIV-positive men 163, 167
  HIV-related 161, 175
Stroud, Angela 42
structuralism 3–4, 7–8, 10, 19
structure 3–4, 19, 118, 124
structure of talk 102
stylistics 13, *see also* Bakhtin school
subjectivity 38, 83
  collective 91
  co–subjectivity 91
  gay subjectivity 170n16, *see also* identity gay
Swedberg, Richard 15
Swidler, Ann 15, 18, 122, 162
switchings 106–8, *see also* White, Harrison
symbiosis 183, 200, *see also* posthumanism
symbol, *see* sign symbol
symbolic gender oppositions 187–8, 193, 196, *see also* gender ideologies
symbolic interactionism
  American 54, 58–9, 63
  American pragmatist roots 52
  Blumer's 56–7
  and *Homo sapiens* 65–6
  interactionism in general 54, 56, 60, 66
synchronic/diachronic 153
syntactico–semantic system 6–9
syntagmatic relations 8–9, 127 *see also* signification Saussurean tradition
syntax 23, 120–1, 123, 127–31, 147
  cultural, *see* cultural syntax
  rules 123, 128–9

## T

Tavory, Iddo 14, 15, 18, 57, 67, 122, 162, 166n8
Taylor, Charles 6, 90n11
taxonomy, *see* binary classifications
technological embodiment 185–7
telementation metaphor 16–17, 17n10, *see also* signification Saussurean tradition
Telhan, Orkan 185
temporality 24, 108, 110, 140, 142, 144, 149–51, 153–5
text, *see* computational text analysis; culture as text
textuality 3–4, 11
thick description 55, 123n6, *see also* Geertz, Clifford
thirdness 12n3
Thomasson, Amie 76–9
Timmermans, Stefan 14, 15, 166n8
Tittenbrun, Jacek 59, 65
Tovar, Virgie 33
transhumanism
  body as machine 188, 191, 194–9
  datafication 182, 191
  frameworks 182, 194–9
  male rationality 190, 192
  masculine-identified practices 186, 190–1
  masculine oppositions 188, 192
treatment optimism 163, 163n4
Treichler, Paula 162
triad
  action 99, 103
  *divide et impera* 105
  and pointed displays 111, *see also* Goffman, Erving
  and side–directed behavior 105–6, 108
  as social form 105, 105n16
  *tertius gaudens* 105
trope 126
Trubetzkoy, Nicholaj 31
Tuomela, Raimo 83
Turner, Victor 120, 122, 125

## U

unlimited semiosis 10, 16–18, 150, 164, 170, 170n15, *see also* interpretant
unmarked condom practice 163, 163n3
utopia 144

## V

values 18, 62, 87, 125, 145–6, 148
Vaughn, Diane 45
verbal utterance 96
*verstehende Soziologie* 54, 61, 68
Volosinov, Valentin 13, 187, 199

## W

Waugh, Linda 16n9, 31
wearable technology 182, 184–7, 190–1, 197–9, 200, *see also* transhumanism, posthumanism
Weber, Max 39, 54, 54n1, 55, 61–3, 65, 122n5
"We-mode," *see* "I-mode"
Wherry, Frederick 122
White, Harrison 5, 12, 14, 17, 106–8, 165, 167
White, Hayden 133
Whorf, Benjamin 7
Wiley, Norbert 2, 60, 62–3, 65
Williams, Raymond 18
Wissinger, Elizabeth 24–5, 184, 192
Wittgenstein, Ludwig 12

## Z

Zelizer, Viviana 122
Zerubavel, Eviatar 21, 31, 34–5, 130